Henry Scott Holland

Creed and Character

Sermons

Henry Scott Holland

Creed and Character
Sermons

ISBN/EAN: 9783743423077

Manufactured in Europe, USA, Canada, Australia, Japa

Cover: Foto ©Lupo / pixelio.de

Manufactured and distributed by brebook publishing software (www.brebook.com)

Henry Scott Holland

Creed and Character

CREED AND CHARACTER

Sermons

BY THE REV.

H. S. HOLLAND, M.A.

CANON OF ST. PAUL'S

"In Thy Light, shall we see Light"

RIVINGTONS

WATERLOO PLACE, LONDON

MDCCCLXXXVII

PREFACE.

Sᴇʀᴍᴏɴs that are brought together in a volume
embody a new motive, over and above the direct
aim with which each was separately preached. They
profess that they are united together by more than
the mere cover of the book. They claim to suggest
a single and paramount idea; to convey a single
impression; to communicate a single impulse; to
verify a single supposition; to witness to a single
source; to promote a single interest; to work under
a single direction; to tend towards a single conclusion.
They trust that their partial and piecemeal treat-
ment of their subject will correct itself by help of
juxtaposition; so that they may lose their unhappy
appearance, as loose and sketchy fragments, and may
visibly be seen to cohere into a valid and substantial
consistency.

What is this inner and masterful Unity which, it
is professed, binds all into a whole?

The answer is presumptuous; but it is presumptuous
only with that presumption which alone entitles a

b 2

man to preach. Every Christian preacher, of necessity, undertakes the responsibility of representing "the Mind of Christ." Such a responsibility, if he were, indeed, loyal to it, would, of course, be the secret, not of his pride, but of his abject humiliation.

"The Mind of Christ." That is what ought to be felt, and recognised, as the Beginning and End of all sermons: and this, not as a vague commonplace, but as a Presence, that, growingly, with ever more masterful pressure, with ever intenser force, pervades, utilises, covers, vitalises, absorbs the entire and undivided attention. Ever it ought to be felt emerging out of the background of silence, which lies behind the word and voice of the preacher—felt as an Energy, of which the preacher is but a tool; felt as a living Cry, of which his voice is but an echo.

"The Mind of Christ." This is no formal rule of thought, no text-book to be expounded. It is the expression of a single personal Self, conveyed into us by a vital and personal Spirit. It must exhibit itself as personal—that is, as a living individual Being, self-consistent and self-identical. Nothing that results from it can be casual, accidental, detached. Everything will tell of a certain, fixed, and entire Personality, pervading, encompassing, animating all. "The Mind of Christ" must, if it be shown at all, make it manifest that it is a substantial and organic Thing, which has a character of its own, which acts and speaks in a manner of its own; and all its outward expressions must, necessarily, illustrate this single and identical mode of handling life.

Now, this is what we are so strangely given to ignore. We discuss Christianity as a set of theological ideas, which have more or less value; or we examine into its facts and records, by which it subjects itself to historical criticism. But we seem to forget that what it claims to be is a living Kingdom of Christ; by which it means that it attempts to assimilate to itself the entire body of human affairs, whether internal or external, whether private or social, so that they shall obviously and visibly display the dominion of a single Master-Mind, "the Mind of Christ." The validity, indeed, of this dominion, its potency, its authority—these depend on the literal reality of certain historical facts. If Christ did not rise again the third day, no such dominion can exist. But, if the dominion exists at all, then it exists in the form of what I have spoken: and, if so, then it is, throughout its length and breadth, the manifestation of a Personal Will in action upon the affairs of earth.

Now, how does a will show itself in action?

It shows itself in two forms, which we call mind, and character.

Every act that it does exhibits its inner "*mind*" —that is, its normal and original set of intentions, motives, aims, ends, presuppositions, instincts, imaginations. And, then, it exhibits its "*character*"—that is, its own peculiar mode of combining, selecting, furthering, co-ordinating this set of intentions. A will is individual and personal in that its peculiar mode of combining these motives is absolutely unique: the act that results bears the stamp of an unique character.

The Kingdom of Christ is the manifestation of Christ's sole Will: and it must embody these two forms. It is the display, on earth, of a certain body of motives and intentions, peculiar to Christ, co-ordinated into a certain characteristic combination, peculiar to Christ. Where do we find the first of these two forms? In the Creed of the Church. Where the second? In the ethical ideal of the Church; in the Christian character.

We are accustomed to abstract these two from each other for logical and temporary purposes; and this abstraction has had disastrous results. We all know them. They make the sickness of the hour. For men are sick, and miserable, and weak as soon as their thought has no definite relation to their moral practice; and yet the absurd and ignorant commonplace, that Christianity is a separate matter from its Dogmatic Belief, persuades men to accept a false division, which attempts to break up the undivided unity of the man, to sever the inseverable. No wonder they find themselves enfeebled, and disturbed, by such an impossible divorce.

Christianity, if it is anything at all, is the Will of its King; and, as a Will, it necessarily appears in its double form, as a Mind that thinks, and as a Force that acts: but it is one and the same Will in both, whether it thinks, or whether it acts; and if there is one thing that is absolutely certain, it is that its acts will be totally unintelligible unless they are seen in combination with its Mind. Its intentions, aims, ends, presuppositions—these, most assuredly, enter into the decision by which it combines them, and inserts them into the field of action. And the Creed of Christianity is, simply, a summary of its presuppositions and motives; its moral action, its character, is the sheer and necessary outcome of the Will that selects, and relates, and co-ordinates that particular set of presuppositions and ends. Christianity is a certain spiritual temper, which thinks and acts in a definite manner; and that temper is the outward expression of a self-identical Will, that creates and vivifies it, which is "the Word of God."

Now, surely, if this be true, it is high time to clear out, once and for ever, our wasteful and fatal confusions on this matter. Surely, it is the first duty of all, who presume to teach and preach, to help in the clearance. And it is in an attempt, however weak, to discharge this duty, that I have ventured to call this little book by the title given it.

I desire to offer, by that title, a challenge to all

who may happen to read these sermons, to say whether they can possibly contrive to conceive a separation between the Creed herein pleaded, and the Character herein portrayed. They may freely criticise the work offered them; or they may discuss the practical possibility of a moral character other and higher than the Christian. But can they ever unravel the threads which knit the Character which we know, in its developed form, as Christian, from the Belief which appears, at every single point of the character, as its inherent and vital groundwork? Can they detect, as they read this book, the transitions by which the Creed passes over into the Character? Can they mark the point at which it ceases to be Creed, and becomes Character? "I live; yet not I; Christ liveth in me." There is the law, which accounts for every jot and tittle of Christian Ethics. And the question which I want to put home is, By what process are you going to drop out of that law its theological and retain its ethical value? The Character built on belief in that law combines the uttermost of self-abnegation with the uttermost assertion of vigour and vitality. That is a subtle combination to affect: yet, on its possibility all Christian Character depends. How are you going to attain that moral combination, without giving it its dogmatic background; or without the effective use of those motives which belong to the theological doctrine of Grace? Yet, unless that peculiar combination is possible, the Christian Character is impossible; it must cease out of the earth.

I am not asking how much would remain if Christ were withdrawn. There are other moral ideals, by which men have built up fair and seemly lives: and they would do so again. But, at any rate, those ideals would never produce that particular mind and habit which we call Christian. It would be a different combination of motives, with a different resultant temper. The vision of the Christian citizen, as St. Paul and St. John knew him, and described him—*that* would have gone for ever. It goes when the Creed goes. Nothing can help that.

" The Thing committed to us " is the whole " Mind of Christ; " and Christ cannot be divided. We might be persuaded, if we laid hold of this truth, to guard the Deposit more faithfully and more consistently.

CONTENTS.

Contents.

V.

The Fellowship of the Church.

PAGE

VI.

The Witness of the Church.

VII.

The Resources of the Church.

VIII.

The Mind of the Church.

IX.

The Ministry of the Church.

CONVERSION.

X.

The Solidarity of Salvation:

XI.

The Freedom of Salvation.

XII.

The Gift of Grace.

XIII.

The Law of Forgiveness.—I.

XIV.

𝕿𝖍𝖊 𝕷𝖆𝖜 𝖔𝖋 𝕱𝖔𝖗𝖌𝖎𝖛𝖊𝖓𝖊𝖘𝖘.—II.

XV.

𝕿𝖍𝖊 𝕷𝖆𝖜 𝖔𝖋 𝕱𝖔𝖗𝖌𝖎𝖛𝖊𝖓𝖊𝖘𝖘.—III.

XVI.

𝕿𝖍𝖊 𝕮𝖔𝖒𝖎𝖓𝖌 𝖔𝖋 𝖙𝖍𝖊 𝕾𝖕𝖎𝖗𝖎𝖙.

NEWNESS OF LIFE.

XVII.

𝕿𝖍𝖊 𝕭𝖊𝖆𝖚𝖙𝖞 𝖔𝖋 𝕳𝖔𝖑𝖎𝖓𝖊𝖘𝖘.

XVIII.

The Energy of Unselfishness.

THE CHRISTIAN LIFE HERE ON EARTH.

XXI.

The Activity of Service.

XXII.

Character and Circumstance.

Apostolic Witness

THE STORY OF AN APOSTLE'S FAITH.

B

THE STORY OF AN APOSTLE'S FAITH.

"We beheld His glory."—JOHN i. 14.

FAR away down the years, at the close of the first century, an old man sits brooding over the things that he had seen and heard in the cities of Judah and in the fields of Galilee. Forty, fifty, sixty years, and more perhaps, lie now between him and the scenes which he records. Sixty years—and such years!—years of revolution—years of judgment—years in which the old order perished in doom, and the New World rose into victory under the breath of the Spirit of God. He had himself, long ago, it may be, laid up in the Book of the Revelation the visions in which the tremendous drama of those momentous years moved toward its final and critical act. Yet, now, his look is not forward into the silences that delay the trumpet-blasts of Divine action. His eyes turn ever back, overleaping the crowded interval,—back to those wonderful days when he walked behind the feet of the Master—the days when he touched, and tasted, and handled. Still his whole being hangs upon those sealed memories. Still he ponders, and weighs, and wonders, and broods. For we are listening, in these first verses of St. John, to an old man's broodings. No one can mistake their tone, or be insensible to their atmosphere, as the verses fall on the ear with their solemn weight of measured monotony, serious as a winter's eve, in which the stars silently offer themselves to our eyes, one by one, in seemly order and in noiseless ease. So the great words detach themselves from his lips, single, slow, deliberate, unhasting. Round and round the story his spirit has searched and laboured, and waited, until word could set itself to word, and phrase to phrase. No time could be too long in which to collect into one brief passage the sum and substance of all that revelation which was made known to him in the Name of Jesus Christ.

So he sits, and slowly speaks, and round him are clustering close a crowd of anxious listeners. How strange that crowd would once have been to the fisherman of Bethsaida! It was a crowd gathered out of all those who are scattered abroad upon the face of the earth—keen Greeks, and fervent Syrians, and cultivated Africans, with perhaps a Roman magistrate, or a Gaulish slave. Every kind of alien blood is there, but none, or almost none, of his brethren, the children of Abraham. The Church in which he rules is wholly Greek in tone, in temper, in habit. He has had to forget his own country and his father's house; and that house is now shattered, and that country wrecked, and all the old scenes of his far home are darkened and desolate; and never will he walk at all in those dear, familiar places, where first he looked up from his nets and saw the Master, and heard the call, and left all, and followed Him. Ah! how long ago! though it be to him but as yesterday. And now he sits alone, perhaps, in all the world of those who saw the Lord! Alone and very old, and the question is daily pressing, Can it be that he, too, is to die, as all the rest have died—James, his brother, fifty years back, and Peter, whom he loved—can it be thirty years since Peter died?—and Andrew and Philip, so long His companions on the coasts of Asia? And will there be no one left on earth of those who were His friends, who will be there to greet the Lord when He comes again, as they had seen Him go?

Yet what was it the Lord promised, when Peter pressed Him by the lake-side, on that awful dawn, when they whispered, "It is the Lord"? Was it not that he, John, should be there alive, tarrying long until the glad day when He should come again, and their joy should be full?

So he had half thought, so many had asserted, and yet it was not quite that. No; but only that perhaps it might be so, if Christ willed that he should so tarry.

And would He will it? Often he had prayed for this to be, and cried, "Even so, come, Lord Jesus." Yet now it seemed otherwise. Now it seemed as if, after all, he would die without seeing it. So it felt to him; so it looked; it must now be very near. And much as he and they had longed for the other to be true, yet still he keeps reminding them that his dear Master had never said, "He should never die," but only, "If I will that he tarry."

Surely, we are let in, as we read these last words of St. John's Gospel, to the very heart of the thoughts that were moving about the circle who sit round the feet of the dying Apostle! Will he die or will he not die? That is their incessant anxiety. For they had hoped so much; it is the close of all that burning longing for the coming of the Lord which St. Paul could hardly curb, nor St. Peter quiet, in their new converts. And now, the last argument for the quick coming is being withdrawn—the last hope to which they had clung is fading. "Surely," they had said, "surely John, at least, will live to see it. Surely, the Lord cannot fail His word—the word that He pledged to the brother who lay upon His Bosom!" And the old man stills and soothes their passionate assertions. Nay, the Master never said that. All He said was, "If I will that he tarry till I come;" but He never said, "He should not die."

So they sit, and cluster, and watch—his dear children—his children not after the flesh, but after the Spirit. Their anxiety is daily increasing. Many questions are abroad. Never since those first few months at Jerusalem had there been any rest from questionings and doubts. But now, at the closing days of the century—now, more than ever, they swarm and thicken. It was an age like our own—restless, ardent, disturbed, speculative, revolutionary. Brains were alert, and imaginations kindled. Meteor-hopes were flashing and vanishing; strange voices shook the people and passed. All was seething, agitated, alive. And the little flock of Christ stood in the very thick of the flood; the rains beat down and the winds roared against the house that their faith had built. The Rock was under them, and the house must stand; but, for all that, it is an anxious hour within the frail and trembling shelter, as they listen to the rush of the storm. The Rock was under them; but could they touch it, and be sure? The faith is theirs, their joy and their possession. Yes! but oh! that they could be quite, quite certain that they had a firm hold on it in its uttermost and invincible verity! And lo! just in the very crisis of their sorest distress, they feel that he is dying—he, John, the last of all who could say "I touched, I tasted, I handled." And they gaze and gaze—and cling wistfully to him, as once more he goes over the old, old words which he had said a thousand times before, but which they ever and ever yearned to hear again. We can almost feel them pressing him to tell them yet more, to tell them all, as he tenderly puts them by—"Nay, my children, if I were to tell you all that Jesus said and did, why, the world itself would not contain all the books that would be written."

"Oh! then, tell us just how you learned to believe," they seem to say. "How was it? What was it? It is no easy matter, as we find it. It is no brief and ready affair. We believe, but we are sore pressed by difficulties that beset our belief. We believe, but we cannot say surely and clearly what it is that we believe. Men ask us; puzzle us; distress us. And we see so many fall away in perplexity. How can we be sure that we hold the faith in a way that will never fail us? that we hold it as Jesus meant us to hold it?" Such is the mood to which the fourth Gospel addresses itself. Not written against opponents, nor to confute heresies; it never argues, never reasons. It assumes a circle, an atmosphere of faith; it addresses believers. But the faith is troubled; believers are anxious. The Gospel concentrates itself on the effort to reassure and enhearten a belief that cannot afford to be childlike and simple any more, but must test its foundations and make proof of its security. "Beloved," the Apostle has had to say to them, "believe not every spirit, but try the spirits whether they are of God: because many false prophets are gone out into the world." And so now, "These things have I written unto you that believe on the Name of the Son of God" —why?—"that ye may know that ye have eternal life, and that ye may, in this fuller and more certified knowledge, believe on the Name of the Son of God."

So they sat and looked up into his face—that harassed, yet loyal, band of faithful disciples. "Once more let us hear it—once more before he dies. Let him tell us yet again, let it sink into our souls; for very, very soon there will be no voice in all the earth that can speak of Bethsaida, and of Capernaum, and of the sorrowful hour in the upper chamber, and of the Agony upon Calvary, and of the wonder of the Resurrection morning!"

So they clustered and clung; and we—we know too well their sad anxieties, their miserable sense of orphanage, their eagerness to make quite sure. We, too, would join our voices with theirs. "Oh! speak to us too, yet once again, dear master, our father, blessed John; we are sore harassed; we are troubled with many thoughts! Thou hast seen; thou hast lain upon His Breast. Make us sure with thy own sureness. Speak once more, and tell us. What was it that thou didst touch so nearly and love so dearly? Tell us wholly; tell us plainly. We would have thy experience: we would possess thy perfect witness!"

"We beheld His glory." That is the Apostle's deliberate answer; that is his description of the process which gained him conviction. "They beheld." They used the help of both eyes and mind; for the word suggests that they saw as men see when they let their minds follow their eyes—when they watch and think and learn as they look.

The Apostles had had no brief and unsteady sight of the Master. Nay! They had had time given them to rest their gaze upon Him, and to continue looking, as He moved, as He spoke, as He went up and down with them. In many moods and varied scenes, in hope and in fear, in exaltation and in depression, by day and by night, alone and in a crowd, as a Prophet in the glare of the public sun, as a Friend in the secrecy of confidence—in a thousand incidents unforeseen and surprising—in all they had been close, very close, to Him, and had looked with all their eyes, and had hung upon Him with all their souls, and had meditated over all that they saw, and had pondered and had brooded, and had done this slowly, by degrees, habitually, moving forward step by step to this great conclusion. So they had seen; in this sure and tested study of Him, they had lived and walked; and what was it they found by so looking?

They found a most wonderful thing. Within His flesh, deep down in the heart of His Being, there was a secret—a secret that lay hidden, and yet that could be seen and known by those who had the eyes of habitual and patient faith. It was like a Presence within a Temple—like a vision of God within the Holy of Holies—like that glory behind the veil of the sanctuary, girdled by the intervening courts, yet felt to be true by all, seen at sacred moments by privileged priests, who could bring report of it. So, within the Body of the Master those friends of His discovered His secret, His verity. It was there, as a hidden flame, which at intervals leaped out and reddened all the sky. And the secret, the verity, was unlike all that they had ever heard of in men. And yet they were not without experience of the highest human excellence. For they had been under the sway of that greatest of all earth's great ones—John the Baptist. He was not only a prophet, but more than a prophet; it was he whom the Lord Himself placed highest of those born of women. They had known the full splendour of that heroic spirit, who moved all Jerusalem and Judæa, until men mused in their hearts whether it were not the Christ Himself. Yet the secret of Jesus was totally divided, by irresistible and unhesitating distinctions, from everything, however high and pure, that could be found in him or any other. When once they had known it, it was simply impossible to confuse it again with any of those gifts which grace and ennoble human character.

No! of one thing they were convinced. That which they found in Him was something that had not been in the world at all before Jesus came. It was not merely a higher form of that which had been already in others, even in the highest—in the Baptist, or in Moses. As they had known all that the Baptist could do, so, too, they had felt all that Moses could bring them. He had brought them a great gift. He had given them a law from God. But this peculiar grace and life which they now had received came into the world in Jesus Christ, and Him only. So strange, so new, so marvellous, so incomparable was this deep secret on which they had found themselves gazing.

And what was it, then, this secret? How could it be told, this discovery? "Well," the Apostle says, "it was nothing short of the supreme vision of all visions. It was (and we, as we waited and watched, became more and more certain of it)—it was the disclosure, the unveiling of God Himself. It was in character, in substance, in reality, God's own glory. Whatever men have found God to be,—whatever our fathers of old time felt God to be, as He shone in upon their hearts through the splendour of the Shekinah in the Tabernacle of Moses,—that same thing Jesus showed Himself to be and mean to us who so closely studied and loved Him. We saw Him, saw Him long, saw Him very near, saw Him very carefully; and what we saw in Him was the glory of God—the glory as of the Only Begotten Son of the Almighty Father."

"Ah! but how could you be sure of that? What proofs have you? What experience? Could you have been mistaken?"

"We had both outward proofs and inward experiences," the Apostle answers. "Outwardly, there was John. He asserted what we assert. He came for the very purpose of declaring it, and he made his declaration with unfaltering courage, and with unconquerable force. John stood and cried, and said, 'Lo! there standeth One among you Whom ye know not, the latchet of Whose shoe I am unworthy to loose!' He, the highest of prophetic seers; he, who saw furthest of all yet born of women into the ways and the mind of God—he gave us the first witness. He first made it possible to believe it.

"And, then, we had our experiences; and of these we cannot conceivably be mistaken. For, indeed, we received within our own selves this secret of Christ; we had it given us; and we took of it; we shared in His life, in His substance. Of that very power with which He was filled, of that we ourselves partook, through faith. 'Of His fulness we all received.' It was in us, and at work, and alive. How could we mistake it? It made itself manifest in us in its double form—in grace, which is the new energy; and in truth, which is the new reality. We became what we had not been before. We found ourselves vitalised with the sonship of God; authorised and enabled to become new creatures. We looked at our old selves, and we knew this without a doubt, that not of them, not out of their impotence, had these strange and novel capacities sprung. No! Not of anything that could be found in us—not of blood, nor will of flesh, nor will of man. These could not account for it. The power that was within us was the Name of God. The light that shone out from us was the glory of God. We had it; we held it; we felt it; we were quickened, renewed, endowed by it. We moved in it, we fed on it. We could not hesitate, or doubt. To doubt? How was it possible? 'As many as received Him, to them He gave power to become the sons of God.' The power was there in them, and they knew it—they were born of God."

Dearly beloved in the Lord, we, too, to-day, sit clustering in Christ's Church, and still we keep our faith; but our hearts are anxious and troubled, as were the hearts of those who clustered around St. John at Ephesus. We are harassed by loud and importunate inquirers; we are harried by sharp attacks, and great gusts of doubt sweep over us and through us; and we shake as dry and shivering leaves whirled under naked skies by wintry winds.

Oh, if only we could but have once heard him speak! if but once we could have listened to that voice, that tarried so long behind its Lord! So we pray, so we think; and yet we have the words it spake, certified to us by those who sat round him long ago. "This is the disciple that testifieth of these things, and wrote these things: and we, we who sit listening round him, we know that his testimony is true." So those dead voices still speak to us, reassuring our trembling belief; and he, too, the old man now so soon to die, he positively assures to us, before he goes, the clearness and the certainty of his testimony. "He who saw it, he, and no other, bare record; and his record is true, and he knoweth that he saith true." And from that hour to this the continuous Church of Christ, One and Apostolic, outliving all times and changes, hands down from generation to generation that certified and sworn testimony, and declares, with unbroken and unhesitating voice, to all who will take or read, "This is the disciple, John, who testifieth of these things, and wrote these things; we know that his testimony is true."

We doubt the book; we cry for the living man. Yes. But these same suspicious fears would haunt us still, even if we were listening to the living voice. Is it not an old and dying man, we should be saying, talking of days very long ago? Can we trust his memory? Can we commit ourselves to his assertions? How can we tell, how can he himself tell, what changes he may have brought into his story through fifty years of brooding imagination? No, dear people: we can never get back behind all perplexities, and scruples, and doubtings. No living voice would save us from them. For the living voice asks for faith— just as much the dead book; and faith is faith. It cannot escape from its conditions. It must always, to the last, remain an act of confidence, of confidence in two things—of confidence (1) in human honesty, (2) and in Divine truthfulness. If we are not prepared to give God and man this confidence we can never push through our difficulties into the peace of belief.

Argue and discuss as we will, finally we must find ourselves facing a simple assertion, " God said," over against which can always be heard the lurking whisper of the serpent, " Hath God indeed said? " And the assertion that we face is the assertion always of a man. God's Word reaches us through the human minister. The act of faith in God's Word, therefore, asks of us always an act of trust in a man—in his loyalty, in his capacity, in his sincerity. Always we must have in co-operation with the " God spake " the human witness who asserts, " I that saw it do now bear record; and I know that my testimony is true." And, therefore, whether through book or through voice, it does not matter. Finally, we can but pass by unanswered all your swarm of questions, and challenge you with the direct appeal—Will you trust John, who lay on the breast of his Lord? Will you trust the disciple whom Jesus loved? Will you trust the corroborating Church which declares to you " This is the disciple John, who wrote these things : we know that he saith true "? Yes; and if he, John, tells you things which amaze and stagger, will you still trust, oh doubting and bewildered souls—will you trust an old man of ninety years, who has put his witness to all those violent and terrible tests which had for sixty years assaulted the infant Church of the first century? Who could know if not he who had touched and tasted and handled? Who could know the worth and the certainty of faith like him to whom it had been a living and life-long experience, approved by persecution, attested by his joy, made evident in the perfect beauty and grace of his Christ-like love?

Such a one as John the aged, the beloved, it is who says to you, on the very verge of the grave—" I saw it; I saw His glory; and I tell you, it was the glory of the very Son of God.

" We beheld it." The belief, personal and proved, of individual believers is the final proof and testimony of the truth as it is in Jesus.

This is the fruit of our faith towards our fellow-men, to be able to say to them, " I have seen; I can speak; and I know that I say true."

And this is the crown and honour of a Christian old age, that it should be able to offer before all men the flower of all conviction, the witness of a prolonged and approved experience. And such a flower of blameless and beautiful witness he certainly bore who has passed so swiftly from ruling this great Church of London into the sleep of Christ.[1]

My brethren, it is no light task to make old age a gracious and beautiful sight. But he had so made it. In him it was most tender, and lovely, and benign. In him it was no time of pitiful decay; but rather it came carrying with it a yet sweeter goodness, a yet gentler dignity, a fatherliness that was always fair, and yet now seemed to win a yet fairer gift of kindly sanctity. To the very end he grew in grace; and round his last years, which are (in so many) such sad shadows of brighter days, there gathered yet more peace, and love, and goodwill, and gladness than ever

[1] Dr. Jackson, Bishop of London.

even in the days before. No one could look upon that life, or on that face, and not be absolutely certain that here before him was one who had gained firm and serious hold on spiritual things, one who could draw on some deep wells of piety, and thankfulness, and peace.

So he stood here, last Sunday[1]—he, whose body is already committed to the dust, and whose soul is now wrapped in silence. So he stood in this pulpit, full of the gracious tenderness of age; and all that tenderness and all that grace he offered as a witness to the faithfulness of that Master to Whom he had for so long, with unshaken loyalty, surrendered himself.

Could he have been mistaken in his surrender, in his belief? Only if you could be mistaken in the kindly beauty of temper which was its fruit. If the fruit was so sound, can the root have been corrupt? If the issue be so fair, can the belief be false? Do men gather figs from thorns or grapes from thistles? Nay, indeed! Up through the long seventy years he had served a Master Who had never failed him, and now old, and on the very edge of death, He was there to deliver the unwavering witness. He had seen —had seen the inner secret of Jesus; and lo! it was the glory, the glory of the only Son of God! This was his record, and he knew that he said true, and that record which he delivered here alive among you last Sunday he now utters out of the homes of the silent dead. Death has sealed the record, death that tries all. In the vivid hour of death we see what

[1] January 4, 1885.

it is that endures when God shaketh terribly the
earth. Oh, my brothers! you, too, are dying. But,
verily, you may yet, while you stand here, before you
taste of death, see the kingdom come among you of
eternal life. For Christ is still with us; Christ is
still strong; Christ may yet be seen in glory. And
those whose lives are enriched by prayer and ennobled
by grace shine before us as stars to confirm His glad
Epiphany.

Oh, follow where the star is leading! Follow and
trust the Wise Men, full of years, full of experience,
who are bowing down before a new-born Child on a
Virgin Mother's knee, and are offering there the sweet
gifts of a beautiful old age—gold, and frankincense,
and myrrh.

THE STORY OF A DISCIPLE'S FAITH.

*"𝔗𝔥𝔢𝔫 𝔴𝔢𝔫𝔱 𝔦𝔫 𝔞𝔩𝔰𝔬 𝔱𝔥𝔞𝔱 𝔬𝔱𝔥𝔢𝔯 𝔡𝔦𝔰𝔠𝔦𝔭𝔩𝔢, 𝔴𝔥𝔦𝔠𝔥 𝔠𝔞𝔪𝔢 𝔣𝔦𝔯𝔰𝔱 𝔱𝔬 𝔱𝔥𝔢 𝔰𝔢𝔭𝔲𝔩𝔠𝔥𝔯𝔢, 𝔞𝔫𝔡 𝔥𝔢 𝔰𝔞𝔴, 𝔞𝔫𝔡 𝔟𝔢𝔩𝔦𝔢𝔳𝔢𝔡."—*JOHN xx. 8.

JOHN, the beloved disciple, has given his witness, has made his confession. What he once touched and tasted and handled, that he has declared unto us. It was the shining, the epiphany of God the Father which he and the Twelve had discovered, tabernacled close at their side in the body of Christ. " We saw His glory, the glory as of God Himself." So he pronounces. Yet still his listeners sit on about his feet. They hear great words, but these words are the end of a long and anxious meditation. The Apostle in these leading verses is giving them his completed conclusions; and they have accepted the conclusions, they hold them fast. But it is not enough to know what they ought to believe, though that is much—they must also know the process by which the conclusion is to be reached. They must reproduce in themselves the living story of its formation. They must be conscious of its stages, its degrees, and its growth. They cannot afford to be as reapers entering into the labours of others who went forth weeping with good seed. They must feel their own faith grow, first the blade, then the ear, and so at last, in ample richness, the full corn in the ear; and therefore they went on wondering. "Let us hear it all," they say: "tell us of that day when first it came to you that something wonderful was there. Tell us how you slowly learned the great mystery; and then tell us when and how it was that the full truth broke from your heart and from your lips. Tell us this, that so we too may say with you and with ten thousand times ten thousand: 'Worthy is the Lamb that was slain.'"

Here is the question that St. John sets himself to answer; and you can see that it is so by this—that he begins his Gospel, not with our Lord's own beginning, the Baptism by John, but with the day on which the disciples began to believe on Him; and he ends it, not with our Lord's own ending, His Ascension, but with the first completed confession of Jesus by an Apostle,—the confession of Thomas. This achieved, his Gospel is done; he has nothing to add but one scene that to him was full of tender personal interest.

The fourth Gospel tells how the Apostolic faith was built and established. Let us carefully turn to it, for it is a revelation of the Apostle's own heart. The old man himself is bidding us draw near and taste of his own experiences. He unlocks his soul to us that he may help us to mount up into his assured peace, so calm, so strong. He sits there murmuring always his "Come, Lord Jesus, even come!" and round about him, enthroned in the majesty of age, is that mysterious silence in which the voices of the Spirit and the Bride say, "Come." And yet he can turn from that upward vision and bend his eyes back on us—on us so perplexed, and troubled, and hesitating, and fearful, and bewildered. He can yearn to make us have fellowship in his joy. "Little children, it is the last hour. Even now are there many anti-christs. And now, my little children, abide in Him. My little children, let no man lead you astray, for this is the true God and eternal life; and therefore, O my children, keep yourselves from idols." So tender, so beseeching, is his fatherly love!

And in the name of that love he sets himself to tell the story of his own conversion; how he had begun. He can recall every tiny detail of that first critical hour. It began on the day when John the Baptist cast off the hopes that were so eagerly bent upon him. For he it was, the Baptist, and not the Lord Jesus, who first woke in their hearts that spiritual movement which became Christianity. He it was who first evoked the cry of faith, and passionately they had given him their souls,—they, and all who, seeing John, mused in their hearts whether He were the Christ. Even the Pharisees of Jerusalem felt the excitement and shared the hope; and it was to their deputation that the Baptist made his great repudiation: "No; I am not the Christ; no, nor Elias, nor the prophet. I am nought but a flying cry in the wilderness, a cry that floats by on the wind and perishes. Not I, but Another—Another Who comes after me; yea, Who is now standing among you, even though you know it not." So he confessed. He denied not, but confessed; so brave a soul he had! All those hearts

were at his service, a world of devotion all lying there
at his feet; but he would not be tempted. He knew
his own limits; he would have none of it. He confessed, and denied not: "I am not the Christ."

And then came the great moment. It was the very
next day after the great confession—so exact is the
Apostle's memory. The very day after, John saw
Jesus coming towards him, and a wonderful word
broke from him: "Behold the Lamb of God, Which
taketh away the sin of the world." Taketh away the
sin! Oh, the peace of such a promise to those who
had been washed in Jordan, and had repented, and
had confessed, and yet found their burden of sin as
miserable, as intolerable as ever! The words haunted
them; and when, the day following, John uttered
them again, two of them at least could not rest.
Their hearts burned to know more. Who is this
strange visitant—so quiet, so silent, so unobserved?
He makes no sign. He says no word. He invites no
attention. He does not even stop to look. He just
passes by; and, lo, He is already passed—in another
moment He will have gone. They must act for themselves then. They must force Him to stop and tell
them the secret. So two of them that heard John
speak followed Him—two of them, and John the beloved who now tells us the story was one of the two.
And now that they followed, He, the stranger, must
turn and speak. Then, for the first time, He looked
upon them with that look which again and again had
power to draw a soul, by one glance, out of the night
of sin into the life of eternal light. He turned and

saw them following, and it was then they heard His voice first speak,—that voice which by its cry could raise the dead. "Whom seek ye?" That was all. And they,—they hardly knew what to say,—only they must see Him, must go with Him; and they stammered out, "Rabbi, where dwellest Thou?" And He said, "Come and see."

Come and see! It was all as quiet and natural and easy as any ordinary interview. No one could have seen anything unusual. Just a few words of salutation,—just three short sentences that could be said in half a minute. And yet that sealed their lot for eternity. That was the moment of decision. "Come and see." They went and saw. So intense is the Apostle's memory of that blessed hour that he can never forget the very hour of the day. It was just ten o'clock when he got to the house. They stopped there with Him that night; and in the morning they were sure of what they had found,—so sure that neither of them could rest until he had hurried off with the good news to find and bring his brother. Andrew found his brother before John could find James; or else it was that both went at once to seek for Peter, and Andrew found him first. Anyhow, when Peter was found, both were prepared to assert, "We have found the Christ." And so they brought the great chief to his Master; and in a moment the Master knew what He had won in that loyal, loving soul, and He turned those deep eyes upon him, and named him by his new name. "Thou art Simon, the son of Jonas; thou shalt be called Cephas."

So it all began. The very next day after that, the Master Himself added one other to the number—Philip, a friend of Peter's and Andrew's—and Philip brought Nathanael; and these were that little band whom the Master took with Him from Jordan to Cana—the seed of that great Church which was already reigning from Babylon to Rome.

" And what next," so the listeners ask, " what was the next step made ? " Three days later, at Cana, for the first time, came that strange secret of which the Apostle had spoken. The glory shone out with a sudden flash from the deeps within Him ; a word of power leaped out. Very few felt or knew it. But as the few saw there the white water redden into wine, they knew and felt the wonder of that change which had passed over their own being. That word of power was at its work within them, transforming them from out of sickly impotence into splendid energy. They saw now the full range of the Lord's authority, that it would be the same to Him whether He spoke to matter or spirit, to body or soul; whether He said, " Thy sins be forgiven thee," or " Rise up and walk." As water into wine, so the old passed into new.

Thus the light flashed ; thus the secret made its first disclosure. It vanished again, for His hour had not yet come ; but they had seen it, and this is John's enduring record, remembered by us this day,[1] that there first, at Cana, Jesus manifested His glory, and there His disciples first believed in Him.

And what next did they learn ? It was at Jeru-

[1] Second Sunday after Epiphany.

salem, the Passover feast. The Master made His first entry and startled them—for, He Who was so quiet and reserved, burned with a sudden fury as he looked upon the Temple of Jehovah. Very, very rarely did He show Himself excited or disturbed—but then He was terrible. He bound together a scourge of small cords: He drove the cattle in front of Him: He dashed over the money-changers' tables. And John can recall still the look of the coins as they poured down upon the pavement. And they, the disciples, wondered at the violence of the emotion, until a word from an old Psalm came into their minds, and they remembered how it was written that the zeal of the Lord's House should be in a prophet's heart like a devouring fire.

At that time too, the Lord Himself gave a sign and spoke a word, which the disciples could make nothing of. It was about the Temple being destroyed and raised again in three days. They forgot it; but afterwards, "when He had risen from the dead," the old words came back to them, "In three days I will raise it up," and they remembered then how He had spoken them two years before His Death, and, as they remembered, they believed.

It was also at Jerusalem, on that first visit, that they began to understand the Master's marvellous insight into the depths of human character. For at that feast there was a great show of belief in Him in many, and that belief looked to the disciples very strong and genuine, and everything seemed promising and confident. They longed for the Lord to go forward, and to seize the opportunity, and to trust Himself to the larger movement. But He surprised and disappointed them. He held strangely back. He would not trust that which was brought Him. He had no faith in its strength : and, as they watched, they saw that He was right. They saw that He could penetrate deep beneath outward show, and could estimate, and weigh, and judge, by some flawless balances of His own. Nothing could disguise itself from Him. He knew exactly where He was, what He could rely on, what would fail Him; and this He did without the helps that other men have to use. He did not have to wait and see how men would act or behave. He knew all about them before they acted. Nor did He need information about them from others. He could read out their secret somehow from within Himself. And this power of searching the heart—what was it but a privilege of God only, of Jehovah Whose " eyes are in every place " ? So at Jerusalem, at that first feast, they found it to be with Jesus, Who " knew all men, and needed not that any should testify of man, for He knew what was in man."

How can we stop to follow the Apostle through all the wonderful story? Yet just one thing we cannot pass over—the awful hour of crisis in Galilee. It came just when all looked brightest, when the people were rushing round Him and would have made Him a king. They would have gone with Him to the death. But He—He threw it all away to the winds. He hurried off the Twelve in a body across the lake, for they had caught the crowd's enthusiasm and could not be calmed. He scattered the crowd;

He fled back Himself alone into the dark hills; and on the morrow, at Capernaum, He broke it all down by a word which staggered the rising belief. It was a saying about His Body and His Blood,—a very hard saying. Not only were the Pharisees furious, but His own followers were dumbfounded. They could not bear it, could not believe. They fell away, and walked no more with Jesus.

"And you, O disciple dearly loved, what of you and your brethren?" "Most terrible, most bitter that hour, my children," the old man answers. "We walked trembling, quaking, behind Him. We were cowed and disheartened, until He, the Master, felt Himself the chill of our dismay, and He turned to us and challenged our failing faith. 'Will ye also go away?' Oh, the shame of being open to a charge of such meanness! The very tenderness of the question and of the reproach recalled and recovered us. We knew nothing. We could explain nothing. Every clue was lost. The darkness was thickening over our heads, our hearts were failing for fear, our souls were sinking in the great waterfloods, earth was falling from us, struggle and anguish and doubt shook us with wild alarm; and yet, even so, as He turned His eyes upon us, the old unconquerable faith woke and stirred and quickened; and with a rush, as of a mighty wind, it lifted us; and out from Peter's lips broke the words which saved us—the words which sealed us to Him for ever: 'Will we go away? Nay, Lord, to whom shall we go? Thou hast the words of eternal life!' So we spoke with burning hearts, and yet through and through us still those strange eyes of His pierced. Deep below all our emotion He penetrated. Quite calmly He weighed its worth; and in one of us even then He detected a rift which would widen and worsen. One of us, He knew, hung back from echoing Peter's confession. One spirit there was there that could not throw off its dismay, one dark spirit in whom the hard saying was the seed of bitter and poisonous fruit. 'Have I not chosen you Twelve, and one of you is a devil?' He spoke of Judas Iscariot who should betray Him."

So they followed and clung, the trembling band; clung through all the harrowing days in which the Jewish enmity hardened itself into the hate of hates; clung, even though their souls fell away from the rapture of Peter, to the desperate wail of Thomas: "Let us go with Him that we may die with Him;" clung, even through the terrors of that last evening, when they sat shaking with the very shudder of death, and the Soul of the Master Himself was trouble-tossed, and there was the scent of treachery in the air, and the end was very near, and He spake dim, dark words that they could not follow,—only they knew one thing, that He was to be taken from them, and they sat shrouded in a mighty sorrow such as no assurances even of His could lessen or lift. One moment there was indeed, even then, in which they seemed suddenly to lay hold of His meaning. "Now we believe," they cried. "Now we are sure that Thou camest forth from God." So they cried, and yet He met their professions with a sorrowful hesitation.

"Do ye now believe? Yea; the hour is all but come when ye will all flee and leave Me alone." How sad and cowed they felt at the rebuff! Were they, then, never to rise into the joy of clear and entire belief? Yes; it came at last—the blessed joy of perfect assurance! Let John tell how it was reached by him.

Two points he singles out for himself as marking epochs of his own conviction, and in them both we are let inside the workings of his innermost mind. And how curious, yet how natural, is the working! For in every hour of agony the mind becomes strangely and fearfully alert to very little things. It is sensitive to sudden and ineffaceable impressions. It is startled into the swiftest and subtlest activity by the tiniest touches of detail. Often in the supreme moment of a dark tragedy, the fibres of the imagination seem to close round some minute incident, such as the ticking of a clock in the hush of a death-chamber; and never throughout the long years that follow can it detach that tiny incident from its memory of the black hour. And so with St. John.

He stood below the bitter Cross, and he saw the nails beaten through the hands and feet, and he heard the last loud cry, and yet still his despair hung heavy as death upon his soul; until, just at the touch of the soldier's spear, there broke from the dead side a little jet of blood and water. What was it that he saw and felt? What was it that so startled him? Why could that little jet of blood and water never pass out of his sight? Why should it haunt him sixty years after, as still his heart wonders over the mysterious witness of the water and the blood? We cannot tell. Perhaps he could never tell. Only, his spirit woke with a start. Only, a strange tremor shook him, and somehow just then, just at that little pivot moment, he must break off all his story, to declare with abrupt and quivering emphasis: "This is the disciple that wrote these things. He it is who saw the water and the blood, and he knows that his record is true."

And once again, in the haste of the Resurrection morning, what was the moment and what was the scene which turned his despair into belief? It was the moment at which he stooped down and saw within the empty tomb the folded napkin and the linen clothes. What did he notice? why, that the napkin that had been round the Master's head was not lying with the linen clothes, but was rolled up in a place by itself. A tiny, tiny thing! Yet somehow it was that which he saw and never forgot. It was that which he could never omit from his story of the Resurrection— the rolled-up napkin lying apart from the linen clothes. Was it the sudden sense that struck him of order and seemliness, as of a thing premeditated, intended? Was it the reaction of detecting the quiet tokens of deliberate purpose there, where all had seemed to him a very chaos of confusion? Who can say? Only just then a key was somehow turned and a bolt shot back somewhere within his breast, and a secret flashed in upon him, and a thrill of insight rushed over him, and his blindness fell off as it had been scales, and a quiver of hope shot up like a flame, and a new light broke over him, and he passed at one bound out of death into life. "Then entered in, therefore, that other disciple which came first to the tomb, and he saw and believed."

My brethren, where do you stand? How far have you come in this pathway of faith? Are you yet at the beginning, looking wistfully with hungry eyes, after a hundred gallant human heroes who point you this way and that? Are you musing in your heart which of them may be your guide and master, which is the Christ? Good, and fair, and high they may be; but they must all confess it, they cannot deny it,— they are not the Christ. And all of them who are honest will earnestly assure you, "It is not I, but Another." Oh, and that Other even now standeth among you, though you know Him not yet; and there is a voice gone out upon Him which has gone out upon none other ever born of woman, with this witness, "Behold the Lamb of God Which taketh away the sin of the world!"

Consider it. What an assurance! Who is there that has ever been brave enough to accept such a salutation without a whisper of protest, without a shadow of a scruple? Who is this that dares to stand up before the entire mass of his fellows and say, "Come all who are weary and heavy laden—come all who are burdened sorely with sin —come all to Me—I will give you rest." Who is He? Look at Him. He is passing even now before you. Follow Him. He is very quiet, and still, and silent—but follow Him. He will turn at last, and speak, and invite you—invite you a little further. "Master, where dwellest Thou?" "Come and see."

O Jesus, Lord and lover of souls, there are many of us laden with sickness and sin, so many that are sad with doubt and fear, that are asking, " Master, where dwellest Thou ? " Oh, let them even come home with Thee and see.

Go and see. Abide with Him, talk with Him. Wait upon Him. Learn His words. Take up His Gospels. Read them with care, with silence to yourself, with thought and prayer. Abide with Him one night at least, that you may in the morning be able to tell your fellows, " I have found the Christ." And after that, suddenly, now and again, a light will flash, and a glory be made manifest to you. Some touch of divine benediction will break out of the secret silence, some sudden joy, some gift of power. It will be with you as at Cana when the water ran into wine. Yet this, when it comes, remember, is not the end. It is but a pledge. You may not cling to the blessings and the gifts of faith. They flash and disappear, and you will not be surprised to find that you have yet a long road to travel—a road of disappointment, of increasing failure, of gathering pain, of enlarging doubt :—doubt, why not? Doubt of the ways and the methods of God, doubt of the path as the darkness encompasses, doubt of Christ's meaning, of His wisdom, of His readiness, of His care, of His guidance. The obscurity may even deepen as you advance along the road of faith. The storm may grow blacker and fiercer, —for the higher your faith in God, the darker will be your despair at His failure to make His Name good. And you will find Him strange. He will seem to make so little way in the world, He will seem to miss opportunities. It is very hard to believe in One in Whom others believe less and less every day. And then it is, when all are falling away, and the hard sayings of theology begin to harass and repel, then it is that you must call with all your might upon the inner faith, that you may have the heart of fire which will feel but one thing—will feel that though the world fall into ruins and though the power of God Himself be hidden, yet there stands the Christ still facing you with the question, "Will you go away? Will you fail as others fail Me?" Then it is that you must be bold to send out your faith in the one passionate cry, "Lord, Thou art here, and that is enough! Thou hast the words of eternal life. To whom can I go? Though all men forsake Thee, yet will not I; and in spite of all, I believe, and am sure that Thou art the Christ, the Holy One of God." That is the faith which is felt indeed as a rock under the feet, and to such faith the love of God will make itself more and more manifest. You who will so trust Him in the black night, you who can walk on, knowing nothing but that Christ goes before you, you who immutably cling with the violence of an ineradicable love to Him Who has enthralled you,—you will find yourselves carried on day after day, you know not how, until at last you find yourselves enclosed in some upper chamber with the Master. Yes, and there the secrets of His love will be disclosed, and the mysteries of His counsels and the hidden wonder of His victory and the strange glory of His consolation. You will not know or understand all;

you will feel yourselves held in the grasp of a wisdom
that reaches far and away beyond your little day. You
will inquire with stammering lips as Philip and Judas
(not Iscariot) and Thomas stammered in the upper
chamber before you, and the answer that He gives will
be but dim; and yet you will know enough to make
you absolutely sure that the truth as you held it in
Jesus is the truth that holds the world in one in God,
and you will be able to cry, in glimpses of peculiar
manifestation, "Lord, now speakest Thou plainly and
speakest no parable. Now, I believe and have known
and am sure that Thou camest forth from God."

And yet, even that faith, the faith of roused feelings,
may lapse again; even that moment of blessing may
lose its power over you. Yes, for only when you
become convinced, not only of your possession of a
Teacher Who once came on earth from God, but more,
of a Lord living on the far side of death, living in the
might of a Resurrection life, able to stand by you in
that life-giving might as you abide here with the
faithful in the upper chamber, able to feed you with
His life now from that home of His beyond the grave
—only then, when you so receive Him, and take of
Him, and taste Him, and know yourselves quickened
in Him—only so will your last doubt pass away from
you—only so will the close of the crown of your faith
be obtained, and you will end—as the story of St. John
ends—with the cry of doubting Thomas when his last
doubt scattered, the cry in which the perfected
Apostolic faith at last saluted its risen Master, " Jesus
Christ, my Lord and my God."

The Church in the Gospels

THE ROCK—THE SECRET—THE FELLOWSHIP —THE WITNESS—THE RESOURCES—THE MIND—THE MINISTRY—OF THE CHURCH.

SERMON III.

THE ROCK OF THE CHURCH.

WE are Churchmen. We believe in the Holy Catholic Church. What is it so to believe? and why do we believe it? We are apt to be content with partial and arbitrary answers to such a question. We are Churchmen by historical accident perhaps: we found ourselves born so, and we see no reason to regret it. Or we are Churchmen by preference, because it suits us. Or we are Churchmen because some organisation of Christians is expedient and useful, and history has shown the Church system and rule to be the most practical, and the most enduring. Or, again, we have a higher reason,—we are Churchmen because we believe that the technical validity of the Sacraments is assured to us most clearly by an Apostolic Ministry. And yet none of these answers, not even the last, goes back to the very root of the question: "What is it to believe in the Catholic Church?" For belief is nothing if it is not practical; it must of necessity penetrate the life and colour our character; it must lay hold of heart and soul; it must touch home on the central core of our spiritual being. How is our

life, then, made different by believing in the Church ?
What is the mind which such a belief prompts and
builds and directs? What is the will which it animates and the desire which it enkindles ? What is
the character, the tone, the activity which issue
instinctively out of so believing ?

And in answering such primary questions we need
not concern ourselves at all, as yet, with the discussion and justification of a particular Church system
and ministry. We go back behind any such inquiry ;
and, believe me, this is a vital matter, for, unless we
do so, any such discussion is bound to be inconclu-
sive. For there is a background on which all arguments for a particular system rest, a background of
assumptions, anticipations, expectancies, to which all
such arguments make their appeal.

What is it, then, this background? Before we ask
why we should trust a special Church system of orders,
we must be sure that we expect already to find some
system and some organisation. Now, where do we
get that preliminary expectation? How is it that
we Churchmen find in the very act by which we
believe in Christ Jesus, a reason for expecting a
Church? Why should our individual and personal
union with Him feel marred and stunted and meagre
unless it can realise itself in some organisation ?
This is the expectation, the anticipation, which forms
the mind of the Churchman ; it is this mind which
he brings to the discussion of a threefold Ministry. " I
believe in Christ Jesus" seems to him to open out of
itself, without effort or strain or change, into " I believe

in the Holy Catholic Church." And this belief affects, or ought to affect, not his head only, but his heart, his life, his character; and, more than that, it ought to affect, indeed it must affect, his conception of our Lord Himself.

Let us take this last point to-day—belief in a Church affects our belief in Christ Jesus; it involves, that is, a particular reading of His Life-work, a particular conception of His purpose, of His mind, of His desires, of His plan while He was here with us on earth. If we include the Church in the Creed, we must mean that the story of our Lord's Life includes and involves the story of the Church, and that we could not read the Gospels themselves without seeing there the origin and the necessity of Christ's Church. Now, do the Gospels, as we ordinarily read them, convey that to us? Let us consider them.

There is a familiar picture which the Gospel story leaves at first sight upon nearly every mind, a picture so easy, so natural, so satisfactory, that it is but too apt to arrest the imagination and entangle the understanding. " Jesus of Nazareth went about doing good." That is a story we can lay hold of. He is in Galilee among the hills and the fishermen, far from the heartless and harsh city, far from the disputing schools and the narrow priestcraft of Jerusalem. He lives among the villages, and simple country folk are flocking after His Feet; all the long evening He stands at some quiet door, and they bring the sick and the maimed to the blessing of His touch, and all are made whole. He sits on some hill, and words fall from His lips that enthral and pierce and quicken. And He forbids none to come near; if they be but weary and heavy laden, all may come unto Him; let them be but children, they shall not be forbidden; let them be but suffering or diseased, and, and even though He have not so much as time to eat bread, He yet will heal them all: so gracious, so tender is the Son of Man—so He calls Himself,—the name of compassion, of sympathy, of human-hearted-ness, and brotherly kindness. The Son of Man!—yes, and Son of God, we cannot but name Him, for some Divine, unearthly presence is there within Him. "Never man spake like this Man." "Never before have we seen it in this fashion." "With power commandeth He the unclean spirits, and they obey Him." "He speaks with authority, and not like a scribe." "What manner of Man is this, Whom even the winds and the sea obey?" "No man could do such miracles unless God were with Him." "Son of Man," so He names Himself: "Son of God," so we may gladly name Him, we who are drawn after Him as those crowds of old were drawn, we who carry to Him still our sicknesses and our sores, and listen as of old to the voice with which He speaks as never man spake. Son of Man and Son of God, so our hearts salute Him; for indeed they cannot help it. But do not press us (so we cry) with inquiries what our words may mean. It needs no commentaries, no definitions, no theologies to know the sway of Jesus. We cannot tell what He is; we only know that we were blind and now we see, we were deaf and now we hear; or at least we follow with the crowd behind Him and know that He has a fascination such as we find in no other.

That seems to us the Gospel story in its main import. The sower scatters the seed, and is careless where it falls. Jesus defines nothing, organises nothing, asks nothing of the believer,—nothing at least, we say, but a blind emotion of the heart towards Him—faith. He says little of Himself and almost nothing of a Church; it is to the loose multitudes that He devotes Himself. There is His home, we think; His work, His happiness. He is slain as soon as He leaves the simple folk in Galilee, and ventures to approach the city and its misguided priests. So He lived and so He died, and the work of the Lord is still continued in this ancient and patient fashion by the written records of that life on earth; and still, wherever they are scattered abroad, men's hearts are stirred, and their souls shake, and their spirits rise and follow, as again the old words fall with comfort on their ears.

"Jesus of Nazareth went about doing good." That is a true, a gracious, and a blessed memory. But why stop at the beginning of the story? Why not touch the rest? If we only read on, we shall find what will surprise us, as it surprised St. Peter and the rest. "He went about doing good;" but why is it, then, that the Lord flies from this good work of His?—for He certainly does. The very first day of it He escapes alone to the hills, and His disciples have to go and find Him. All men are searching for Him; why is He not to be found? And more and more, as the days go on, He withdraws, He escapes, He hides Himself beyond the lake in heathen hills. He does not seem to want these crowds any more. It is only because He cannot be hid that they find Him, and when they find Him He scatters them; He goes further and further afield away from them; away among heathen Greeks, away to the borders of Tyre and Sidon, among those to whom He is not sent, and for whom He cannot do good works. He enters there into the houses, and will not have His presence known. He does all He can to avoid publishing His works. He takes the sick aside, He charges them to tell no one; yes, and He rebukes them, we are told, with real passion, for their eagerness to make Him known. And this strange avoidance of what we suppose to be His main aim and work steadily increases and sharpens. He seems at last to feel the work of healing to be almost an interruption, an obstruction. It obscures His true meaning, it hides Him from the people. They eat of the loaves, and in their wonder at the miracle see no sign, attain no understanding of Him Who stands in their midst. And then, what is that startling cry at the foot of the hill of Transfiguration, when the father pleads for his boy ? —"O faithless and perverse generation, how long shall I be with you, how long shall I suffer you ? " So He speaks, as if weary of their dulness, who come to Him only under the stress of some blind hunger, and only want Him to cure their ills. While, indeed, He is there, their cries cannot but enter into His ears and His compassion must be at work. But how long, how long, is He to be with them, and they to see no more in Him than this ?

And then there come those fearful words about the parables,—what do they convey? "Lord, why speakest Thou to them, the crowd, in parables?"—"That seeing they may not see, and hearing they may not hear." These stories, so easy and taking, these are a hedge, then, a barrier between Him and the loose crowd. He uses them because He is forced to refrain from too open speech. He must probe and examine his hearers. He needs a sieve through which to sift those only who can hear with ears. Blessed the ears of those who press in behind and listen, who have their appetite whetted by the beauty of those tales. But there are those who, until they obtain ears to hear with, must of necessity remain without. Because they are without He speaks to them in parables. What is all this?—and there is more. As the days go on He sets Himself to throw off the crowds that dog His steps; He shakes them back with hard sayings, until they fall away, as He seems to expect. He turns round upon them with hard and repellent commands: "If any man will come after Me, let him take up his cross; let him hate father and mother and sister and brother, yea, himself also, or he is not worthy." And He puts sharp tests to those that offer to come with Him; He will have no follower who cannot live as He does, in a worse case than the foxes or the birds. He cannot let His disciples even go back to say "Good-bye" to father and mother, or perform the last rites of the grave: that is to look back from the plough—that is to go back from life to death. And He bids the crowd, all of them, to count the cost before they join Him; for it is a large work, and it will be ridiculous to begin and then fail to finish; it will be a bitter war, and it will be pitiful to yield at the mere sight of the foe in his array: so to start and fail is more demoralising than never to have started at all.

What is all this? We may wonder even as His brethren wondered in faithlessness. "Why," they said, "this secrecy? No man can do such things as these and not desire to have them published." We may wonder, out of our very faith, as St. John wondered in the early days in Jerusalem, when men flocked about the Lord and were ready to believe and follow. They looked so sincere and so hearty in their faith; and yet, to the Apostle's surprise, Jesus gave them no encouragement, would not rely upon them, would not open out to them. No, He did not commit Himself unto them, so John noted; and he perceived that the Lord read deep, that He knew by a strong intuition what was in men, and saw reason to distrust them.

So those close to Him wondered; and, as they watched Him, they saw a new and marvellous thing: His inner Heart, His deeper Mind, they saw, was concerned with something far away from those Galilean crowds. For them His love and tenderness do indeed stream out in help and consolation, but He holds a secret, and He walks with some hidden motive, some purpose, some plan, some work not here, not amid those hills. His eyes are set elsewhere, His being is bent upon another goal. This Galilean time is but a delay, a pause in the great work set before Him, and His very success almost interrupts Him. He takes pains, therefore, to avoid it, to break it, to hide Himself from it, because He is bracing Himself to some strange, hard task. What is it, and where? Look how it sometimes possesses Him! Now and again the disciples catch sight of that secret intent, and feel its tremendous pressure, as the Lord strained, as it were, under the awful responsibility. "I have a baptism to be baptised with; how am I straitened until it be accomplished?" He has a cup to drink, so harsh and so bitter, who can drink it with Him? He who would follow whither He is set on going must be ready for a cross, and not for a throne. And we know what that secret of His is. It is the exodus, the Decease that He should accomplish at Jerusalem— that secret of His Transfiguration. It is on this, that He is always pondering; it is for this He is ever preparing. He is but in Galilee through compulsion, because He can walk no more in Judæa for fear of the Jews, because He has no honour in His own Judæan country. St. John asserts this plainly, but the other Gospels tell us as plainly that He is in Galilee only that He may return to face that death already decreed of God, and determined of the Jews; He is in Galilee to be withdrawn from His foes for a time; and, ever as those foes from Jerusalem dog His steps, He retreats and He hides, for as yet His time has not come. "I go not up to this feast." He goes not up; but His thoughts are ever in Jerusalem, and everything is being steadily shaped for that great day of His which draws on apace, when once more He will tread the streets of the Holy

City, and the deed commanded of the Father will be done, and the cup of the Father will be drunk, and the work will be finished, and the Son of Man will attain the end of His coming, and will be glorified. "Behold, we go up to Jerusalem, and all things that are written concerning the Son of Man shall be accomplished"— so He spoke to them incessantly and insistently. "From that time He began to say unto them, Behold, we go up to Jerusalem;" and when at last, all things being ready, He moves forward in this intent so long repressed, towards His baptism wherewith he has been so terribly straitened, He is so possessed with the exultation of achievement that His disciples can but creep behind Him, cowed and alarmed; for lo! He seems transfigured, and there is something terrible in His Face; He moves even as He who should come from Edom with dyed garments from Bozra, He that travelleth in His strength, mighty to save; for "they were on the way going up to Jerusalem, and Jesus went before them and they were amazed, and as they followed Him they were afraid."

"Behold, we go up to Jerusalem." Here was His great secret, here His burden; this is the commandment He received from His Father, that He should lay down His Life for His sheep. On this He brooded. This was the Will of the Father which was to Him His meat and His drink; this was the baptism wherewith He should be baptised, and how was He straitened unto the day of its accomplishment! This was His secret; but not one word, not one whisper of all this to the Galilean crowds; not one syllable stole out to tell the secret that worked within—not one word. He moved among them tenderly and pitifully; He helped, He healed, He forgave; the mere sight of those unshepherded multitudes was enough to stir His compassion: but His Heart was hidden from them, and they knew and guessed nothing of His Mind. They knew nothing; and therefore He could only give them according to the measure that they had. Pity, infinite pity, He gave them—but Himself He never gave; He could not commit Himself unto them. His work, His mission, His purpose on earth,—how could they receive it? how could they understand it? They were far too occupied with their own needs, and hunger, and pains. They had children cast by devils into fires, they had boys lying sick of fevers, they had wants and sorrows and miseries of their own, and that is what occupies them. How can they take time and trouble to consider exactly Who He was Who stood there in their midst? And what could it matter by what Name He should be called? How could they decide whether He be the Messias or not? Why! He Himself is content with the vague title " Son of Man," and never calls Himself Messias. Why should they press questions which He never asks? Surely they may take Him as He stands, and as He offers Himself. Call Him by what name you will, call Him John the Baptist, Elias, one of the prophets,—that is enough—He is ready to save. Send out some passionate cry,—" Lord, come down to my child ere he die "—send it out and He is sure to come. Follow Him and He will fill you with strange bread on the hills; follow Him and listen, and feed, and be content. So the crowd followed, careless of what name they named Him, and therefore the crowd was unserviceable to Him. He would not use it, but held it off; He got Himself hidden from it, He never committed Himself to it.

For, indeed, He has work to do, urgent, vast, and awful, before the night draws on. Why is He here? He is come, not to heal a few sick folk only, but in the mind of those eternal counsels which reach from the beginning to the end, He is come to cast the stone from Heaven which shall break all the kingdoms of the earth and grind them to powder. He is come to gather into one act the entire story of the world, to fulfil all things that are written in Moses, and the Law, and the Prophets. He is come, laying His Hands on the courses of the stars, on the motions of the earth, on the empires of men, on the wars of the flesh, on the tyrannies of sin. He is here, as Samson, lifting the gates of death from the house of evil; He is here wrestling with principalities and powers; He is here to beget the new race of men; He is here to build the new House of GOD, the Temple of His Body. To build! How can He build on that loose and shifting rubble, on that blind movement of the crowd, so vague and so undetermined? To build on this is to build on the sand; and He is to build for eternity, and in the face of Hell. He is looking far ahead to the days of tribulation, when the strong winds will blow, and the great floods sweep down upon His House. There must be no sand under His Eternal

Temple. He must have rock, sure and steadfast, and that Rock is His own Name, the Name of the Christ made known and made alive in the heart of man. His Name,—confessed by men's lips, sealed upon men's souls, embodied in men's being, apprehended by man's spirit, His Name eaten as a food and drunk as a drink, so that men may become what He is, and may carry on His work, and may fulfil His life, and may bear His message, and may fill up His sufferings and drink of His cup,—His Name, so taken, is the One Foundation that may endure unto the end. And this Name is just what the crowd are most indifferent to. This is just that which they neglect, and confuse, and ignore. John the Baptist, Elias, Jeremiah, one of the Prophets —any name will do: what use in precision?

Where, then, can He find building ground? Not in them who bring Him but sand; only in those Twelve, selected, prepared, set apart from the crowd, led off with Him in lonely places, men who could be trained at last to penetrate His secret, to apprehend His life-work, to name His Name. "Whom say ye that I am?" "Thou art the Christ." Oh, the great opening, the relief of the soul! The Spirit of the Lord, so hidden, so repressed, leaps forward out of its secret place, out of its loneliness, out of its silence. At last, at last, He is through the sand; He has touched ground; He can begin. "Blessed art thou, Simon Barjonas; and I say unto thee, thou art Peter, and upon this Rock of My Name, now first apprehended, I will build My Church; and so build that the gates of death shall not prevail against it."

We said, dear brethren, that the question whether Christ organised and founded the Church would tell right home upon our own conduct, and indeed it is so; for it sets before us that searching question—" Are we among the crowds that follow, or with the Twelve who apprehend ? " If we stand among the crowd, we are as loose and rotten sand on which the Lord builds no Church, for the rock on which He builds is the clear confession of His Name. To stand among the crowd —is it not so at this hour with hundreds of us ? We stand among the crowd, swept along by the Christian movement, carried to church and back by habit, by inclination, by instinct, listening, wondering, blessed, comforted; and the old familiar words of Heaven and Faith hang pleasantly about our ears: but never once does Faith get hold upon us, never once do we feel its decisive grip. All life long we may be in that dream. We are as those who listened to parable after parable by the quiet waters, as the Lord taught them from a boat. Like them, we sit impressed, charmed, even enthralled; but like them, too, we have never once broken through our dream, never once pressed our way in with the Twelve there in the house, with them who are pushing their eager questions : " Why, why dost Thou speak to them in parable ? Tell us what that parable means." To how many in this church to-day is Christ still speaking in parables ? To how many is His whole Life and Death and Resurrection no more than parable ?

" But He will be merciful," we say; " surely He will not be hard upon us, because we cannot name His

Name with precise certainty; He will be good and tender to those who have followed Him hither and thither." Yes, He is very good, and His compassions fail not, but are new every morning. Very good He will be to you, very tenderly He will feed you, and if you call upon Him in trouble He will hear you, and if you bring Him your sores in faith He will heal you; but one thing He will never do—He will never " commit Himself unto you," He will never tell you His secret, never unburden to you His heart, never reveal to you His Name and mission, never ask you to share in His baptism and drink of His cup. All this will be hidden from your eyes, and you will never know or understand the eternal counsels, nor the secret of the select friends, nor the mystery of the Church, nor the joy of His service, nor the splendour of His glory, nor the hidden life with the ascended Lord in Heaven. He will hear you, He will save you: but He cannot do more; He must pass you over in pathetic silence; and you will never know what He wanted of you, never know His disappointment in you, never suspect your own failure. You are without; you have never found your way in, and seeing Him you will see not, and hearing Him you will hear not.

And yet you may find the way to Him, you may hear, and understand, if only you will get through the shifting sand, if only you will dig down to the rock. Search yourselves through; ask, examine, probe,— " What do I think of Christ? Whom do I say that He the Son of Man is? What does He mean? What is His mission? What is His task? What is there behind the charm, the goodness, the patience? What is it He darkly hints—this death at Jerusalem, and this call of me to Himself? What does it involve? How far will it go? How much does it require of me? What use may I be to Him?" So examine yourselves, so press down to the deep of your being, so probe home, and you will find the rock at last, the rock of a clear confession, the rock of revelation from the Father, when faith is no longer an instinct of flesh and blood, but a spiritual apprehension. You will see with clear eyes, you will hold with firm hands, you will confess His Name, "Thou art the Christ;" and the blessing of Peter will fall upon you: "Blessed art thou, My son, blessed art thou! Here is the rock on which I can build; here is a stone laid for My Eternal Church."

SERMON IV.

THE SECRET OF THE CHURCH.

"I have manifested Thy Name unto the men whom Thou gavest me out of the world."—JOHN xvii. 6.

WE are asking, What is it that the Gospels have to tell us of a Church? And this, not in a few rare texts, open, as all isolated texts must be, to discussion and hesitation,—but in their inherent and vital teaching, as expressed throughout the length and breadth of their consentient record. And we put this question in its most crucial form if we ask it thus—Do the four Gospels imply that our Lord Jesus was content to throw the truth down upon the open area of the world, and to leave it to make its own way, to shape its own course, among the listening crowds, undirected and unorganised? Did He discharge His message without taking securities who should hear it? Was He as a sower who sowed His seed without asking where it fell?

Here is the salient question, and the answer is absolutely certain and precise. *Some* seed there was He cast out loose among the multitudes, to fall where it would; *some* general offer of Himself He made to all who passed by, to all who drew near: but such offer, such message, was only experimental, suggestive parabolic. It acted as a test, as a probe, as a sieve. It operated as a judgment between man and man, between those that had ears to hear, and those who hearing heard not. His full significance was never told the crowd. No, not even though the pathetic appeal came up from the bewildered Jews, "Tell us plainly, art Thou the Christ?" It could never be told plainly. It could never utter itself in words that would be plain to those who were not in the moral condition of His sheep, and who could not, therefore, know His voice. His Name, which is Himself, could never be committed to the floating crowd. Nor was His inner secret ever once cast down loose to take its chance. On the contrary, the Gospel story is the record of the pains and anxiety with which the Lord sifted, selected, prepared those few to whom this, His vital and essential message, should be committed. Where else but in this lies the terrible interest of the Gospels? We are spectators at a living drama. We watch the Lord passing through the multitudes, as they sway beneath and about Him, like great tides that roll, and swing, and lapse, and roll again, under the quiet eye of the moving moon. We know the silent secret that He holds deep buried—His Death at Jerusalem—on which His entire Will is unerringly bent. We know; but those crowds know nothing, suspect nothing. Who is there that will ever believe the report? Who will be found to understand, and share the tremendous news? To whom will the arm of the Lord be revealed? We wait, and watch, as one by one they are detected, detached, elected. Two there are, first, who followed that silent Teacher home, and abode with Him in His own house. And each of these has a brother to bring on the morrow. Strange things they learned, alone there in the house with Him; and they could tell what they had learned: "We have found the Christ." Andrew findeth Peter. And, then, there is one on whom our Lord's eye has already fallen: "Jesus findeth Philip;" and Philip, once brought, can bring another, the Jew without guile. The work is beginning, but a whole year will pass before four of these, who so heard and learned, will be summoned to the intimacy of discipleship, and will be shaped for the great work. And not yet, even to them, is a word said of the inner secret. Much is first to be done: fierce trial; bitter experience; sharp agonies of judgment. These four are called, and, after the long night's prayer among the hills alone, He adds eight others; and with these He walks. Keenly He watches them, searches them, prepares them. Even now, do they know Him? Dare He trust them? Have they discovered His meaning, His Name? Who can say? Far apart He leads them, out from among the troubling noises of the town, far from the perplexing dishonours of the home-country. Will they stand? It is a terrible, a searching hour! All men have misunderstood, the most faithful are falling away; and bad as the case looks to them now, in Galilee, He has worse to tell them, of the desperate things that must be done in Jerusalem. How will they endure it? Are they not already touched, tainted? Not only are all baffled, saddened, cast down, but one of them, nor

he the least, has even now lost heart, doubted, dis-
believed: "Have I not chosen you Twelve, and one
of you is a devil?" One of them is gone, is lapsed,
is weighed, and found wanting. The Lord feels it,
knows it. What of the rest? "Will ye also go
away?" It is the crisis of the drama; and now that,
through the great confession of Peter, eleven at least
are found worthy to receive, and hold the unburdened
secret, the care of the Lord intensifies. With ever-
increasing anxiety He devotes Himself to the single
task of preparing those few for the ultimate revelation. The Gospel now becomes little else but a story
of their slow and reluctant training. With growing
emphasis He unburdens His secret, and for long they
cannot accept it. "They understood none of these
things, and this saying was hidden from them, neither
knew they the things that were spoken." Very slowly
they are made ready, chastened, purged; until that
last awful hour was reached when, with feet washed
clean, with hearts made pure by the word implanted
—alone with Him in the upper chamber, apart, hidden
from the world, they receive the uttermost secret, no
longer in parable, but in plain speech; and share in
the New Covenant, and take of His Body, and drink
of His Blood.

That is the story. There can be no doubt about it.
It is perfectly simple, plain, familiar.[1] How is it, then,

---

[1] Cf., for instance, article by Dr. Edwin Hatch in *Contemporary
Review*, June, 1885 [on "Canon Liddon's Theory of the Episcopate"]:
"We believe that if organisation had had the importance which many
attach to it, that importance would have been marked in the Sacred
Record. The main facts of that Record are clear enough for those who
in any sense accept it."

that we allow people still to assert and believe that our Lord cast His word loose among mankind—that His message was independent of all embodiment, of all organisation? Yet the exact contrary holds. His message, His secret of Redemption, is never given except in an organised form. He occupies Himself with little else but the framing and perfecting of its Tabernacle. This Sower is very far from being careless where His seed falls. There is a seed He keeps in hand until He is quite sure of the ground; only to a certain plot will He commit it—a plot deliberately selected, painfully prepared, by shrewd and wise husbandry, dug, weeded, harrowed, watered. His spiritual force has to be held back, until it can effect a lodgment, until it can secure for itself an organised home, until it can house itself within a body. And that body, that home, can only be built of living men, who can apprehend His true Name. To discover such men, to choose, call, stablish them, this is the life-task of Jesus Christ, as recorded in the Gospels. Give Him but twelve men, so found, chosen, and secured, and He is ready to go up to Jerusalem, and die, and be seen no more. Nay, though even of those twelve there be but three who can be shown the vision of the King,—though there be one, the son of perdition, who is hopelessly lost,—yet eleven have been won—eleven men who have received the deposit. This is what has been given Him of His Father, and this is enough. Give Him but these, who are to Him not as servants, but as friends, who can understand Him, feel with Him, live and die in Him, and His

Church is based on a rock. He can leave the world, and go unto the Father. He can lift up His eyes, and say, "Now, O Father, glorify Thy Son. I have manifested Thy Name unto the men whom Thou gavest Me out of the world: Thine they were, and Thou gavest them Me; and I have given unto them the words which Thou gavest Me; and they have received them, and have known that I came out from Thee. I pray for them; I pray not for the world, but for them whom Thou hast given Me. O righteous Father, the world hath not known Thee; I have known Thee, and these have known that Thou hast sent Me."

There it is! there is the rock on which all is built—these two strong facts, "I have known Thee," and "These have known that Thou hast sent Me."

A knot of men, selected, set apart, elect, precious, on whom alone the final attention of the Lord is concentrated, to whom alone His inner heart commits its secret,—here is the seed-plot of the living Word. Here is the issue of the Gospel story, the fruit of the Lord's earthly mission. This is what He left behind Him on earth when He died.

But, then, the objection starts at once. Is not this to curtail God's mercy? Is not this to circumscribe His love? Will He but save and bless the few—the elect? Does He spend Himself only for those who can be found within the formal limits of a narrow body? Are they to be the sole recipients of grace? Are they to look out from the peace of privilege upon a perishing world?

What a strange and unhappy blunder does such

an objection embody! Yet it is a blunder into which the Church itself has been terribly prone to fall. Let us recall ourselves. First, how did we arrive at our present position? Was it by curtailing or confining Christ's pity and compassion — His work of love? Did we say that these only were to be found at work within the limits of the Church fold? Far, far from it! His mercy, His pity, were poured out freely upon all who could be persuaded to call for them. Everywhere they flowed out. He could not refuse the call of faith, even though it broke through the limitations under which He was at work. Even though He was, during His days on earth, "not sent but unto the lost sheep of Israel," yet the Syrophœnician woman cried and was heard. Far and wide, open and free, His love pours out its abundance. Only let men believe, and all things are possible. His pity cannot but respond to their faith. And His love is unstinted, because His commission from the Father is absolutely unconfined; it is wide and broad as the human race. Not one man can be left outside its range, or untouched by its hope. He would, if He might, "draw all men unto Him." This is the Will of Him that sent Him—that "every one which seeth the Son, and believeth, may have everlasting life." God sent His Son with one only purpose—to save the world the whole world. God so loved the world, the fallen world, the entire world, "that He gave His only begotten Son, that whosoever would believe in Him should have everlasting life." We are not limiting God's love to His Church. No! Yet God's love in Christ found itself limited, found itself cribbed, and cabined, and confined. How? Not by the Church, but by the crowd; by the block of blind and heedless ignorance. Here was the terrible barrier set to love. The compassion of God, so abundant, so mighty, cannot get forward among those crowds. For God's love is limited and measured out by man's desires. Human faith, a human cry,—this is its only door, its one chance of entry. But what then does this crowd desire? What is the measure of its faith? It only wants a relief from some temporary burden, a burden of the flesh! That is as far as it gets. That is as much as it understands or craves. If only it could be healed of its fever! If only it might be given back its health! If only it might be spared the loss of some dying child! Give it that, and that is all it asks. And the mercy of the Lord cannot go further than men ask it, invite it. Yet that Mercy is come on earth to achieve so much more than this momentary relief of a few sick, this short lull in the wild storm of passion and pain. This too, the love of God will give, if prayed for; but not only this. It is burning, there, with consuming zeal, to do a work which the "Father worketh hitherto," from the creation of the world,—a work of which these kind healings are but the omens and symbols,—a work far greater than these, at which they might indeed marvel,—the work of a world-wide and age-long resurrection, by which the hosts of the dead, the very bodies of those multitudes that lie in the graves shall all hear the voice of the Son of Man, and shall rise, and live!

But all this is hidden from the heedless, hungry

crowds. Feed them, and they are satisfied. They see
no sign. They are delighted just to eat of the loaves
and be filled. And His love is shut up therefore.
His compassion is restrained by this meagre belief.
His pity can find but scanty outlet. The barriers of
man's blindness hem it in. It is there within Him;
but it can find no way out. Every door is closed.
What is asked for, it will always give; but these
people ask for so little. Oh that they would but
open their mouths wide, that He might fill them!
But their eyes are shut, their ears are closed, they will
not ask; though He cries to them, "Ask—only ask—
and it shall be given. Seek, and ye shall find. Knock,
and it shall be opened." No; they can read the signs
of the weather, but not the signs of the Son of Man:
though He had done so many miracles before them,
yet they believed not. They could not see Who it
was stood among them, nor guess at the greatness of
the gift, and therefore "the men of Nineveh shall rise
in judgment with this generation, and shall condemn
it, because they repented at the preaching of Jonas;
and, behold, a greater than Jonas is here. The Queen
of the South shall rise up in the judgment with this
generation, and shall condemn it; for she came from
the uttermost parts of the earth to hear the wisdom
of Solomon; and, behold, a greater than Solomon is
here."

Dear brethren, it is not the Church, but the crowd,
which restrains and narrows God's work of mercy. It
is the crowd which cannot admit God's mercy; the
crowd which offers it no room, no free play, no home, no

wide and magnificent range. Christ might have walked up and down that crowd for ever, and still the blessed secret of Redemption would have been held back and forced into silence, unsuspected, unasked, imprisoned. Ah, and worse than that! not only might Christ have stood in their midst unnamed and unconsidered, but He might have died on their behalf and no one would have known it. That love of Christ, which poured out its blood for His sheep, that love unutterable, unmeasured, in height and depth and length and breadth, —that love which surpasseth all knowledge, into the abyss of which Angels gaze and tremble—that love might have displayed itself before the very eyes of that loose multitude, and not one eye have seen anything there but a malefactor, or a thief, hung between two thieves,—blasted under the curse of him that hangeth on a tree—that, and no more! A few poor women might, perhaps, have beaten their breasts; one soldier, in a spasm of pity, would possibly have put a sponge and moistened His dying lips; a centurion might have suddenly cried, "Surely, this is a Son of God!" but the Crucified would have been to men but as "a man of sorrows, rejected and despised; a man smitten of God, and afflicted; from whom they hid their faces." The crowd would have seen and known nothing, even "though it was for their transgressions He was being wounded, for their peace that He was being chastened."

How can this love of God get abroad? How can it find its opportunity? How can it break through its restraints? Only, if it can deepen and enlarge the desires of men; only, if it can persuade them to call upon its treasures; only, if it can endow them with an organ sensitive to God's offer—a channel through which its pity may pass in. Those crowds, so dull and unsteady, cannot admit, for they cannot recognise, the light. They must be given an eye to see with. "The light of the body is the eye. If the eye is but lightened, then the whole body becomes full of light." Here is the law. If this dark body of mankind could but be given an eye that could take in the light, then the entire bulk, thick and gross as it is, would become full of light. And therefore Christ prepares His Church to become the eye of the body. He raises into sensitive life an organ through which He may act upon the whole. If but a knot of men could be sifted out, disciplined, lifted, purged, they might be the organ of distribution by which the gifts, hidden from the mass, might yet reach and penetrate the mass. This is the meaning—the purpose of the Church. The loose thinking, the vague feeling of the crowd, these bar and control the free action of love. The clear and high creed of a compact and organised discipleship, this is what permits the recognition and admits the inflow of the finer and the richer grace. The Church, with its distinct and definite confession, "Thou art the Christ,"—with its disciplined feeling, "Now, we have learned and believed,"—widens, deepens, enlarges the possibilities open to God's love for the entire race. Gifts, otherwise shut off from unregenerate hearts; gifts, waiting for us to take, yet unseen, unguessed, undesired, and, therefore, unused—these gifts are laid open to man, by means of a Church that, holding fast the Name of Christ, can put that Name to its full use and exercise, can measure their human needs by its measureless significance, can enlarge their desires by its magnificent hope, can drink of its spirit, and know its mind, and see with its eyes. So seeing, so knowing, the Church is enabled through the Spirit of disciplined advocacy to raise and expand its intercessions to something nearer the level of God's offers. And, as an organ of such intercessions, wielding the Name of Christ, it can win, for all men, gifts otherwise unattainable — can evoke blessings that, without its availing cry, must remain unopened and unexercised.

Christ's Church, dear brethren, exists in order to make possible, to make known, to make active, the work which Christ, by His Incarnation, Death, and Resurrection, achieved once for all. It was done, it was finished, the task given Him to do. But only through man could it be laid open to man. He needs men to be His instruments, His organ, by which His own activity, supreme and unique, may find channels of entry—may be solicited, evoked, distributed. In securing men who know His true Name, He is securing a seat, a home, into which He can throw His own spiritual forces. They become, through so believing, the means by which His special and personal powers can liberate and discharge themselves. As He is the Light of the world, so they become, in Him, the eye through which the light illuminates the body: " Ye are the light of the world." As He is the sole purifying Sacrifice, so they become, organised into His Name, the seed of all purification—the salt through which the bulk of men are saved from corrupting : " Ye are the salt of the world." In becoming clean in Him, they become the instruments of further cleansing: " If I have washed your feet, ye ought also to wash the feet of others." In confessing His Name, in becoming stones built into His Temple, they become necessarily the seat and sanctuary whence issue the motives, powers, operations, activities of His authoritative Name. They hold the mighty keys of the Kingdom of Heaven ; through their hands the living forces of the Spirit leap out, and find free way over the world. Whatsoever they bind on earth, shall be bound in Heaven. Whatsoever they loose on earth, shall be loosed in Heaven.

Read, I pray you, the last prayer in St. John : and see whether every word does not obtain its meaning, in the light of this office of the Church to the world. What He Himself has been in the world, that is what they will now become. They are His organ of communication with the world, the material of His manifestation.

Dearly beloved, the study of the Church drives questions home, indeed, upon our personal life. We are of the Church, called, elect, precious, not that we may receive more, but that we may give more. Blessed, indeed, to receive ! but more blessed still to give ; and that is our blessing, the blessing of the Church ; we are in it for this supreme purpose, that we may be used by Christ ; to be vehicles of His message ; to be instruments of His purification. We are there, in order that His energies may discharge themselves through us; and, to-day,[1] His Spirit leaps out, as of old, to lay hold of us for His service and work. That Spirit is essentially a quickening Spirit, quickening the dead; a purifying Spirit, purifying the unclean; and "so is every one who is born of the Spirit;" to be born of the Spirit necessitates our being what the Spirit is. We, too, if we are His begotten, must quicken dead things, must purge corrupt things.

What is it you are doing, then? Here is a practical question for Whitsuntide. Being of His Church, "ye are the light of the world." What light is going out from you, now and every day, to those who have not the joy of your secret? What radiance can they see about you? What good cheer do you bring? Is there any one dark soul, that brightens at your coming—and brightens, not with your own light, but with that light which you hold in you from Him Who alone is the Light of the world? His light it must be. Is there any one to whom that light passes, through your ministry?

"Ye are the salt of the world." You are the purifying elements lodged in a world that without you would fall away into corruption. That is your office, your function, your purpose, as members of Christ's Church. Can you recognise that purpose, that office, in your daily life? Can you see that that is why you are alive, why you are baptised and redeemed? that that is your use, your justification? Ask yourself—Is there any society into which Christ's purity finds its way opened

---

[1] Whit-Sunday.

through you—a society, which, without your presence, would begin to stink and putrefy? Is there any corner of the earth, however tiny and obscure, which you serve to keep clean for Christ? You cannot escape this question, for you are salt: that, you were made by Baptism; that is your nature in Christ—to be the salt by which mankind is kept sweet, and clean, and fresh. You are this salt. Christ counts on you for this. This is your high calling: very high it is! Salt is good; but what if the salt be unserviceable—if it lose its savour—if it cease to purify? What a desperate case! It is good, then, for nothing; it has to be cast out, and to be trodden under foot! You are salt. Oh, be very sure, that your savour is fulfilling its service!

My brethren, the burden of this world's vast woes is laid upon us. By being of the Church, we are the materials through which Christ has to act upon it. On us He counts, to give Him His opportunities, to carry His succours. No doubt His compassion will struggle to make way without us. But, believe me, there are treasures—and they are His richest—which He cannot unseal but through the compact fabric of an ordered Church. There are secrets—and they are His deepest and His sweetest—which He can only unveil through the channels of a disciplined and organised Faith.

Every one of us, by being in Christ's Church, then, is under strict obligations, undertakes responsibilities, towards the ignorance, the suffering, and the sin of a world that cannot see the Form of God, as we see it, nor hear the Voice to which our ears have been

opened. Each of us, lay and cleric alike, is constituted
by Baptism a light-bearer to those who sit in darkness, a Christ-bearer to those who lie in the shadows of
death. We dare not delegate this, our true priesthood,
to the Clergy, nor leave it all to be done by our
sisters. If Christ has washed our feet, then we are
bound to be found washing the feet of our fellows.
Surely, those who need us are not difficult to discover; any one who wills can find them. Very near
to every one of us are so many who are plodding
so wearily along dry and forlorn paths, without a
hope and without a home; and it is we who might
so easily lead them in, and make them sit down, while
we gird ourselves with the linen towel, and put water
in a basin, and lay cool kindly hands about their sore
and tired feet. Very near to every one of you they
can be found; and you are charged with their succour.
For we have an unction from the Holy Ghost. We
are the hands and feet on earth of Christ in Heaven
As the Father sent Him, so He sends His Church
"into the world." And to each of us, the voice of
Pentecost is, to-day, uttering its eternal commission;
the Spirit of the Lord is upon *thee;* and *thou* art
anointed to preach the Gospel to the poor. Thou art
sent "to heal the brokenhearted, to preach deliverance
unto the captives, and recovery of sight to the blind,
to set at liberty them that are bruised."

THE FELLOWSHIP OF THE CHURCH.

"If, therefore, the prisoner of the Lord, beseech you that ye walk worthy of the vocation wherewith ye are called, with all lowliness and meekness, with longsuffering, forbearing one another in love; endeavouring to keep the unity of the Spirit in the bond of peace."—EPH. iv. 1–3.

THERE is a ghost that haunts our economic and political thinking, which has again and again to be laid; and, once more, in our day, men are engaged, both in thought and action, in the task of shaking themselves free from its unhappy influence.

We had slid into supposing, as many before us have supposed, that each individual man is, in his inner life, a solitary and separable being. The long story of social growth may, indeed, have sown about him many subtle intimacies with his fellows; but at least (so we thought), in the secret recesses of self, in his germinal instincts, in his primary impulses, in his root desires, it is himself that he must regard, and not another. And this being so, each individual will be at his best, it was argued, and at his strongest, when he is set free to build his own life, to consider his own interests, to shape his own career, to secure his own happiness. In all this his course will be straightforward and vigorous,

his development will be sound and solid and healthy;
for he will be obeying and freeing the promptings of
his truest nature, and, in following the line of his own
richest efficiency, he will be also making himself most
beneficial to the general good.

Consideration of his neighbours, of their works and
needs, this, it was allowed, there must, indeed, be;
otherwise, no combination would be possible, and he
and all gain by combination; but still this consideration of his neighbour, however expedient and necessary,
cannot but hamper, delay, disturb, traverse his own
power and energy of action. He would be going forward with higher freedom, with less obstruction, if this
consideration had not to take place.

Yet neighbours are very numerous, and their consideration grows ever more complicated a matter as
civilisation advances, and there is ever slowly rising a
huge and rigid system of law, which enforces and
determines this consideration of the neighbour. This
is the object of law—to compel the individual man,
driven forward by his inherent self-regard, to remember his fellows, to allow them their chance, to suffer
their intrusion in return for the room they leave to
him. Law, then, is expedient, is essential to general
well-being; but, nevertheless, its office is to limit,
curtail, traverse, in the interests of others, the free
motions of individual activity. Law is a necessary
evil; so far as the man by himself goes it obstructs,
forbids, confines him. It weakens his independence, it
fetters his natural bent and play.

But if this is so, in what a dilemma do we find

ourselves! For law increases its range as civilisation advances; and must civilisation, then, be ever weakening, more and more, the natural man, ruining his independence, imprisoning his best forces?

Yes! the logical Frenchman said. Cities are but hospitals. Civilisation is a sickness. It distorts and hampers and clogs the free nature of the man. To know him in his vigour, in his beauty, in his truth, you must carry him far from the fettering crowds, and plant him down in some wide homes where his noble savagery will display itself unshackled.

No! said the thoughtful, practical English. Each of us gains more than he loses by submitting to the limitation imposed on each by co-operation with his fellows; nevertheless, the less there is of law the better. Law is the necessary negative, forbidding a man to disturb his neighbours; but in so forbidding it does hamper him, and the aim of the law must be to hamper him as little as possible—to turn loose, whereever it is practicable, the real man, and leave his native energies to work their way out unchecked.

So we learned to think; and so thinking we naturally looked askance at any attempt to push forward the realm of law. Our political task, we said, is to discourage and diminish the activity of law,—until we all suddenly began to discover that our premisses were so partial as to be false to facts. How have we discovered this? Chiefly, I think, by the violent irruption of a radical force, of which this system of thought had made no account—the force of nationality. It was as if history had made a plot to undermine our theories. For as fast as we forgot to consider the influence of nationalities in binding men together, the spirit of nationality began to stir itself with vigour, with insistence, with violence. We have been forced to see ancient and orderly systems of society shattered into fragments by this upspringing force. It has under our eyes re-fashioned Europe and recreated history. And, in spite of our philosophy, it has won, again and again, our enthusiastic sympathy. Yet this spirit of nationality —what is it? How can our theory account for it? It is a sense of fellowship that lies deeper in a man than all calculations of self-interest; it runs in his blood, it is bred into his bones; it will carry him whither he would not; in its name, on its behalf, he throws to the winds his own obvious gain, his own private career, his own personal happiness. Down within his individual self is a self, it appears, that is not solitary, but social; under the impulse of a common brotherhood, powers are evoked in him, energies discharged, far, far beyond the narrow efforts which he will set moving on his own behalf; he will do and dare far more for his fellows than ever he did for himself. We did not know what was in him until this breath of patriotism passed over him—this passion of community awoke within him. A dull and vacant sluggard in his own interest, he is set aflame with heroic ardour, now that it is the interests of others that he serves. Lo! now he is alive; the man in him is freed, and set in motion. What can hold him down? He lifts the iron gates of selfishness on his shoulders, and bears them away as a very little thing; he snaps the strong cords of self-regard like withes. Here is a passion that, indeed, moves mountains; and it is a social passion, a passionate sense of fellowship, of blood, of community, which, far from finding itself fettered by law, is only then made free when it has won its way to legal and social recognition. We are driven out of our old position. Law, a social fabric, a State system —these cannot be treated as uncongenial and obstructive burdens. Nay; these are the natural outcome of what is in a man ; for the desire for national existence is certainly in a man, and it is this desire that builds States and creates laws.

Here is a force, then, which has insisted on being heard and considered. And we who are here gathered to-day [1] know well its meaning and its power. I will not speak of the bitter and baffling experience through which we are learning the passion with which the national sentiment of Ireland is set on building its own house and its own habits. Rather I would appeal to its victorious efficacy in ourselves. We English know, if any know, the tingle in the blood, the springing tears, the light and the lift in the heart, which speak from within our very souls of the bonds that bind us to our own people and our father's house. We know, if any know, what it is to "kindle as a fire new stirred" at the sight of English eyes, at the grip of an English hand, at the comfortable sound of English voices and an English tongue. Even if we, of the old country, have now and again lost sense or touch of that which was too

[1] Preached on anniversary of Queen's Accession before members of Colonial and Indian Exhibition.

familiar to us to make itself felt, you who have gone out to build far homes under other skies, you have roused us from our slumber ere the jewel that we held so sleepily had slipped out of our idle and careless hands. You knew better than we what it would be to lose that, which was to us hidden only because it was so very near and so common. You, standing outside our dream, you knew, you retaught us the full honour of the English name—the high passion that belongs to the possession of national memories and a national story—of a common blood and a common home. Home! Ah, it is far away over the sounding seas that we first learn the music of that name! To be home in England, amid the old folks at home! Your hearts know well what those simple words carry in them. Home! what is ever like home? We cannot say why; no words will ever tell to others what we mean by home. It is an air in which we breathe as we never breathe elsewhere; it holds us as in a charm; it lays kind hands about us; it enfolds us; and everything within us wakes and springs and grows at this sweet and tender touch. At home, we are ourselves; we move in freedom; we are alive; we open upward as a flower. And then—an English home—the very thought of it is a benediction. Nothing else can ever win from us the look that comes up into our eyes as we stand in strange lands and drink in news from home—as we stand and think of quiet farms that grow old amid the English uplands—of new-mown hay that lies sweet in river-meadows—of the piping of the blackbird and the thrush over dewy

English lawns—of primroses and cowslips that are growing as of old in the fields and lanes, where our child-hands have plucked them in days that are long gone:—

> "Green fields of England! wheresoe'er
> Across this watery waste we fare,
> Your image in our hearts we bear,
> Green fields of England, everywhere!

Yes, wherever we English scatter we carry the same associations with us; a life is in us, which is one and the same in all. The same call stirs us all; the same past embraces us; the same names are to us as household words; the same heart beats in us. And whence is it, I would ask, that our hereditary Throne wins the secret of its strength, but out of its inherence within the very core of our familiar traditions? Its story is inwoven into the very texture of our memories; it gives substance to our national imagination. This Throne of ours is rooted in English soil; it belongs to England as naturally as her hazel hedgerows and her willowed brooks; and, by overshadowing Providence, at the very moment at which we are learning to prize its ancient interests, and its wide significance, it has been dignified and endeared to the hearts of the people by her whom we remember before God to-day, by her who was already a Queen before many of your new homes were even named; and who, through all these long years—years of shock and change, of tumult and wreck—has lifted high a name unblemished by any suspicion and untouched by any reproach.

Here, then, is a great tradition, embodied in the name of England—a tradition which dividing seas

cannot quench, nor any floods drown. It endures as
a force at work within us, which no calculations of
self-interest can prohibit or deter. It forces its way
forward, in spite of all that can be done to frighten,
or chill, or numb, or paralyse it. And in so doing it
is the everlasting and invariable assertion, that the
passion for brotherhood lies deeper in us all than the
passion for self; that a man's individuality must have
its roots in some wide fellowship; that he is never
fully free or alive unless he can feel himself embodied
in a corporate union with his brothers. For their civic
companionship is to him no obstruction, but the ex-
pansion of that old sense of home. Through their
presence there becomes possible that growth of custom
and habit, of law and of order, which is as essential to
him as the air he breathes. In company with them
he builds again, wherever he and they may find themselves, the old social system which is familiar as the
very tongue they use in common. His political fabric
is an English affair: it springs from him, it belongs to
him with perfect spontaneity; for it is an expression
of his English heart, of his English temper, of his
English training: without it he would be but half an
Englishman; he would feel homeless and unhoused,
as an exile on an alien earth.

Here, then, in nationality we have the surest
evidence that the deepest, the most radical elements
in man are not individual, but corporate; not solitary,
but social. And faith, dear brethren, man's faith in
God, is much deeper and more radical than all else.
Down in the innermost heart of hearts lies the source

and root of faith; we cannot be surprised, therefore, to find that faith, too, bears this social and corporate character. This is true of all faith in God; its earliest and strongest forms are all of them national. And when it attains the fulness of the Christian faith it retains its inherent social character. Christian faith cannot be a solitary affair of the isolated individual man; it cannot, by the necessary and essential law of its being.

For, first, its object, God Himself, is no self-contained Being, living to Himself alone. He, according to the Creed which Trinity Sunday commemorates, finds His life in an eternal intercourse. He is not a solitary God, Who chooses to enter into relations with other creatures created for that purpose. His Godhead itself consists, from all eternity, in personal relations, such as express themselves in the family and the home—it consists in the communion of Person with Person, in the interpretation of Person by Person, in the identification, through the vital bond of love, of Person with Person.

The God on Whom faith fixes itself, then, is social; the Absolute Life is in its very essence a life of community, of combination, of co-operation. And the faith which is fed from such a source, which is inbreathed by the Spirit of Divine union, that Spirit of love Whose being is knit up into the Being of the Father and the Son—that Spirit which proceedeth out of that blessed home in heaven to build a new home on earth for God the Father among His children, for God the Brother in the midst of His brethren — such a faith cannot but be social and corporate to its very core. It must hunger after community; it must pine for brotherhood. And, therefore, Christ our Master never imagined a faith which should not include and involve a Church. Therefore it was that in His eye the direct personal, individual confession of one single man—the one and only man who as yet had apprehended His full Name —carried with it the principle of fraternity, the germ of a community. Peter cried, " Thou art the Christ; " and our Lord saw in that confession the structure, the foundation, of a whole society. " Thou art Peter: on this Rock," of My Name so confessed, " I will build a Church."

The object of faith is social—a Triune God; and the inward motives of faith are social also. Yet it has been so easy to blunder here! Just as politically we have so often slid into supposing that each individual man is by nature alone, and has then, for practical purposes, to unite himself to his neighbours in a State, so we have again and again imagined that each individual man in his faith, in his religious character, stands and acts alone, and has afterwards, for reasons of expediency, to unite himself with other believers into a Church.

And just as, in the first case, we dreaded the State, as hindering and obscuring the natural man, so, in the second case, we fear the Church, lest it should dim or fetter the vital faith of the solitary spirit.

But if man himself is inherently social, then, we found, his being frees itself, delights itself, enlarges itself, in a State. The problem of "Man *versus* the State" has ceased if man is the State.

And if man's faith is inherently social, then it must need a Church in which to grow, expand, bloom, flower, ripen. It is obstructed and cramped, not by being incorporated in a Church, but by being left alone without a Church.

My brethren, I am not discussing at all to-day what particular form the Church ought to take. I am but pleading that some form of Christian Church there is bound to be. I am but pleading that our personal faith in Christ hungers for some brotherhood. How can it do otherwise? Its roots are dug deep into the soil of fraternity. It starts from the profound community of being, which knits the believing soul into the race-sin, the one age-long sin, which is one and the same in all, the sin of its brother Adam. And, again, its hold on salvation stands in the same racial community, which knits its own tiny life up into the one act, one and the same for all, of its Blessed Brother, Christ Jesus, in Whose crucified Flesh the entire race died, in Whose risen Body the entire body of mankind is raised to justification. Through its complete identification of its own lot with that of its fellows each individual soul is both lost and saved—lost in Adam, saved in Christ.

Here are, indeed, the springs and seeds of an ineradicable brotherhood; and it is this root-brotherhood which ought to find its voice, its life, its freedom, its joy in the Church of the faithful. The law of its salvation necessitates its finding itself knit into a fellowship—the fellowship of the new human society, which is the Body of Christ. Its innermost instincts make for corporate life. It is become a member of Christ's Body. Where is this Body? It must find it, feel it, or it will wither and spoil.

Listen to the great invitation: " Beloved, ye are come by faith in Christ unto a city, the heavenly Jerusalem, into an innumerable company of angels, to the general assembly and Church of the First-born —to the spirits of just men made perfect."

Ah! there is what our souls yearn to behold! There is the companionship for which they sicken!, We want, by the very fact of believing, to find ourselves embraced in a great society, incorporated in a united mass.

The Church of God may be shivered in fragments, and we may find ourselves thrown by history into some strong group of believers, cut off from the main body; and we must be true to our historical position, and long history cannot be undone in a moment.

But, at least, we may be sure, and we may recall with penitence and sorrow, what it was that Christ our Master intended and founded. Faith was not to be solitary and homeless. Nay! it was just a country, a home which Christ promised it; a home on earth; a home for the redeemed spirit, with all the delightful rest and security of an ordered household, where each man had his post and office, and the porter watched at the door, and the steward brought out meat in due season. It was a home in which all was arranged, allowed for, remembered; and round about the soul would be kindliness and brotherliness and goodness and peace—for in this sweet home all would conspire to help all, and the foot would not complain of the head, nor the head despise the hand; and the air would be charged with tenderness and sympathy, and any one who was in pain would know that all were suffering with him, and any one who was made glad by good would be sure of neighbours to whom he could run ever and cry, " Rejoice with me, I have found that which I had lost;" and every prodigal, creeping back in shame, would feel the whole house ringing with music and cries about him, as they say one to another, " Bring forth the robe and the ring; for lo! this our brother was dead and is alive again; was lost and is found."

It was a home into which they were brought, those Ephesians and Colossians—so the Apostles promised their converts,—a home, wide, manifold, crowded. It was a nation into which they were admitted—holy, elect, precious; a nation, one throughout, gathered out of all nations and kindreds and peoples and tongues; a nation in which all divisions had ceased, all separations, all solitariness. In it there was neither Jew nor Greek, bond or free, male or female; for all, who were made originally of one blood over all the face of the earth, had now recovered their broken unity in the one Blood of the one Man, Christ Jesus.

How blessed, how untiring, the joy of this great companionship! Those who once had known all the loneliness of aliens, the misery of strangers and exiles, without any holy commonwealth, without any hope, are now no more strangers and foreigners, but are "fellow-citizens with the Saints and of the household of God; are built into a holy temple, fitly framed together," laid upon the strong foundations of the Apostles and the prophets. They have a city in Heaven, which is their dear motherland; "Jerusalem on high, which is the mother of us all." There their citizenship lies; and on earth they walk in all the virtues of the holy citizenship, in the habits of delightful intercourse, in the beauty of fellowship; "with all lowliness and meekness, forbearing one another in love, endeavouring to keep the unity of the Spirit in the bond of peace."

Ah! why is it that this great Bible language sleeps in our ears? Why are we content to let it die down into the mist of poetry—into the hollowness of metaphor?

It was no dead metaphor—no vague allegory—to those who heard the Lord and the Apostles tell of a family of God—of a household of Christ—of a country, a kingdom, a holy nation—of a temple fitly framed—of a body compacted and entire. Yet what meaning, what reality can our broken Christianity give to words like these?

And are we content that they should have no meaning? Are we content to shut ourselves up in the narrow question, "Am I saved?" Shall we fasten our eyes on nothing but our own private interest in Christ—our own personal receipt for getting to Heaven, as if that were something that concerned no one but ourselves?

Surely, now that the great unities which underlie human life are pressing forward so vigorously, we shall discover again those yet stronger and wider unities which underlie the Christian faith—unities wide and full as humankind. We shall hunger again for the joy of Christian fellowship—shall pine for the spaces and the fulness, for the heights and the depths of the Kingdom of Christ—shall send up to Christ His own last prayer that we all may be one, even as He and the Father are One; that yet again the day may be given when we shall all be one Body, as well as one Spirit; one baptism, as well as one Lord!

And, until that blessed day be shown us—alas! so far off—what can we do but strain to exercise among ourselves those virtues of the city and the home, which should blossom out of the unity of faith,—the virtues of those who walk as neighbours in a heavenly country, as children in a holy home,—the virtues of love, peace, goodness, loving-kindness, charity—" with all lowliness and meekness, forbearing one another, honouring one another, endeavouring to keep the unity of the Spirit in the bond of peace "?

THE WITNESS OF THE CHURCH.

"This Jesus hath God raised up, whereof we all are witnesses; there=
fore being by the right hand of God exalted, and having received of the
Father the promise of the Holy Ghost, He hath shed forth this, which
ye now see and hear."—ACTS ii. 32, 33.

"FOLLOW Me and I will make you fishers of men."
Christ, we have seen, Who so promised, was Himself the
great Fisherman Who threw His net over the multitude, and drew to Himself out of those crowded waters
those who had been given Him of the Father. They
were but eleven. This was all that was left Him in
His basket when He had sat down on the beach and
had sorted the good from the bad. Only eleven who
could be trusted to understand Him as friends, only
eleven to whom He could commit His secret and tell
His Name. Eleven, but they were enough. Now let
Him die. "Arise, let us go hence; now is the Son of
Man glorified and God is glorified in Him."

So much we have seen, and yet is this all? Has our
Lord, then, founded His Church? Has He set His
faith in motion? Far from it. Nothing that our Lord
did during His life on earth was enough to establish
a faith in Himself which should survive His Death.

People who have taken but slight measure of human sin, talk as if His faultless Life and His heroic Martyrdom were sufficient to account for the existence of Christianity; but the answer to this is final. Our Lord's glorious Life, His heroic Death, did, as a fact, fail to effect that belief in Him which starts a religion. At the end of His career, not even the Twelve retained their conviction: they all forsook Him and fled, and Peter, the chief confessor, is chief in denial. He who had said, "Thou art Christ," now protests with oaths, "I know not the Man." Here indeed was no rock on which Christ could build His Church. The mere Life on earth ended with nothing yet achieved, with no body of believers established. The few to whom the secret was intrusted were secure of nothing, they were still loose and incoherent as the dust of the ground, for the word of the Lord was not yet spoken which should take of that loose dust and fashion it into a living and consistent body.

And we know why this must have been so. Our Lord lived His Life as a Jew born under the law, within the limits of the old dispensation. He had not yet done the deed which should end the ancient story, and constitute Him the King and Priest of the new Covenant for all mankind. Not yet is He lifted up so that He could draw all men unto Him. Not till the Jews had destroyed their own Temple can He be set free to raise the temple again, the temple of His body, to be a house of prayer and praise for all nations. His secret is shut away within Him; His spiritual forces lie hidden, repressed; His Hands are bound, and He may not spread them wide until they have been opened and freed by the extended Cross.

Now, this condition of our Lord's Life on earth lies at the very root of that belief in the Church which we have been considering in these sermons. Christ, we see, cannot reveal Himself in His full significance, or royalty, or power, until after He has been perfected through suffering, until after He has carried the blood as our Great High Priest in within the Holy of Holies, and won our remission of sins. Of all this kingship, this priesthood, His actual Life among us was but a prophecy and a symptom. Christianity lies hid within the womb of Judaism. We can feel something is near, we become conscious of a new presence, ominous, awful, mysterious: there is more to come, we can be sure; yet we know not what; for all still sleeps in silence; only from the silence reaches us the promise of strange things. The prohibition stands: " If I go not away, the Comforter will not come unto you," and until He comes, the Church is not endowed with her power from on high. If the Lord had only left us the Sermon on the Mount, and the memory of a martyrdom, there would never have been a Church of Christ at all. The risen and ascended Christ—here is the only intelligible account that can be given of the existence of our faith. From beyond the grave the living Master works; from thence He discharges His office, He liberates the Divine energies; it is from thence He issues to act, to comfort, to redeem, to hallow, to perfect.

And how is it to be done? By a Spirit; and that

Spirit will, indeed, in its work for Christ, "move whithersoever it listeth," so that we shall "hear the sound thereof
and yet not be able to tell whence it comes or whither it
goes." But does that mean that this free Spirit will fly
and flit hither and thither as an unembodied influence,
touching souls here and there among mankind in that
confused mass? Was that a method by which our
Lord could expect to reverse the current of human
history, to uproot ancient societies, to shatter vast
empires and immemorial religions? Was that casual
and accidental process one by which the kingdoms of
the earth would ever become the kingdoms of Christ?
Have we not seen how profoundly our Lord while on
earth distrusted such loose methods of action? We
have watched what He did; how it had been the work
of His Life, to prepare a nest for that Bird of God; to
build a house in which the Spirit should abide. For
that Spirit, if it is ever to act firmly, steadily, consistently, enduringly, must be given an instrument, an
organic body. So alone could its influence be effectual;
and effectual, you will observe, not in the secret recesses only of the believing soul, but in the plain face
of the unbelieving *world*. For the Spirit when it
came was to convince the world that Christ, Who had
gone to the Father, was nevertheless alive; He was to
convince the world through the Twelve that Christ
had indeed been sent from the Father: "I in them
and thou in Me"—so He prays—"that they may be
perfect in one, and that the world may know that Thou
hast sent Me." "When He, the Spirit, is come, He
will convince the world of sin, of righteousness, and of

judgment." It is an organ by which to act upon the dark and faithless world, a world which has no eye to see Him, and can only see and know Him through those whom He has glorified by His name,—it is such an organ that Christ needs. And such action to' be effectively done through this organ, must of necessity, therefore, be visible. It must push and press and force its way in among the affairs of men; it must be vigorous and obvious and undeniable; for it has got to convict the world of its sin in slaying Christ, of its true righteousness now hid from it in the ascended Christ, of its own inevitable judgment in warring against Christ, in whose undoubted victories, worked through the Church before its very eyes, the world itself cannot help seeing the proof that its own master, the Prince of this World, has been indeed judged and defeated. Christ hid in Heaven needs a body as well as a spirit by which to manifest His living rule. He needs a body through which He may make Himself intelligible to men, and even to unbelieving men; make Himself felt, certified, effective, enduring. This body He must have, and that body He has with pain secured Himself. And now into that prepared body His Spirit issues from Him, to gather it up into organised life, to inhabit it, to unify its capacities, to regulate its aims, to quicken its impulses, to fix its offices, to direct its gifts, to correlate its functions, to shape and distribute its parts, to feed and govern its entire frame.

A Spirit-bearing body—that is the agency which the ascended Lord has organised for His Spirit's service on earth, and its office, therefore, is clearly determined for it by the conditions of its existence, and that office is summed up in the one word, "witness." "The Spirit of truth proceeding from the Father shall bear witness of Me, and ye also shall bear witness,"—and so the Apostles say, "we are witnesses of these things." The Church is the witnessing body; it proves Christ's case, it testifies to His victory, and this it does, first, before God the Father. It manifests His glory by justifying His method of Redemption; it bears witness before God that He has not sent His Son in vain. And, secondly, it has to witness in the face of men, to prove, to convict, to convince, so that even an unbelieving world may believe that the Father did send the Son.

And in accomplishing this conversion of the world, the Church has two points to prove and testify,—first, that Christ is alive and at work now to-day on earth, and that He can be found of them that believe, and manifest Himself to those that love Him; and, secondly, that He is so by virtue of the deed done once for all at Calvary,—by which the Prince of this World was judged, and the world was overcome, and man given access to God.

What proofs can the Church offer for these two points? It has three proofs to give. First, its own actual life. This is its primary witness that Christ is now alive at the right Hand of God the Father. Its one prevailing and unanswerable proof is, "I live, yet not I, but Christ liveth in me." "I know, and I can testify, that the life I now live in the flesh is only possible to me by the faith in the Son of God, Who loved me and gave Himself for me." This is the cardinal testimony. " Christ is alive, otherwise I should not be alive as you see me this day."

And then this personal life of Christ in His Church verifies and certifies to the world the reality of that old life on earth, of that Death on Calvary, of that Resurrection on Olivet. The fact that the man at the Beautiful Gate has this perfect soundness in the presence of all, the very man whom they knew and saw so lame,—this makes it certain that God did send His Son Christ Jesus to be a Prince of life. And, therefore, the living Church bears a book about with it, the Gospel book, the Apostolic witness, the witness of those who so beheld, tasted, handled, the Word of Life, of those who were actually there all the time in which " the Lord Jesus went in and out amongst us, from the Baptism of John to the day on which He was taken up." This book the body of Christ carries ever before it, declaring to all, " This record is true, and we know that these Apostles spoke true ; we are here to prove it, in that we have tasted and touched the present power of that Word whose story they saw and recorded."

And again, the body carries with it a third witness ; not only the Apostolic record, but the Apostolic Rite, the act commanded by the dying Christ to be done for ever as a memorial and a witness until His coming again. Ever that society rehearses this deed of the new covenant, that deed which is the seal and pledge to men for all time, of the one covenant sealed with Christ's Blood once for all, even on the night of His Betrayal. Ever this rehearsal continues until Christ comes again, and every such rehearsal verifies, to all who take and eat the bread, that great Sacrifice which the Lord offered when in the upper chamber among the Twelve, "He took bread, and lifted up His Eyes to Heaven, and blessed and brake."

Here are the three prevailing witnesses by which the body testifies to the Resurrection of the Lord. The present life—"I live, yet not I, but Christ liveth in me." The unshaken record—"This is the disciple that testifieth of these things, and wrote these things, and we know that his testimony is true." And the memorial act—"As often as we break the bread we show forth the Lord's Death," we witness to it, we offer the one unfailing and unflagging proof of it until His coming again. And this witness never grows old; it is renewed from generation to generation. We are witnesses of these things, you and I; every one of us discharges the offices of this Church; every one of us, who claims membership in that Church, is required by that membership to become a standing proof on earth of God's truth in Heaven, a living and undeniable evidence of His love in Christ, a sacrament, a visible sign and pledge of the present energy of an unseen fact; and this proof, this evidence, this pledge, we are to give the world, so that the world may be able to see and know that God certainly did send His Son to be its Saviour.

My brethren, by believing in a body, in a Church, we find, once again, that our faith lays upon us responsibilities. It gives us a call, a vocation; it sets us each a task. And is not this just what our religion most lacks ?   There is so little sense of purpose within us, no purpose in our religious life. Religion comforts us in dark hours; it is a pleasant refuge from the cares and worries of life; it is a comfortable habit; it is a refreshment in weariness; it is a solace and security in the face of death. Yes, but is it the one thing that gives us a living reason for being alive ? Is it that which sets us on an aim worthy and enkindling, for which it is well worth while to live ? Does it come to us as something which lays upon us a service—a service of delightful freedom under the eye of a Master Who waits ever to say, " Well done, well done, thou faithful servant ? " Is not this exactly what we lack ? Is it not the absence of all sense of responsibility that keeps our religion so low, so poor, so dreamy, and so unreal ? A religion that is merely personal is bound to be cloudy and dull and meagre. We never can fix our attention or interest on ourselves for long without finding it a strangely wearisome occupation. Nothing comes of it; nothing grows or springs or quickens. Whether in religion or in other matters, we are never alive or alert unless we serve another's purpose, another whom we love and honour. We are never happy or strong until we are given some task to achieve, a task to which we can gladly devote every power that is within us. And if Christ established and built a Church, this means that He has a work for it to do; it means that every member of that body has, by believing, a definite, an urgent, a glad and proud task set before him.

Have you found this task, then? Have you found that your faith sets you to work? Does it endow you with a public responsibility? and, if not, do you wonder that believing seems to you a sleepy and a cloudy affair, not very real, nor very important, nor very interesting? And that task is to witness; and do you doubt whether you have any call to witness for Christ? Can there be any single believer in this church who is not urgently called to give this witness of which we speak? For what is this witness? It is the evidence you can give by active personal union with your Lord, now alive at God's right hand, of the authority of the Gospel record and of the Gospel Eucharist. You give your witness by your capacity to say, "I know that that record is true; Christ did rise from the dead, for it is He Who lives in me to-day. I know that the blood of the new covenant has been taken within the holy place to work reconciliation, for I have tasted and have drunk of it, and lo! I am reconciled to God."

And is there no one, then, who needs that evidence from you? Can you find no one near you who is struggling with doubt and perplexity as he reads that Gospel story, and cannot dismiss the memory of all the sharp and searching criticisms that necessarily encircle books that are now eighteen hundred years old? How can he be sure who wrote them, and when? And then the strange things they tell of—how can he take so much on such slender authority, the authority of those brief fragmentary pages, nameless, uncertified? How can a book ever convey certainty? How can a dead writing speak? How can he trust his soul to it? How can he answer and dismiss the hideous crowd of perplexities that encumber these books and their authorship and their authenticity? So he ponders, bewildered and unsettled, and the story of Jesus fades from him into an intangible and ghostly vision; and it is your witness and your evidence that alone can recover him his footing. He might break through his dream, he might grasp again the realities of his faith, if you were but ready to speak up to him and cry, "Christ did rise, believe it; those trembling women did find His grave empty, those eleven scared disciples did behold Him among them breathing peace; for not only is it written in the Book, but I, too, have seen, and have felt, and have heard. I know Christ dwelleth in me, and the life that I live is the life of that risen Christ: I can testify that that testimony is true."

Or is there no one who looks out upon the scenery of this bewildered earth as upon a dark and melancholy plain where "ignorant armies clash by night;" one who can see nothing there but confused suffering and unjust penalties, and an immense and terrible woe; and no light breaks through to him, and no voice speaks, and he can but cry out his bitter protest: "Is God indeed to be found there? Is there a Divine Judge of all the earth? Where are the signs of His love? There is no God; or, if there be, He is a God of cruelty and hate?" And what if your witness were ready at hand?—if you could but whisper, "I know that God is love, I know that in

Him is no darkness at all, for I have drunk of that love, I have known and believed the love that God hath for us, and amid all the darkness and the pain I know for certain—as you, too, may know if you will —that the love of God has been manifested to all who believe that Christ Jesus is the Christ born of God ; every one that so believeth hath the witness in him " ?

Or you may find yourself standing by one whom some strong sin has fast bound in misery and iron. It is a habit inevitable and masterful, and he loathes it ; and yet he returns to it. He is caught in cruel bonds, the soul is secured ; and though he hate himself and weep tears of shame, he cannot break loose ; and he can find no peace, and he gives himself over to the horrid thing. Now is your time to speak, to cry to him, to deliver your testimony—" My brother, you may be free, for Christ is not dead—He is risen ; He holds the keys of death and of hell ; there is no prison gate He cannot open ; He is here in our midst ; He, the great breaker of bonds, He is strong as of old to set free the captives ; He can thrust in His hand amid all that tangled net, and snatch the bird out of the snare of the fowler."

My brethren, it is for us to be sure that we know, by blessed experience, that Christ was manifested to take away our sins ; to know that He hears us whatsoever we ask ; to know that whatsoever is born of God need never sin, for God keepeth him, and the wicked man toucheth him not. " We know, we know," —so St. John keeps declaring in his old age—" we know,"—and that is the message that you have to carry on your lips; that is your needed witness—" We know that it is true."   It would be a miserable thing to find yourself standing over some brother, with your human heart indeed yearning to help him, and yet to find yourself speechless and impotent just because you had never taken the trouble to learn, when you had time, the happy lesson which would enable you to say to him the one word that can now save him: "I know it.   I know that what I say is true.   I have never found it fail me."   God grant us, brethren, grace to learn how to give this evidence on His behalf: that we may fulfil the purpose of our Regeneration by offering proof to the world that " this Jesus hath God raised up, Who now sheddeth forth this Holy Spirit, as all can see and hear."

THE RESOURCES OF THE CHURCH.

"When Jesus then lifted up His eyes, and saw a great company come unto Him, He saith unto Philip, Whence shall we buy bread, that these may eat? And this He said to prove him; for He Himself knew what He would do."—St. John vi. 5, 6.

WHAT is it to which we pledge ourselves by the Feast of Whitsuntide? To this above all—that the Church, in which we profess our belief, was brought into actual existence, not by any one while living in our midst on earth, but by some One already gone out of our sight beyond the cloud of death. Whitsun Day reminds us that the Church of Christ was not created until after our Lord had been hidden in the glory at the right hand of God.

Our Church first dates from Pentecost.

But what had our Lord done on behalf of His Church before He died? He had, as it were, cut or squared the stones out of the quarry, and shaped them for the building. They lay there, marked and numbered, twelve, with Peter in the midst—stones, indeed, but not yet living stones, fitly framed together by the Spirit Builder; the stones were shaped, but not yet made alive. The faith in the Name of Jesus, which

H

should become as a rock against which the gates of hell should never prevail, was as yet totally unfit to bear the slightest storm, and was splintered into fragments on the night of the threefold denial. Nothing of our Lord's work upon the Twelve stood the shock of Calvary. "They all forsook Him and fled." Nothing had been achieved when our Lord died on the Bitter Tree. If His mission had ended there, there would have been no such thing as Christianity in the world.

Yet, though nothing was achieved, all had been prepared; and as the Church of the Resurrection looked back, out of the light and glory of the Spirit, upon those old days in Galilee, the Will and the Intention of their Hidden Master started out into intelligible clearness, now that the clouds of their former ignorance had been dispelled : and in His words now so tenderly treasured, in His acts now so vividly recalled, they caught sight of the Will with which He was even now looking down from out of the heaven of heavens, and directing and governing His Kingdom. With their eyes on the Gospel story, they could read out the mind and the heart of Him Who now moved, as a living flame, amid the seven golden candlesticks. And so St. John reads deepest into the secret of those early sayings of the Master, as he sits, widowed and alone, drawing near to his end, in solitary awe, far down the years, amid a wondering Church,—St. John, now become the fisher of men, as his Master had promised him, a fisher in such strange seas, amid those Isles of Greece, where ever leaping wave spoke of Pagan stories and of Pagan dreams—St. John, now guiding, chronicling, completing with a master hand, that secure and marvellous organisation of the Episcopate, which should become the one Net, which should never break, whatever the multitude of fishes that should be drawn into its meshes, so delicate, yet so strong,—St. John himself, now shepherding, as his Master had bade Peter tend and feed, these swarming thousands, and thousands upon thousands, who had poured out of those terrible Pagan cities to follow the wonderful teachings of Christ, drawn after His feet, as the Galileans of old, bearing their wounds and their sores, that He might still touch and heal,—drawn after Him, they know not whither, to find themselves exiles or strangers, driven out of the homes of men, hungry and astray and homeless and forlorn on windy hills of fear, but forgetting all, risking all, heedless of the morrow, if only they might move on after Him, rapt and possessed, and might feel His healing hands upon their heads, or might sit and wait and hear and wonder; happy though they had lost lands and wives and children and friends ; happy though they had lost the whole world, yea, and their own lives also, if only they might sit at their Master's feet, and listen and listen for ever and for ever ! There they sit, hearing from John all that he can tell of the loving Lord in Heaven—and he, the Apostle, is responsible for them all. He must see that they are fed ; he must make them sit down in the pastures, that the food of the Lord may not pass over any, but reach to all, men and women, young or old, rich or poor. And as he sits there, old and venerable, uttering authoritative doctrine, or organising and ruling the beginnings of the Church, he sends his hearers back to the old days with the Lord, the days when he was, in his blindness, being so sweetly disciplined for the latter times of vision and udgment, rich with the manifold experience of fifty miraculous years.

And, as He looks back to single out the emphatic acts and words, one day there is, in the Galilean ministry, and one day only, which he cannot bring himself to omit. That Galilean time had been carefully recorded by the other Evangelists : as a whole, he could safely leave it untold; but this one day is too prominent, too decisive, too vivid, to be passed over. Though all have told it, he will tell it too. It was that wonderful day, the day of the feeding of the five thousands on the wild upland country beyond the Lake.

And why must he repeat the familiar story ? Because it was that day on which, for once, and once only, the Lord let the secret of His Church disclose itself in public, and anticipated the happy hours of Pentecost, and set in action ˙His chosen Twelve. The people were gathered and seated on the grass, and the command had gone forth, " Give ye them to eat." How could the disciples do so ? What had they to give ? How could they buy bread there, in the wilderness ? They — poor, ignorant fishermen — who were they to be charged with this tremendous task ? Nay! they had but one thought—how to get rid of these hungry multitudes. Their advice was so plain, and so prudent : " Send them away lest they starve in this desert, send them to find food for themselves in the villages."

"Send them away." That was their contribution to the problem—a very rational and practical bit of counsel. Yet the command stood, "'Give ye them to eat!' You are My chosen ones. You share with Me this burthen. You Twelve and I, we must see to it together that these poor wanderers go not away starving. It will be on your heads, as on Mine, if they faint by the way; you may not send them away at your peril. Rather 'give ye them to eat!'" So He spake, and lo! it had to be done; and, what was more surprising, it was their own private stock that was required for the task. It must be bread of their finding, be it but five barley loaves. Yet, as long as it is theirs, it will be sufficient. Our Lord waits for this. He acts only through their own meagre supply. And then, through them, the miraculous food must travel, through their hands, borne by their feet, under their twelvefold ministration. The bread that was eaten passes down through this specified channel to the expectant people; "He distributed to the disciples, and the disciples to them who were sat down:" and so to the last, even the cleaning of the tables as it were, is all theirs. They must see to it that all is fitly ended or thoughtfully stored. "Gather ye up the fragments," and back each of the Twelve returns, with his own basket, from the division to which he had ministered. "They filled twelve baskets with the fragments of the five barley loaves."

No wonder that no one of our Evangelists could forbear from telling of that first Eucharist of the ministering Church. And to St. John above all, looking back over the years, it must seem that every gathering experience had but served to manifest what was the Mind of Jesus under which he had unwittingly moved on that memorable day.

I. That old perplexity of the Twelve as they faced those hungry multitudes—had it not been, for many a long day since then, their one doubting question? What swarms of unknown people had poured out behind them as they told of Jesus! From place to place, from tribe to tribe, they had travelled; the cities had emptied for them, and temples had grown desolate. And what new and strange people they were, of unknown tongue, of alien blood! Wild heathen from the Uplands of Derbe and Lystra, passionate Gauls, dreaming Asiatics, hot Africans, quick Greeks, and serious Romans, and rough runaway slaves, sober philosophers and Syrian enthusiasts, and those of Cæsar's household, and rich ladies about the palace, and all the poor and helpless out of a hundred different towns—out they had come, leaving the customs of their forefathers and the sanctities of their immemorial faiths, out they had come, through strife and scorn, through sword and flame, to follow the Lamb whithersoever He goeth! And amid them all stood the Twelve; and, at the heart of the Twelve, stood Peter, and John, and James: and ever they watched the swarms that gathered about them from the East and from the West, from the North and from the

South. And still the Master from the hidden home within spake, with His old familiar tones, the un-daunted command, "Give ye them to eat!" And their food—this Gospel message, their stock of the Bread of Life, their little story of the old scene in Jewry, their service of bread and wine which they broke and poured and gave with the same simple words as of old, "This is My Body, this is My Blood"—would it then really suffice for all these strange new-comers? Would it never fail them? Would it feed all? the cultured as well as the ignorant? the slave as well as the philosopher? Would it strengthen all who were timid? Would it lessen all the savagery of life? And again, this Church of the Twelve—so small, so slender, and gathered into one single upper room in Jerusalem—would it widen to their immense opportunities? Would their own might, their own wisdom, hold out always under the pressure of their tremendous burdens? Would they find some whom they could not include or satisfy? So they must have wondered, and yet year after year found them still advancing—and still that wondrous food held out. They arrived at no heart to whom it could not bring the same peace as to their own. And it could never fail; always it was there still in the basket, enough and to spare; always at each hour of storm, when all seemed hopeless, and resources had all vanished, they looked, and lo! some unexpected supply showed itself; some little lad there was, just at the right moment, found standing, no one knew how, or whence, with his five barley loaves and two small fishes. So it had been always; they had had to begin with whatever was at hand : always they had, in the faith of their mission, acted as if all would be well, and had " bade the men sit down " wherever grass could be found ; always they had expected the food to be found them to give : and never had they been deceived. They looked into the basket, and still there was bread ; nor did they ever come to the end of the store. At the close of each evening, they had something yet to spare ; they had frag-ments to gather up into their baskets—enough for the morrow over and above that which had been eaten. " O that men would therefore praise the Lord for His goodness, and declare the works that He doeth for the children of men ! For He satis-fieth the empty soul, and filleth the hungry soul with goodness."

II. My brethren, the story of the Church as St. John saw it at the close of the first century has been its story always. It is its story at this day. Now, if ever, surely, the old scene repeats itself. There lie the multitudes, spread out before the eyes of the Church ; there they lie, scattered and astray over windy hills, homeless and hungry. And they have nowhere at all, in this dreary desert, where they can buy bread. *Bread for the body*, first ; that is hard enough to win. God knows how many will faint by the way ; many who have come from far, and have had nothing. Bread, literal bread for the body ; this is their first, their vital need ! Wherever can we buy that bread for them ? Yet here, too, the message touches us sharply, "Give ye them to eat!" That miracle was no allegory. It saved these worn bodies from starving, and it lays everlastingly the burden of its literal message upon a Christian Church: "Give ye them to eat." You are the Church of the Father, Who feedeth the hungry. See to it that these little ones are not starved. See to it that they "do not faint by the way;" that life is not made impossible or relentless to them; that at least they know among them the presence of a Church that is pledged to discover a means of allaying this their terrible hunger, in the Name of Him who made it responsible for their needs by His charge, "Give ye them to eat."

And *bread for the soul*—bread from Heaven, the blessed Bread of God. Ah! whence can they buy that here in the wilderness? Whence can they ever win it but from us? Look! how their spirits faint within them by the way! How they sicken, and fail, and die, spiritually starved! Such a miserable death! so sickly, so weak, so white, so nerveless do their poor souls become; their spiritual life sinks almost without an effort, as they wander lonely, beggared, unhoused; and ever the long bleak path stretches on and on, through the stony wilderness, through which their worn spirits travel, and never once will it bring them within sight of a spiritual homestead, where their weary souls will lie at rest, and be sweetly nourished and refreshed! There they are, round and round us, on all sides, round us at home, in cities that terrify us by their monstrous growth—abroad in colonies, that are filled before we have discovered their very names.

There they are, and they are starving. And still the voice within the Church, the voice of the Unseen Master, cries on and on, "Give ye them to eat! Give ye them to eat!"

How can it be done? Dear people, we have this comfort that we cannot feel more powerless or more perplexed than the Apostles on the hills of Decapolis. "Whence can we buy bread at all here in the wilderness? Why, two hundred pennyworth of bread would not suffice, that every one should have a little." We know that perplexity. We know the ring of that excuse. And yet there is one solution absolutely forbidden us—"Send them away into the villages to buy bread for themselves." How obvious the advice sounds! It is so sensible, so rational. It commends itself so easily to us. Are they not responsible, these multitudes, for being found in their distress? Why did they come without forethought, without provision, so foolish, so reckless? We never brought them here. They must look to it for themselves. We are very sorry. Why should they not have remembered that there would be no food for them here? Why is all this burden thrown upon us? Why do these crowds still swarm and swarm about us, as if there was no limit to our charity and our powers? We cannot help them. We have not the means; it is a human impossibility. Nay, we are ourselves in a bad way; we, too, are in the wilderness. We must do what we can to feed ourselves. It will cost us all our time to secure to ourselves our spiritual food, to pay for our Church and clergymen. How can we manage the greater task, if we can hardly struggle along with the small one?

Yes, it is perfectly sensible and intelligent and plain, and yet the Master brushes away every syllable of it aside, as a man brushes a mote out of his eye; His ears do not hear this apologetic pleading, as unswervingly His Will bends itself to the other task set before it. They must be fed. "How many loaves have we? Is there really nothing? Cannot some bread be found? Is there no one with five loaves and a fish or two? That will do to begin with. Make the men sit down."

Two points, two rules, are here given us; two rules, in which we catch sight of the means wherewith the Lord governs His household:—First, He cannot begin until we men bring Him something. His material comes from us. The law of the Church is the law of the Incarnation. As He saved us by stooping to use human means, by confining Himself to our resources, so it is still: something of ours He must have whereon to work: He will use no more than we ourselves possess. What can we bring Him? What help is in our hands? It matters not how small; it matters not how casual or incidental. It may be a mere chance that a lad is there who happens to have in his basket five loaves and two fishes. But it must be *our* bread. Give the Lord this, and He is ready; He is free to act: "Make the men sit down."

Our second rule is this: However little we can start with, at any rate the Church accepts the entire task set before her. All these people have got to be fed;

and they were intended to be fed by her. Not one item of the responsibility may be declined. Not one of those hungry millions ought to be sent away to find food for himself. Yet how impossible it all looks! How can we feed them all? It is not only the poor in their numbers that alarm us, but the few, the learned, the cultured. How are we going, with our simple Gospel story of sin and its cure, to satisfy them all? Whole worlds of new knowledge, new interest, new skill are opening, yet even out of these men come to our spiritual hills, drawn to the voice of our Christ, hungry and faint for His living and undying bread. How can we in our poverty, in our inexperience, hope to embrace their aspirations, or crown their discoveries, and find for them food more spiritual, more enduring, more alive, than all the delights of art, all the splendours of the service which they have left behind in the pursuit of the better thing which is theirs in Christ?

"Make the men sit down!" That is the answer. Believe that you have a message, an office, to them, as to all. Decline nothing, offer to fulfil every human hope. Pledge your own souls that though you know not how, yet that He will prove Himself sufficient for all. Give the Lord your loaves, and make the men sit down. Give what you have, however tiny. Believe in the power of the Gospel, however immense the task, and then—oh! we know what happens. The Spirit that rushed down at Pentecost, as a wind, and as a fire—He comes down as of old, to fill with motion, to quicken with heat; He fulfils; He achieves; He enlarges; He multiplies; He spreads Himself abroad; He rushes mightily; He flashes as the lightning from one end of heaven unto the other. He takes of Christ; He discloses new wonders; He opens out strange secrets. He brings us the strength of God. What is there He cannot perform? He brings us the Wisdom of God. What is there He cannot conquer?

One word for members of the Church. Let them, each one of them, do just one thing and that thing only. What is that which is close at hand to you? What is that which you can begin doing to-day for Christ? Some one little thing, quite definite, near, practical, direct, and immediate. Some help you now hold in your hands. What is it? Look now! How many loaves have you that you can give up at once before you leave this church? Some home duty, already yours, but never yet taken and offered; or some chance help that opportunity throws in your way. Is there not something; some lad with his basket— unexpected, suddenly disclosed? A very little thing, after all,—five barley loaves and two fishes! Yes, contemptible! What are they for so high a task? Plain common bread, just what everybody has; and a tiny fish or two, to season it. But that is enough for the Lord? He will begin with thát. Offer him that. He will take it, contemptible as it may look, and in His hands it will miraculously increase; and He will give thanks; and give it you back. The change will begin; the spirit will be at work. The leaven will stir within the lump. Out from this little spot in your life, that you have given to Christ, for His sake only, out from it the leaven will spread. Dedicate it to Him, and the entire self will become quickened, revisited, illumined; for the thanksgiving of Jesus will work like light, like heat, from the sacred hearth in the centre; and the whole man will be subdued into the mighty working.

SERMON VIII.

THE MIND OF THE CHURCH.

" And Jesus took the loaves; and when He had given thanks, He distributed to the Disciples, and the Disciples to them that were set down;
and likewise of the fishes as much as they would. When they were
filled, He said unto the Disciples, Gather up the fragments that remain,
that nothing be lost."—St. John vi. 11, 12.

THE mind with which our risen Master for ever
influences the living Church from His throne through
Heaven is to be detected in glimpses and flashes through
the records of His deeds while still living as a Jew
among Jews. And this because the acts and the
words which then He did, make known to us a single,
and definite Person, possessed of a certain final character, type, mind, will, purpose. Just as a man is
always the same whatever he does and wherever he is,
changing his time without changing himself, so with
the Lord. His personality reveals in one set of circumstances what He for ever is; and this is why we
are justified in considering actions done on earth as
typical of His eternal activity in the Church. What
He was then that He still is; and we therefore read
the gospel story, not merely as a record of past facts,
but also, that so reading, we may look up to high
Heaven, like birds that sip at pools and lift their

heads,—may look up and say, "Lord Jesus, I know Thee now, as Thou art before God in glory." And here, in the miracle of the loaves, He seems to have let His secret, repressed till then, break out for a moment—the secret of His Church. He allows Himself to exhibit for one short hour the plan and purpose wherewith He looked to use after Resurrection those Twelve whom He had chosen. Here, then, we can look close into His mind; here, then, we can see, indeed, the mystery of that anticipated Kingdom. We can watch the Master as He founds, and builds, and orders. Let us look at Him closely.

First, what is the motive from out of which He sets Himself to ordain a Church? It is compassion for crowds. It had been compassion for crowds that had first bent Him to call and send out those Twelve. "When He saw the multitudes, He was moved with compassion, because they fainted, and were scattered abroad as sheep having no shepherd," and He called unto Him His Twelve, and gave them power to heal and to preach. So it had been; and now it is the starving of the crowds that impels Him to set those shepherds in motion. Compassion for hungry crowds— this, then, is the everlasting secret behind the Church of Christ; this is the motive which puts all in action; this is its primary spring and source; this is the form and fashion in which God makes Himself known through the Church. The Church is the steady witness and abiding proof of the compassion of God —of God, the great God and Father of all, Whose eternal character displays itself in helping them to right who suffer wrong, and in feeding the hungry; Who never, at any time, left His compassion without witness, in that He always sent upon all rain from Heaven; and now that same God sends from Heaven His Son that He may build for the poor and needy a city in the wilderness and gather Himself houses like a flock of sheep. So wide, so universal, is the compassion of that One Father, Who made all to be of one blood, sending His rain upon the just and upon the unjust, and making His sun to shine on the thankful and the evil.

Let us consider this in its depth, and width, and height. It is the compassion of the entire Godhead that builds the Church—the compassion of God, the great Father, made known to us through the tenderness and tears of a human heart, in flesh and blood, in Jesus Christ, His Son, our Brother. That compassion, as it is in Christ Jesus, offers itself in a shape that enthrals and subdues with a touch of human kinship; but, nevertheless, it is, still, in Him but a revelation of that supreme compassion which moves the Father to send His Son into the world. The compassionate mercy of the Father sends His Son; and it is made manifest and sealed to us in that hidden, yet felt Spirit, whose very Name is given Him for His pity, the Advocate, the Spirit of Consolation, the Comforter.

The Ministry of the Church, then, issues out of the deep compassions of the Triune Godhead. And what is the active force which animates, and sustains, and fills, and advances it? Thanksgiving. Jesus, taking the bread, lifted up His eyes, and blessed and brake—

all which St. John sums up in the words, "Jesus gave thanks:" He made His Eucharist. The thanksgiving of Jesus was the power that was infused into the bread, by which it swelled and grew and multiplied and sufficed. The thanksgiving of Jesus is the breath of the Church. Just as His compassion is the form in which His Godhead looks out upon us through the Church; so, in thanksgiving, Jesus makes known to us the perfection of the Creature, the crown and glory of His Manhood. As God He comes down in pity; in the name of mankind He looks up and gives thanks.

And consider how solemn is the act. For the entire creation grew together to reflect and repeat the glory of God; and yet the echo of God slumbered in the hollow bowels of the dumb earth until there was one who could wake up the shout by a living voice. Man is the first among the creatures to deliver back from the rolling world this conscious and delicious response, the recognition of the Father Who begat him. He, and he alone, is Nature's priest, her spokesman, her mediator. It is his part, in the midst of her silence, to lift up in her name the voice of thanksgiving. The life that passes into him from its far home in God is redelivered out from his lips back again in the sound of thanks. Through thanks it completes its circle, moving from God to God. In that thanksgiving man makes the discovery, the full disclosure of his sacred origin. Always he is in God and exists by God, but in thanksgiving he sets his own seal to the work of God within him; he gives back love for love; and there is no other end to which man ever ultimately sets himself but this of thanksgiving. It embraces all his possibilities, and satisfies all his aspirations. Man lives for this and this only—that by word and by deed he may give thanks unto God.

And Jesus Christ is the Crown and Sum of humanity, and this one thing, therefore, He does, He gives thanks for ever and for ever; He takes all our loaves, takes all the poor, scant, pitiful offerings we can bring out of our niggardly baskets, and over all He lifts up His eyes to Heaven and blesses the Name of the Lord. And the thanksgiving is mighty; it works and stirs in the heart of the Church; it warms, quickens expands, and lo! the strange, unceasing change begins. Under its working dead things live, and dumb things speak, and blind things see, and dry things soften, and every stone becomes bread, and frozen things yield, and run, and sing, like rivers among the hills, and all silent things shake themselves loose and break into vigorous life. The breath of the Lord fills His Church as He spreads His Hands abroad and offers His great Eucharist. And we, too, stand with Him. We are empowered by His intercession, we are authorised by His brotherhood; we, in Him, complete the perfect office of a redeemed mankind, and all our growth and all our force come to us out of the heart of those hours, those blessed hours, when with Angels and Archangels, and all the company of Heaven, we, too, take our place and mingle our voices in amongst the thousand times ten thousand who, as the sound of many waters, sing the new and eternal song of the Lamb, and cry to one another and say

"Holy, holy, holy! we praise Thee; we bless Thee; we give thanks to Thee for Thy great glory!"

Compassion is the motive with which the Church is built, and thanksgiving is the force by which it is made alive; and what is the nature and character of its activity?   Order, organised order, is the stamp of Christ upon His Church. "Make the men sit down;" arrange them, distribute them; they are very hungry, and they are in crowds, there will be confusion if care be not taken; there will be a rush and scramble, and some will get too much and the weaker will get nothing; see to it that every one—woman and child—has a bit; "make them sit down,"—sit down in squares like flower-beds (in twelve squares probably, one for each of the Twelve), and keep the men apart from the women and children; and find them grass, and set them in rows, like plants in their beds, so that the ministers can pass in and out among them.   And when that is done, and all is ready, in quiet and care He divides the bread to the disciples, and they divide to the people; and, at the end, He bids them clear up everything, store it away for the morrow, that nothing be lost.   How seemly, and orderly, and measured, and steady, and wise!   Do we sufficiently remember how incessantly our Lord loved to talk to those twelve whom He had so methodically sifted and selected, of order, place, and regularity, of servants in households, each in his separate lot,—one the porter, and another the steward, so that in that regulated life the food should all be brought out in due season? How He loved to tell them of the monotonous steady forethought of the banks and warehouses! "Yes, be ye, too, good bankers," was the word He is reported to have said to the Twelve. "Be as he who, for many a long day, while his lord is far away, works out the dull work of turning five talents into ten, and two into five." How he loved the soldier-faith of the centurion who saw that the spiritual kingdom was directed and ordered by graduated authority from end to end, just as he himself had learned under the formal discipline of the army, where each stood above the other in regular sequence, and all action was easy and thorough so long as each in his place took the commands from those that stood higher and passed them to those beneath, who came and went at his bidding! How He loved to parallel His Kingdom to the laws of natural growth of seeds, of corn, and leaven,—growth which is the triumph of organic and compacted and constructed life! Our Lord loved order, loved method, loved system. He loved to use harmonious means. He loved the precision that is involved in all creative artistic action. He loved the graduated scale of ministers that constitute the perfection of a household, of a city, of a kingdom.

And how, indeed, should we ever believe that He did come from God, if He had left His spiritual work to the confusion of chance, unformed, unformulated, and dis-ordered, while every fragment of God's natural world speaks in another language altogether, speaks of methods and modes of arrangement, of forethought, of combination, of organisation, precision, direction, co-ordination? In nature everything is systematic, and everything is definite; everything must be done in one way, and in that way only, or it cannot be done at all; there are lines and channels, all laid down and fixed. And as we pass up and out of the natural world, we are bound to expect no breach between the manifestation of God in nature and His revelation in Christ. Here, too, in this new region, we shall instinctively look for the same Mind to be at work, with its peculiar joy in the beauty of order. And so it certainly proves. The type, the ideal, that we were familiar with in the lower level, prevails also in the higher. As we pass out of the natural kingdom we find ourselves moving through a spiritual country which is governed and controlled, where words have a fixed meaning and offices have fixed rules, and there are roads and paths, and the broad highway, and mutual services, and ordered ministries; and, ever as we walk, we see descending out of Heaven in all the comeliness of bridal grace the Holy City, set four square, with three gates on the east, three on the west, three on the north, and three on the south, and the length and the breadth and the height of it are equal, and the walls are measured with a golden reed, according to the measurement of an angel, one hundred and forty-four cubits, and there are twelve foundations, and twelve gates, and every foundation is a separate jewel, and every gate a single pearl. That is our vision, towards which our pilgrim steps are set; a vision in which law and rule are no temporary necessity, but the eternal glory of God's holy Name. Yea, and even to us, even in the earthly courts of that great Kingdom, the sweet strength of Divine order reaches, and we, by faith in that vision, can joyfully recognise the echoes of the Heavenly Kingdom in those distributed ministries, and regulated offices, by which the Church admits, and encompasses, and feeds us, allotting to each member its separate part, under the sanction of that law, "which has its seat in the bosom of the Lord, Whose voice is the harmony of the world, to Whom all things in Heaven and earth do homage, and all with uniform consent admiring her as the mother of their peace and joy."

That is the Church, and each soul within the Church must reflect and embody the spirit of the Bride. Each one of us is set to display these three graces of the Church—compassion, thanksgiving, and order. This is our high calling, and no one may decline or fall short of it wilfully. We are called to careful and trained activity; and we may not hang back at the doorway through which we enter. We cannot arrest our spiritual life at the forgiveness of sins. Never, indeed, will the penitential under-current cease to flow; for ever we sin, though "we walk in the light," and the sprinkling of the Blood of Jesus must ever renew the blessing of our first pardon. But, beyond our pardon, there is a new life wherein we walk in the glory of the faith of Jesus Christ. And this redeemed life must be the life of citizens who can move with clear eyes and steady steps through the measured streets and by the appointed gates of this clean and comely City, the new Jerusalem. Discipline, thanksgiving, compassion,—these are our three notes; and we must reverse the order in which they show themselves in our Lord and Master. For we come from below upwards, while He descends downwards from above; and, therefore, for us there must be, first, the discipline of rule before our thanksgiving can be possible. There must be rule,—rule in the entire man : rule in the affections and appetites, that they may yield themselves servants unto righteousness. And together with rule in the affections, rule also in the mind, that our faith may disentangle itself and become articulate where before it dumbly felt, and see where it blindly touched,—rule in the mind until slowly the whole being is mastered, and the heart can move freely in the novel terms, and glow in a rich and outspoken creed. And, again, rule and discipline in the will, that it may bring captive every thought into the blessed bondage of Jesus. Rule in the affections, mind, and will; this there must be ;—and the rule will seem long and the discipline strict, and it may all look at first to us dry and severe. Then begins the wonder : we thought it bondage, and, lo, it becomes freedom ; we seemed to be crippled, and, lo, we expand and grow. It is the new man in us that strengthens and makes increase, and moves and warms; and within us at last there springs up, as the sound of living waters, as the outburst of a bird's clear song, a strange and transfiguring joy such as we knew not before; and we feel as if our spirits leapt, and danced, and sang ; and we wake as a garden of spices wakes at the breath of the wind from the south ; and there rises the rushing sound of our new praise, and we find we can give thanks to God! We glorify God, we give thanks for His great glory, and give Him worship, and honour, and dominion, and power. So begins our thanksgiving; and, then, out of thanksgiving, we win compassion. As we turn our eyes, full of blessed tears, from the great White Throne, upon brethren and sisters who starve, how we love them, and yearn over them with a new yearning, and our own happiness in God drives us out of ourselves! We cannot bear it alone; why are they not as we are? Oh, that we could tell them what we know! how shall we rest till they have tasted and drunk? And we begin to understand what St. Paul was saying when he cried, "Oh, ye Corinthians, our mouth is open unto you, our heart is enlarged. Ye are not straitened in us, but ye are straitened in your own bowels." So our thanksgiving becomes compassion. Out of our human devotion in giving ourselves to God, we gain a touch of the Godhead to which we give ourselves. We gain this Divine power of pity. We look out upon our fellows with the yearning of the Father— "Oh, that my people would hearken unto Me!"—and our eyes begin to moisten with the tears of Him who wept over the city, and said, "Oh! Jerusalem, Jerusalem." That, when it is gained, is Christian charity,—no light emotion of passing pity, no accident of temperament, but a habit, a nature, a character of life, settled, rigid, and eternal. This is charity as it is in Christ; no fruit of earthly seed which the light winds have sown, but the perfect fruit of that trained and cultivated growth whose root is faith, whose flower is hope,—a fruit which the effort of Divine husbandry has built up into Divine growth.

"Ye are God's husbandry." He would spend His skill upon you, for He desires your fruit. But there is no skill without schooling. We omit and forget the schooling, and because we forget it we see so little necessity for careful scientific training, and our faith remains vague and unstable, instead of a noble spiritual building. The Church, on the Feast of Trinity, asks of us the harder and rarer task, asks us to surrender our unsteady emotion to the rule of Christ's creed, to the discipline of Christ's law, that at the end of the long line of Trinity Sundays, Advent may find us at least one or two steps further on the road that leadeth to perfection.

SERMON IX.

THE MINISTRY OF THE CHURCH.[1]

"Peter saith unto Him, Lord, why cannot I follow Thee now?
I will lay down my life for Thy sake. Jesus answered him, Wilt
thou lay down thy life for My sake? Verily, verily, I say unto thee,
The cock shall not crow till thou hast denied Me thrice."—St. John
xiii. 37, 38.

THE pathos of the last scenes in the Upper Chamber
gathers itself for us into a living picture, as we read
of that ardent offer, and of its serious, far-sighted
response.

All that is beautiful, all that is inspiring in human
loyalty, in human affection, in human hope, in human
courage, is working in the heart and in the eyes of
the eager Apostle, as he looks up into the Face that
he loves so dearly; that Face which he would follow
though all fall away, because It had in It the look
of eternal life; that Face which had drawn him under
Its searching gaze down there by Jordan, where first
he received his new name, when Jesus turned and

---

[1] This Sermon needs some apology. Preached at the Annual
Festival of Cuddesdon College, it may well be thought too private
and personal in character to appear formally in a book. Yet I have
ventured to insert it, because it attempts to exhibit, in the region
of the ministry, the working of that very same principle which has
been shown to lie at the root of the Church.

looked upon him, and sealed him His for ever; that Face which had sought him out to call him from the nets and the boats, so that he rose and followed; that Face which had bent over him in full blessing as he made his great confession, and for which he had left all—father, and mother, and wife, and home; that Face which is now clouded over with some dark boding, foreshadowing awful doom, a doom of which He, the Lord, speaks in tones that dishearten, in words that bewilder—speaks of loneliness, of desertion, of failure, of unresisted death, of sad departure, of mysterious end. What is it all? What does it mean? Why should He Who, full surely, has the secret of eternal life, Who has such strange power over winds and sea, over sickness and sorrow, why should He despair of help, despair of deliverance? Whither can it be that He will withdraw? What road is it that He will take alone and undefended? Why should they, the followers, fail to follow? What can ever separate them, Master and disciple—Lord and slave? "Lord, whither goest Thou? and why cannot I follow Thee now?" He has love and he has courage; and he has confidence, and he has faithfulness. Why cannot he follow wherever it be that He goes? "Yea, I will lay down my life for Thy sake." So he looks, so he offers, so he believes, the loyal, eager-hearted man! Who could offer with more confidence than he? He had given himself with a whole heart to the service of a Master loved as no other was ever loved. He had held fast at that critical hour when all seemed forsaking; he had followed Him to

Jerusalem, into the very centre of peril, whither they went that they might die with Him; even now he clutched one of those two swords wherewith he would be ready to strike one blow for Jesus, even amid the hopeless terror of a midnight surprise: surely he, if any, might trust his own faithfulness, might dare to gallantly offer his very life for his Master's honour. What is there that he would not and could not do for Him? Why cannot he follow Him now? He would lay down his life for Jesus' sake.

Ah yes, it is a brave and beautiful offer — the Master does not deny that. He does not refuse or despise it. He cannot but look tenderly down upon the brimming affection, the ardent gaze of him who lays at His feet all that he has to give. And yet His wonderful insight is seeing out and away beyond the impulse that for the moment is so deeply stirred, beyond all that the Apostle himself knew of his own warm feelings and fervent will. He does not despise; no,—but neither does He at all mistake the value of the gift that has been brought Him. He has strange measures by which He gauges it, strange balances in which He puts it to proof. Without any touch of remote anger, without a note of disappointment, in pity rather than in reproof, He is looking away from the warmth of that upper chamber, still haunted and possessed by the wonder of the first Eucharist; He sees another scene, the tumult and disorder of a bois-terous court-yard, the sickness of a sudden despair, the chill of the sleepless night, the rough insolence of the guard-room, the loud laugh of the servants, the light sneer of a maid. What would survive *then* of that ardour which was now so resolute and so daring? That impressionable heart, would it not be as sensitive to the chilling touch of scorn as it was to the glow of hopeful love? That power of affectionate response, which was so precious to the Lord that He rated it above all cool and deliberate resolution of a steadied will, and named it blessed of Heaven, as the best medium through which the revelations from the Father could pass and work,—that very power had its peculiar and perilous collapses; it would be susceptible to adverse influences with the same intensity as to higher calls and finer inspirations. It would flutter down when wounded and hurt, with the same rapid and violent movement as that by which it had shot up, like a lark's song into the height of a sunny sky. So the Lord foresaw; so He pityingly, unangrily pronounced. Beautiful, most beautiful to Him the human devotion, the proffered life, the passionate generosity, the loyalty so ignorant of its own weakness, the confidence so childlike in its simple self-belief. Tenderly He watches it; tenderly He treats it and handles it. "Wilt thou indeed lay down thy life for My sake?" Blessed for that, at least, art thou Simon Barjona! It is the same fervour now speaking that spoke then, by the coasts of Cæsarea Philippi, the words which no flesh and blood, no blind human impulse had made known to him, but the Father Which is in Heaven.

Yes, blessed indeed. But yet there is an austerer lesson to learn, the lesson that would curb and quell that boyish self-confidence which had before now allowed him to become the tool of Satan in the very moment which followed that in which he had been the instrument of the Father Which is in Heaven. He must yet learn why Jesus had taken him aside to speak of going up to Jerusalem, and of suffering many things, and of the shame, and the spitting, and the Cross. He must yet be sifted by that Satan of whom his confident loyalty still savoured. He must learn to know himself, and his own pitiful, shallow weakness; learn for Christ's sake, not only to leave father, and mother, and home, and land, but to hate his own self also, if he is ever to sit chief among Twelve, judging the twelve tribes of Israel. He would learn it in the porch, weeping bitterly, as the cock crew, and the Lord, denied and disowned, turned and looked upon him, with the look that would recall to him this rash vow which now was breaking from his lips in the upper chamber. Yes! though now indeed he feels as if he could lay down his life for Jesus' sake, yet " Verily, verily, I say unto thee, the cock shall not crow until thou hast denied Me thrice."

Why should I speak to-day of a theme so serious and so saddening? Because, on this day, when those flock back to Cuddesdon[1] who here have made their offering of themselves to the Ministry of Jesus, it is good and reassuring to recall the laws that alone can make that self-oblation effective for the Church, and acceptable to God. We have here shown to us in this pathetic scene the relation between the man's own

---

[1] Annual Festival.

offer of himself to Christ, and his true call and election by the Master. St. Peter's ardour, St. Peter's love, St. Peter's passionate professions,—these are no insignificant elements of his Apostleship, of his chieftaincy. His quick, responsive sensitiveness, his gallant audacity, these bring him near to Christ; these play their part; these draw, and stir, and impel him; these answer to that attractive power put out by Christ upon him; these break out in brave utterances that are pronounced blessed by Jesus Himself; these push him forward; these work within: by them he becomes adequate for fuller use, enabled to follow up into the light of the Mount of Transfiguration—to follow in under the black shadows of the Garden of the Agony; by these he presses home his inquiries, his searchings, his appeals, "What shall we have?" "How often shall my brother offend and I forgive?" "Why cannot I follow Thee now?" by these he is urged to this last offer of his very life for his Master's sake. They have done well, then; they have been no contemptible matter at all; and surely, it is they, too, that have won for Peter the love of Christ. Without his rash impulsiveness, without his forward affections, without his boyish self-trust, he would not have been the man beloved, who should be named by his Master, Cephas— the man in whose sample of faith He found the first stone for His Church. Nay! all this is lovely to Him, and dear, and acceptable. All this is the needful material out of which the Apostles are made—out of which Churches are built. But yet, for all that, it is not this human response, this human desire, this human offer, that admits to Apostleship or that can bear the strain of the ministry. "Ye have not chosen Me, but I have chosen you." All that Christ could win of affection and faith from the chosen Twelve during His Life on earth, genuine and loyal as it was, was impotent to form the stuff of a ministry, until it had been taken under the Cross, and touched with the blood of sprinkling, and had died to itself, shattered by the first blow that struck it, and had risen again, a new thing, of a higher type, remade, transfigured, under the strong Hand of Him Who, by His own deliberate act, chose, and called, and established, and sanctified, and anointed, and fashioned it,—by Him Who, in His Resurrection-strength, breathed upon those dead bones that lay dry and broken in the arid desert of despair—breathed into them the Power of the Holy Ghost, and they were lifted, as by a rushing mighty wind, and were lit with tongues of fire, and went whither the Spirit carried them, and spake as the Spirit that was in them moved. Till then—roused, heightened, outpoured though this affection might be—it was but a faithless and fallible thing, with which nothing redemptive could be worked. It might be loved, but it was not trusted by the Lord. His very choice was not in full energy over the Twelve until He had risen from the dead; until the Spirit had come upon them in the might of the Resurrection.

Here, therefore, on this sad evening in the upper chamber, He is but waking a Faith which the very night in which He speaks would shatter into fragments. "Now we believe;" so they all cry, moved by His majestic love. "Now we believe;" so they fancy, caught up by the same brave assurance as St. Peter. Yes, now, under the pressure of the moment; under the movement of roused emotion; in the presence of the Lord, in the hush of the still evening, in the peace of the upper chamber, in the glow of the last farewell, in the fervour of fellowship—now, as our hearts burn within us; now, as we forget the cold, hard, hostile world outside—the taunts, the hatred, the indifference, the jeers, the tumult, the roughness, the violence, the bitterness—"now, we believe." Yea, now; but an hour hence—when the torches flash in, and the swords and the staves menace, and cruel eyes glint round, and there is no time to think, and the darkness dismays, and the Master is snared, betrayed, lost ; and the flood of evil breaks over them, and the blast of the terrible ones is as a storm against the wall,—how will it be then ? "Do ye now believe? Behold the hour cometh, yea, is now come, when ye shall be scattered every one to his own, and shall leave Me alone." Now, indeed, they believe, but then—before even one cock shall crow, that very night—"they all forsook Him, and fled."

There lies, in dreadful accuracy, the story of a human offer—of a human ministry. The emotion, that feels so strong at the good hour, needs but a bad quarter of an hour to collapse and to vanish, to forsake and to flee. No stuff here, on which to rely. No stuff here, which will stand the strain of Christ's work. No, not even if it be tender as St. John's, and brave as St. Peter's. This is well worth our bearing in mind ; for we come to the thought of the Priesthood often through so much of our own—through *our* inclination, *our* good desire, *our* high intention. We have been turned to it, perhaps, not merely by blind habit or a parent's wish, but by eager movements of our own spirit, by the force of our compassion for the poor, of our devotion to Jesus, of our proud will to do what we can for the good of mankind, drawn to the Ministry as to a noble and inspiring task, full of ardour, full of zeal; and as we kneel in glad mornings before Christ's Altar waiting for the Hallowed Food, or in solemn eventides, in still rooms, by the bedside, alone, devout, earnest, we are sure that Christ is with us, speaking to us no longer in parable, no longer in dark hints hard to seize, and in strange sayings half understood, but speaking plainly, with clear, downright decision, making sure to us His meaning, making present to us His love. Then we are all aflame, we could do anything for Jesus, we pledge Him our souls, our lives. "Yea! Now I believe! What is there that I may not do for Thee, Lord? Whither goest Thou? Only tell me and I will follow: why cannot I follow Thee? I will lay down my life for Thy sake."

Ah! how quickly such ardour passes! Amid the stress of toil, in disappointment, in the disfigurement of fatigue, fretted by mistakes, jostled by hate, baffled by stupidity, bruised with scoffs, cheerless, lonely, amazed, confounded, our first love, in the heat of which we had trusted, flickers miserably low, it wavers, and shivers, and dwindles. Our own belief, that seemed to us so confident, somehow fails to sweep everything before it. It is staggered by finding itself so impotent to persuade. We thought that its very fervour would break through all obstacles, that no hard heart would hold out against our eager pleading for Christ. Yet we are thrown back, beaten, despised. Sin holds its own against us, it hardly seems touched at all, or its grip loosened on the world. We preach, and preach, and no one seems one whit the better. The heart of us sickens, the spirit in us is chilled.

Yes, and rightly; for we are learning St. Peter's lesson, learning the cold shudder that crept over him in the loud hall of the High Priest. Well for us, if by the mercy of God we do not learn the bitterness of his tears in the desolate shame of the porch.

Dear brothers, it is not we who choose the service of Christ. "Ye have not chosen Me." This is no light lesson to follow. Not in our own choice, not in our own earnestness, not in our own resolution, not through our own offer of ourselves, not through our own willingness to die, not in this do we fight. Not through this do we serve. Nay! This is the loyalty that forsakes. This is the love that flees. This is the courage that denies. This is the faith that is scattered. This is the service that leaves Christ alone amid His foes. When we are young, we may gird ourselves and walk whither we will; but this is the girding of youth, not the girding of an Apostle. It is a far other girding that we must learn—the girding girt round us by the strong Hand, by the imperial Will of Jesus our Master, in whose hold we shall stand, patient and unresisting as a blind tool, yet alive and quivering as a quickening flame. That Will, steady and invincible, may lift us and bind us to a naked cross, may carry us whither we would not, may bear us against the beating hail of this world's scorn, may thrust us against its merciless spears. Yet, so that we be in Him, we shall not quail or shrink. For the old self-trust will be wholly purged away, and our service will be not our own but the Spirit's service, our courage will be not our own but the Spirit's courage, our loyalty will be the unshaken strength of Christ Himself alive in us. As the moving wheels seen by Ezekiel by the waters of Chebar, we shall turn neither to the right nor to the left, but whithersoever the Spirit moves, thither we shall go. So held, so possessed, we can afford to lie still in God's Hand, to wait, to fail; can bear to learn that our bravest service for Christ may lie, not in busy activity, but in being snatched away from all our works and all our hopes, and lashed to some life-long cross, powerless and dumb. We can endure to learn, it may be, that it will be better than when we were young and walked whithersoever we desired, that when we are old another should gird us and carry us whither we would not!

And yet, though indeed it be not we that have chosen Christ, but Christ that hath chosen us, yet that first human offer, that first pledge of service, is not an idle or ineffectual thing. Nay! it is the very material out of which Jesus fashions that true Faith which is His own creation. God took of the dust of the ground: and out of that dust He moulded the body of man, into which He breathed a living soul. And Jesus takes of this, that is ours, this matter that we bring Him, this earthly material, this human love, this eagerness, this impulse, this affection, this bravery, this emotion—He takes of this, dust that it is, dust without coherence, without solidity, blown hither and thither by every changing gust, whirled on high for one moment, in a pillar, on the wings of some strong storm, and then scattered, loose and ruinous, into a thousand flying fragments, vanishing as a cloud at morn,—this shifting dust, so restless, so impotent, this it is that He takes into His Hands, and uses and shapes, until it grows into a steady and enduring substance, until it coheres, bound and knit into a solid, massive body, which the Spirit of God holds fast together, and possesses, and carries along, and keeps whole and entire. That belief of the Eleven, which the night of the Betrayal so terribly shattered, was itself the condition of that firm belief which would spring up, a new creation, under the breath of Him Who should stand in the Upper Chamber, saying, "Peace be unto you." "Receive ye the Holy Ghost."

As the dust of the earth is drawn upward into the man, so from out of the man's heart is drawn upward that which becomes superhuman. The gallant pledge of the night, the brave promises, all went to naught, lay shivered and broken upon the ground that night. But not in vain; not without fruitful purpose. Unless they had been given, there would have been no stuff upon which the Spirit of the Resurrection could do its work or set its hand. The human passion could not endure the strain of the Apostolate; but it did make it possible that Apostles should be, that the new man should be created. It did open the door to the Spirit's entry. It was because St. Peter offered his life with such impetuous rashness, that he could be raised again out of the misery of the denial into the Apostle that we know in the Acts. He, St. Peter, could not follow Christ now, no! not now; but that very eagerness of his impossible offer made it possible that he, in the power of the Spirit, should follow Him hereafter. Yes! it was the old human love, once so impetuous and now chastened and changed, that our Lord raised, transfigured unto a new thing, as, by the waters of Gennesaret, He called the man once more by the familiar name, and appealed to him by the tender appeal, " Simon, son of Jonas, lovest thou Me ? "

" Ye have not chosen Me ! " No, not at our desire, not in the insecurity of our intention, are we Priests. This first; but then the yet deeper truth—He does choose *us*,—chooses us, one by one, name by name, Peter, John, Matthew, Thomas,—chooses us each for what he is, each with his own peculiar gift, each for his own separate usefulness. So tender He is with us in our boyish forwardness ! We hurry with our proffered aid. We press upon Him our service, and how graciously, how pityingly, how lovingly, how sweetly He checks, and trains, and warns, and chastens us ! " Wilt thou lay down thy life, My son ? Dost thou indeed now believe and know, My child, that I am come forth from God ? Alas, the cock shall crow for thee too, as for Peter ! Alas, the night will find Me forsaken by thee, as by them of old !" So He knows us only too well! Yet, on the morrow, when we have been broken, when we have smarted, when we have tasted the bitterness of our failures, and have sadly learned the sharp lesson of self-mistrust, of self-despair, after we have known the shame and tears óf Peter's porch, have known that in us dwelleth no good thing—ah! then it is by name that He greets us, "Simon, son of Jonas." It is the man that He needs—the man, warm and living, the man, with his separate, individual stamp: a Peter, with his hot impulses ; a John, with his strong, patient, clinging attachment ; a Thomas, with his loyalty still more passionate than his doubt. We, and all that we are, are worth something to Jesus—are wanted with all our gifts, our love, our favour, our faith, our courage ; He values them all. They are needed for ministerial use. They are to be laid out, as talents with the bankers, that He may win from them His profits.

Only, they have passed from us to Him—they are committed to His Hands—transmitted across out of our choice, into His. His choice, His strong choice, is now under them, is in them. In Him they are transfigured, yielded up to Him, to become instruments of righteousness, tools by which God Himself achieves His purpose. He knows what He wants of us. We need not trouble about the result, if only we cling to Him, live in Him, abide in Him. If only we abide in Him ! Then, He does what He will with us, He gets what He wants from us, He establishes us, that we may bring forth fruit : and that this our fruit may remain—fruit that we dreamed not of, fruit that surprises us by its fulness, fruit that is not of us, though it be ours.

My brethren, Cuddesdon is a recognition of this law —that though we may begin by choosing Christ, we must end in Christ choosing us. The man's heart, the man's offer, must first be won from us, drawn out of us, by all that is winning, and gracious, and kindly, and lovely, and tender, in the ministry of Jesus. This is the beginning; and ah! which of us does not know by what sweet entanglement Cuddesdon threw its net about our willing feet? Some summer Sunday, perhaps, we wandered here, in undergraduate days, to see a friend; and from that hour the charm was at work. How joyous, how enticing the welcome, the glad brotherhood! So warm and loving it all seemed, as we thought of the sharp skirmishing of our talk in college; so buoyant and rich, as we recalled the thinness of our Oxford interests. The little rooms like college-rooms just shrinking into cells, the long talk on the summer lawn, the old church with its quiet country look of patient peace, the glow of the evening chapel, the run down the hill, under the stars, with the sound of Compline Psalms still ringing in our hearts—ah! happy, happy day! It was enough. The resolve that lay half slumbering in our souls took shape, it leapt out. We would come to Cuddesdon when the time of preparation should draw on!

So up this hill men come, with a swarm of eager desires all pushing, all compelling—drawn by the cords of a man, burning with the eager offer, "Here am I, send me!" And then, up here, those in office know what is to be done.　The man's heart is taken, but that is not all: the man's offer accepted, but not trusted.　Slowly, in the year of discipline, the secret of the Lord makes itself known.　Down upon the man must come the power of the living Word—the Apostolic choice of the Master.　Down it must come, displacing, thrusting aside, pushing through as a hand, that presses through thorny branches, through sheltering leaves to reach, and grasp, and pluck some wild rosebud that flutters lightly upon a hedge,—so round the heart of the man closes the strong Hand of Christ: His fingers are felt about the soul, and they bend it this way and that, and they sever it from its environing, and they break it sharp off, like a flower; they wrench it away, they bear it apart, bruised sometimes, torn, mangled, un-willingly yielding, alarmed, protesting, disappointed, angry, sad, despairing: and yet, through all this, grafted anew into the stock of Grace, not to wither in the spring hedge with some morning frost, not to be shattered by the loud winds nor slain by the fierce sun, nor washed into ruin by drenching rains,—no wild rose-bud now, but solidly ingrown into the stem of Christ Himself, with the full energy of His new Grace working through it, remaking it into a new and glorious flower, abundant, splendid, enduring, a rose of God's own garden.　Yes—and yet the old natural self is there still: nothing is lost—neither the tint, nor the scent, nor the shaping of the wild hedge-flower; all are there; yet who would have believed the change that has come over them, the fulness of the crowded folds of petals all glowing and all enriched, wealth within wealth of colour, gift upon gift of odorous breath. Ah! this indeed can only be for those whom not only the graciousness of Cuddesdon has drawn up the hill, but who have found there, within, in the hidden places, the sharp knife that cuts and prunes, —have felt the keenness of that sword, which pierces to the very dividing asunder of bones and marrow: it can only be for those whom here Jesus—Jesus Whose compassion and tenderness drew them to His service—has taken aside with St. Peter, apart from the multitude, and told them the inner secret, " Behold, we go up to Jerusalem, and the Son of man must suffer so many things, and be scourged, and slain: and let him that would come after Me, take up his cross and follow Me."

Alas that even now, after all, we most of us have learned the austerer lesson so little! Alas to look back on our ministry, and to recall the baffled self-confidence, the failure, ever and ever, that has dogged our unslain self-love! Still we go on, pledging ourselves, in our old human audacity—" I will lay down my life "—and still, night after night, the cock crows over our rapid denials, over our desperate collapses. Shall we ever learn to walk, not in our own choice, however good, and brave, and high, but in the choice of Him by Whose choice alone it is that we serve at all? A pitiful, pitiful, story it has been to too many of us, as we look back on our tangled ministry! Yet here, at Cuddesdon, back on the old hill, in the dear company of those who love us and are loved by us so tenderly, so unfailingly,—here, where every stone of the church, every voice in our ear, every memory in the soul, speak of the mercy and goodness of a Master Whose compassions fail not, but are new every morning,—here, within this happy garden-ground of God's earth, where everything seems most loving and most holy, and all that is best in us wakes up, renewed like a bird's song in spring: here, to-day, our sorrowful recollections will not be in vain if, like the penitent Apostle of the denial by the old waters of Gennesaret, we hear the persuading voice of the risen Lord once again, with the question that blots out all past shame, and renews us ever again into the blessed renewal of our first love, unspoilt, unstained, and unclouded,— "Simon, son of Jonas, lovest thou Me?"

Name by name, He is speaking now to each of us to-day, "Child of My choice, lovest thou Me?" We have denied Him, denied Him three times, denied Him with an oath; yet still, for every separate denial He has a separate forgiveness, as ever and ever He repeats to us His "Lovest thou Me?" Oh that we may go back from Cuddesdon hill, every one of us, to-day, strong in the renewed communion of which our very denials have taught us to measure the true strength: go back with the voice of the Lord in our souls, re-enacting its choice, reasserting its desire that in Him alone, and by Him alone, we should set ourselves to tend His flock and feed His sheep!

Conversion

SOLIDARITY OF SALVATION — FREEDOM OF SALVATION — THE GIFT OF GRACE — THE LAW OF FORGIVENESS—THE COMING OF THE SPIRIT.

THE SOLIDARITY OF SALVATION.

"As in Adam all die, even so in Christ shall all be made alive. But every man in his own order."—1 COR. xv. 22, 23.

A MAN whom we know, a friend whom we love,—how distinct, and separate, and individual seems to us all that he says and all that he does! Each word issues from some fount of free spontaneity; each act, each movement is charged with peculiar character. No one but he could have said just that—could have made exactly that motion of the hand or of the head. And it is the incessant discovery of this uniqueness, of this subtle yet inexhaustible difference between him and all other beings in the world, that makes the delight and the charm of a friendship. His most marked peculiarities become dear to us simply because they are his and his only. His character stands out to us, cut off, as by a knife, from all else. He is himself and himself alone, solitary as a star. There is not a movement of his eyes, or a sound in his voice, however minute, however momentary, which we should not distinguish at once, with unhesitating and inevitable decision, as a movement, as a sound of which no other human being could ever, in all the ages, be conceivably the author or the owner.

And yet, if we go to his home with our friend, counter-discoveries greet us on every side. There is his father; and we see, at once, whence came to the son that look in the eyes that we know so well. There is his mother; and who can mistake that turn of the mouth, that shade of colour in the hair, which we have delighted to watch in him? And was it not his voice that startled us just now in that young brother? And we almost laugh as we catch sight of little tricks long familiar to us, and that to us were marks and tokens which isolated him from all we had ever known, but which are detected now to be the common heritage of sister and brother alike. And the more we watch, the more we can trace an identity, close, intimate, secret, penetrative, pervading the entire household; until, at last, there is nothing that our own friend can do or say, in which we could not track and note the signs of his parentage, the flavour of his birth, the breath of his home.

Yet is he any the less to us what he was before—a character, a living being, as distinct as a star? Is he any the less free, spontaneous, unique? Nay, his own peculiar distinctness is as real and unwavering and delightful to us as ever. We have not even the shadow of a perplexity about it. Yet how deep our searching might go, how far it might reach, if we pressed home our inquiries into the hidden ground of our friend's life. The county whence he came—the interminglings of Saxon and of Dane, that crossed and fused in the dales that lie about his home—these have shaped and moulded his figure and his face, by the inward pressure of hereditary instincts that are inwoven into the very tissue and texture of his body. Nobody who knew that countryside could doubt for a moment whence had been born and bred the tones in which he speaks, the phrases that he finds congenial.

And Science could take up the very touches which we most love to associate with his presence and his manner, and could show us their exact parallel in un-known populations still living in the ancient homes of the English, on the sandy shores of the Baltic, or by the green waters of far Norwegian seas. Nor is it his body only into which these multitudinous influences have entered; his character, his imagination, his mind —these all have roots that dig deep into the common soil. They are unmistakably English, and English of a peculiar type: nobody but an Englishman could ever dream of thinking after his fashion; nobody but an Englishman would come to those decisions at which he voluntarily and naturally arrives; in contact with a foreigner, every fragment of his being is seen to have received the impress of his national bent.

Now, let us stop again and ask, These decisions of his, are they at all less valid or less genuine because they are the issue of a will that cannot, whatever it decides, escape from the clutch of an English impress, from the fetters of a national type? Far, far from it. It is wholly the contrary. Just as he would have been pleased to have heard it said of some utterance, that issued directly out of his instinctive feelings, "There spoke your father's son," just as he would have been delighted if you had cried at some quick turn of his head, "Ah, how like your mother," so now, his inner freedom, his self-possession, his spontaneity, these all are braced, heightened, intensified, encouraged by the recognition, in them, of an inevitable type; he is not the least alarmed lest his individuality should therefore be weakened, or his identity suffer loss; he is delighted to discover that he is swayed by secret and inevitable forces of which he knew nothing as they moved him, and as they made him. The discovered necessity vivifies his freedom, instead of destroying it; he feels all the more free, in discovering that he is inevitably, and of sheer necessity an Englishman.

Nor does this discovery stop there. Science passes with swift foot from shore to shore, from century to century, and in every land, and amidst every soil, and at every period, she enters upon traces of yet deeper communications that pass, from out of the entire human race and the entire human story, into the brain and into the heart of every separate man and woman in this church to-night. In every motion of our limbs, we are using the stored experiences of bygone generations; we are built up out of their patience; we are the outcome of their toil; the very passions, the very instincts of those dead forgotten peoples are alive in us all to-day, and make us what we are; and, do what we will, we cannot throw off the domination of their hidden forces, for they lie at the most secret places of our souls; we cannot dig down in our life to a spot lower than their influence buries itself; we cannot climb up to any height whither their sway does not follow and possess us; we are dyed through and through with their tints; we are inmeshed in their intricacies; we are wrapped round by their encompassing atmosphere. As we act, as we move, each deed, each motion does but offer a new evidence of that inbred and imbued necessity with which the long past has stored our heart of hearts. And we are not depressed by the discovery. Most beautiful, most cheering, it seems to us, this bonded brotherhood which works in us beyond the seeing, beyond all imagining. Most cheering, to learn the full significance of the words of God, " Thine eyes did see my substance yet being imperfect, and in Thy book were all my members written, which, day by day were fashioned, when as yet there were none of them ; " Most wonderful far-reaching words! Freely, indeed, we walk, and freely move; yet each free motion is a disclosure of the power of the past that is upon us. Far, far back, beyond all sifting, lies the secret of each tiny gesture, of each passing mood, of each incidental trick and turn. Strange symptoms from our fathers' fathers show themselves, now and again, on the surface of our lives, like eddies that tell of deep-running currents ; a whole world of silent force is astir within us, old lives long over, old manners once familiar and dear. Old faces, long buried, look out of our eyes; voices from out of forgotten and unknown graves speak through our lips ; ghostly memories shake us like dumb sounds ; echoes of ancient stories prick and press within the blood; shadows from far clouds cast sudden glooms over our souls, shadows of old wrongs once fierce and sour; or the gleams of buried joys, the loves and the laughter of long ago, quicken the heart to-day as with an after-glow from some lost and hidden sun. Yet nothing of all this burdens us, nothing perplexes. We are ourselves; we miss nothing of our free manhood. We can lift up our heads, and rejoice to know how the Lord has understood our thoughts long before; how He "has fashioned us behind and before, and laid His hand upon us; how there is not a word on our tongues but He knew it altogether; how our bones were not hid from Him; how He covered us in our mother's womb." Far, far more He sees of our implicated heredity than we can ever follow; "such knowledge is too wonderful and excellent for us, we cannot attain unto it." Yet it cannot distress or imprison us, however minute its intricacies, however voluminous its range; for all of it does, as we know well, by the infallible test of daily experience, but feed self-mastery, but enrich our freedom. "How dear, therefore, are Thy counsels unto me, O God! Oh, how great is the sum of them!"

We all of us live one life. Human nature has a continuous being and a continuous history, within which, not outside which, each separate personality plays its spontaneous part. Out of the same earth we grow, like plants out of a common soil, and each of us puts out our own colour, and shape, and scent; but every separate flower, every separate leaf, distinct and individual though it be, is yet fed out of the same juices as the rest, and built out of the same earth. This is the law that governs every fragment of our being: there is no atom of it out of which we can purge away all foreign elements, all natal influences. And it is by this unity of race that we effect a combined advance; civilisation is only possible, because the genius of each generation can be retained and transmitted.

But, then, we cannot accept the gains of heredity and refuse the losses. We are glad and uplifted to recall the noble heritage which is our delighted possession, we are proud to accept all that has been won to our credit, and bred into our blood, by the splendid record of our English ancestry. And why, then, are we surprised, or perplexed, or indignant, if, by this same familiar and habitual law, we all, in Adam, die? How can it be otherwise? What alternative is open? We men form one body; and the generations, as they pass, build up one body: and to prohibit poison, once introduced, from spreading over the whole would be done only at the cost of forbidding that body to perform its functions, at the cost of wrecking its structural life. Let Adam once have sinned, and we, who are in Adam, have the seeds of sin within us. We start with an inherited loss. The laws by which this is necessitated are the laws by which we are men; if they failed, we should be no longer human. They are the laws, again, by which alone we advance, we grow, we win our way to civilised blessing: and how can we suddenly turn round and repudiate them, because they must, if our fathers fail or fall, carry down also the sad working, the bitter story of their shame? "In Adam we all die;" die by our own free act, just as we who are English through the necessity of birth, yet, by our own free actions, exhibit our inherited character. Our freedom is all the more free when it acts under the uplifting pressure of a splendid inheritance; nor is it at all sensible of any diminution because the sin, that it willingly and spontaneously loves to commit, bears witness to the miserable story of a guilty stock.

"In Adam all die!" yet each, it may be, in his own order. Not one, indeed, can escape the losses of his parentage, because to do so would be at the cost of losing all the gains—of curtailing and cancelling his humanity. Not one can win that life which only uncorrupted conscience can ever know. All must die. But each may, perhaps, within that night of loss, have his place according to the gallantry of his protest, or the gladness of his consent—according to the degree with which he either strove to mitigate its gloom, or else revelled in the uncleanness which its darkness served to cover.

"In Adam all die." Yes! but the blessed Eyes of God, as they moved over the mass of multitudinous distress, as they noted the inevitable working of this mysterious inheritance,—still beheld, hidden in this very mystery, the possibility of a redemption. The laws, the conditions of social unity, which spread so far and so widely the poison of a father's sin, carry just as far and as widely the light of a father's honour, the force of a father's purity. A renewal, a reinvigoration of the lost Fatherhood might yet defeat the pressure of the old and sinister disgrace. The blood, once purged, might transmit itself from man to man, from heart to heart, from life to life; and might reach and penetrate, and quicken, and absorb, and renew. Though by one man sin has entered, and through sin, death, yet by Another, Who is the Man in Whom all are made, grace may re-enter and recover the dying race. The transmission that makes for the corruption of all, can be turned to the needs and uses of the regeneration. This is the method of God, to convert the conditions of the curse into the very instruments of the blessing. In Adam, it is true, all would die; but, if that is so, then, in Christ, all may be made alive. If sin has by these methods abounded, grace shall by the same methods much more abound.

So, in the Beloved Son, man becomes new-begotten of God. And now let us measure His task. His virtue must lay hold of the entire sum of man's being. It must imbed itself by roots as deep, and strong, and clinging as those by which sin has dug its dire fangs into the inherited flesh. It must pervade and embrace the entire bulk of fallen and human nature. This it must do; and all Holy Week we have been watching, with the awe of shuddering sorrow, how serious and how thorough was the reality with which this assumption of our flesh was completed. Not only must He empty Himself of His Godhead, and abhor not the Virgin's womb, and be found in fashion as a man, a babe, in a manger at Bethlehem; but everything that is ours He must make His. And ours, now, was a life bound down under a curse, stamped with the brand of shame, smitten with the blight of sorrow, tossed by the anguish of miserable pains, dismayed, beclouded, tormented, stricken through and through with the panic and tyranny of death. And all this He will partake, that He may be verily part and parcel of that solid bulk of our humanity. He read it all over, those sad experiences of a hundred suffering generations, in the record of Scripture. He read there the roll of human sorrows, of human fears, of human bitterness, of human desolation, and not one jot or one tittle of that long human agony would He fail to fulfil, not one throb of pain would He spare Himself, not one tear, not one touch of forlorn despair. All that man had ever felt, He too would feel; He, too, would endure. No legions of Angels should sweep from Heaven to save Him from tasting the last drop of that cup of our terror; no stones of our wilderness shall be made bread for His hunger, lest the Scriptures should not be fulfilled—lest the burden of our iniquity, lest the weight of our inheritance should, in any degree, fail to fall upon Him. So He became ours—our very own. We stamped Him ours by every nail which we thrust through His Hands and His Feet, by every scoff wherewith His Soul was pierced upon the tree of scorn. He is ours by every band, and joint, and ligament; wholly human, wholly knit into our common fate, implicated with us in all our woe; ours by fibre and sinew, by bone and marrow, by tissue and nerve, by the bonds of birth, by the ties of familiar and ineradicable experiences, by the netted meshes of unwoven sympathies, by touch, and taste, and hand-ling, by tears and groans, by agony and bloody sweat, by passion and death, by the bonds of love, by the cords of a man. He is ours. He has imbedded, implanted, ingrafted, insown His own Life into ours; and everywhere, into all corners of our common corporate being, His Presence reaches and is astir. He is ours, wholly ours; and yet, lo! He has brought with Him into our burdened days the new vitality, the freshening splendour of a white-hearted purity, and of a flawless will.

"All are made alive." Ah! we murmur our complaints against the death that is ours through Adam, as if death were all that our corporate unity with mankind had brought us. Yet if God is to be judged, let the Death incurred under original sin be set parallel with the Life involved and inherited under the Covenant of Jesus. For this is our Gospel—this our Easter-news: that as by one man came Death, by one Man also came the Resurrection from the dead. "Christ is risen from the dead," and in Him and with Him the whole race into whose history He has inwoven His Presence and His Name, is lifted, through the Body of His exaltation, to the right hand of God. The entire movement in which we had found ourselves held is reversed. That downward drag, which was upon us all like a weight, that burden of suffocating sin, ponderous, masterful, relentless—this is gone. The set of the strong tide is changed; the dull, withdrawing currents, muddy and depressed, are now running up on the flood, with rush and bubble and press, with gurgling triumph—cheerful, brimming, and immense. The curse of certain failure, that lay, heavy and fast, upon man's wintry world, is become the promise of a victorious hope, vital and young as the Spring.

And *all* feel it; all mankind, who knew the withering touch of the ancient evil, know, in their degree, the power of the Risen Man. Upward and upward we all are drawn; we are sucked up after the movement of that glory: we all live within the range of the Resurrection; we all quiver under its strong pressure, grasped as we all are by the lordship of the New Humanity, Which covers and consummates the entire sum of human existence.

"All are made alive!" for now is Christ risen from the dead, "the first-fruits of them that slept." He, Who was already the Image in Which all were made, is become also, for all, the First-born from the dead. And as that old sin spread out its baneful influence, ring upon ring, circle upon circle, so this new life issues out over the whole, in circle after circle, in ring upon ring.

There is the outermost ring of that dim heathen world which has been brought nigh, in the Risen Christ, to the Father Which is in Heaven, and is ever beloved for His sake Who has made Himself theirs; and thither, amid the thick of those dark swarms, the Blessed Love of God, that must otherwise despair, moves under the drawing of the Brotherhood in Christ; and still it whispers hope among those without hope; and still urges, and still beseeches; and still it lets a face be seen as of God, and a voice still be heard among the trees of the garden. And they, even they, amid ugly and foul confusions, are not insensible to that strange stirring which is the movement within them of the Resurrection—a movement blind, yet prophetic—prompting them to deeds which Christ will yet own as His at the Last Day, though they be done by those who will ask in ignorant surprise, " Lord, when saw we Thee hungered, we who on earth never knew Thy Name?"

And within that ring of outer Heathendom there is the ring of a Christian Civilisation, a civilisation that, for all its miserable stains, for all its dark and bitter shames, has yet this mark of Christ upon it— that, amid all its disasters, it can never lose its hope— a hope, that vitalises; a hope that has in it always the power of a recovery; a hope that can lay its very mouth in the dust of its penitence, and yet can retain its hope. A Christian civilisation is a civilisation that can hope against hope. A civilisation once Christianised can face the utmost reality of the grimmest and direst facts, can face the lies that hold their own, and win; the oppressions that stand rooted in age-long wrongs; the prison doors that the centuries have laboured to bolt and to bar; the graves of all who have died in vain, done to their death under the heels of the ungodly; it can face all this, and live, and hope, in the memory of that day when the eyes of all in a Synagogue at Nazareth were fastened on One Who read of a good time when the eyes of all blind should be opened, and the ears of all deaf should be unstopped, and pronounced that " This day is this Scripture fulfilled in your ears." Therefore it is that we cannot despair, though the Lord delayeth His coming, though the wheels of His chariot tarry, though all things continue as at the first. "How long," we still cry in hope, "O God! how long? How long before we feed our flocks in Carmel and Bashan, as in the days of old?"

And within the ring of a Christian Civilisation is the ring of those over all of whom the Name of Christ acts as a living spell, the ring of all those who cling to Him, and cry to Him, and send up heart and voice to Him, and in His Name cast out devils, and do many mighty works. They call upon Him, and the Lord knows them that are His, and He showers down favour upon them as they look up to Him; multitudes upon multitudes, who are swayed, as the tides of the immeasurable sea, by the magic of His love, as it moves moonlike above them and carries them hither and thither, like mighty waters that shake, and roll, and swing, and murmur, and ebb and flow, and ebb again.

And within this ring, again, its very heart and its very core, is, we believe, Christ's living Church, visible, historic, catholic, at all times and in all places, giving glory to God—a corporate unity, which desires, not only to believe in Him, but to complete its belief by partaking of His very Substance, by transfiguration into His Name, by sharing in His new and quickened Humanity, by receiving of the seed of this new Adam into itself; so that it may be fed with His Resurrection, and be impregnated through and through with His transforming grace, and be knit into His Body by the Presence of His abiding Spirit, and be regenerate by the waters of His Baptism, and may take and eat of His Flesh and of His Blood, so that all who so eat may become one thing, one compact and enduring mass, one loaf, one body, one new man; built up by one force, as living stones into a living temple; a single body wed to Him as the new Bride of the Lamb; growing up into one Head, "from Whom the whole Body, fitly joined together and compacted by that which every joint supplieth, maketh increase of the Body unto the edifying of itself in love"—so that it becomes "the fulness of Him That filleth all in all."

Christ's love beats like a great heart, pulse upon pulse, combating, defeating, expelling that slow death which has crept over the body of humanity. And, thus, "in Christ, *all* are made alive." All: the whole human race is swept forward, is borne upward, by the power of the risen Lord. Where, before, there was degeneration, there is now regeneration. All are made alive: and, if all, then we, too, stand to-night, every one of us, and each one of us, within this new motion. We stand within it; yet, for all that, we lose nothing of our distinct and personal freedom. You and I, we are none the less free to-night, because in Adam, in some old sin, we all died; and then in Christ, in some strange recovery, achieved for and by God, we all were made alive. For our freedom is rooted in those deep, underlying necessities; it drains from them its juices; it sucks out of them its strength; it breaks open out of the powers wherewith these endow it. Just as we won the free exercise of our English name out of the very necessities which had made us English; so, out of our very bond to Christ, we win the energy to become free friends of Christ. Our freedom is born out of what God in Christ does for us, and His action does not, therefore, take the place of ours, nor do instead of ours. Nay, His action on our behalf shows itself in us in the shape of our own free activity on our own behalf. Out of His action we are made free, and the more He does for us, the more we are enabled to do for ourselves.

But every one, therefore, in his own order. The freedom that we derive out of Christ, that is given us of Christ, is ours to exercise, and by its exercise we determine our lot. We determine it, whether we will or no; for we cannot help using the freedom given us in Christ. We have been made free; we have been caught up into the motion of Christ; we have been set loose from the tyranny of sin; we have been reborn into Christ's energy. He draws us, holds us, drags at us, impels us; the cords of His human love are knitted close about our being; and, as He rises, we rise with Him; we feel the pull and the strain, the pressure, the impulse, the rigour of His Resurrection.

Who here in this Church, to-night, is not feeling it, at this very hour? That stir, that throb, that sighing of the soul, that blind leap of the dumb heart—that is Christ, the risen Lord; that is the touch of His Hands laid about your soul—He is at work there. Those are His signs. And they are signs that you are free; that you can act for Him; that you can rise and walk. You can rise—rise from out of all your choking sins; out of all your miserable memories; out of all your dismal forebodings; out of all your horrid past; out of all your ancient temptations that clutch and throttle you. You can rise, you can move, you are free. Christ has risen, and broken your bonds, and you are feeling the pricking and the stirring of His victory alive within your life this Easter Day.

Oh, rise! Rise, as with Him. Lift yourself up; be not afraid. Do not doubt; do not hesitate. The strength is in you—that strength for which you have prayed and have despaired. You are free this very minute to rise and follow Christ for ever and for ever. For in Him all have been long ago made alive. According as you act at hours when the voice calls, and the freedom is given you, will be your lot in the world to come.

For, alas! you must beware; such high freedom cannot but be perilous. It is not yours to choose whether you will rise with Christ or no. All rise with Him; all through Him are dragged through the darkness of the grave, and will stand before the judgment of God. At His voice all must rise again from the tomb. As we *must* have died in Adam, so we *must* rise in Christ.

And what is it, then, that strikes chill as fear upon our hearts? Can it, indeed, be that the freedom regained in Christ — that freedom which is itself the Breath of Christ within us—can itself be turned against the Name of Him Who inspires it; that Christ can be put to use by us against Himself; that we can receive into ourselves from Jesus the power to defile the Body of Jesus; that we can, by the strength that God Himself supplies, take the members of Christ and devote them to shame? Oh, the dread! Oh, the terror! Oh, the awful shame! Oh, the bitterness of the gall! Oh, the grief of the Holy Spirit! Yet this can be. Dark utterances shake us. "Every one in his own order:" we shall rise; but where will that order be, in which we shall have placed ourselves? True, we are all drawn upward into God's light by the necessities of our union with a risen Christ; but what if our approach to God be as the nearing of a great heat, that scorches, and shrivels, and kills? Holiness is as a fire to sin. We cannot safely draw near to God with sin upon our souls. Yet we must draw near, for Christ, our Brother, is sat down at the right Hand of God, and in Him we all are brought nigh. To be brought nigh to God is necessarily to be judged. And in this lies the secret of that terrible possibility, which cannot be excluded by any love of God for us—that we may find ourselves standing hereafter face to face with God, carried thither by the power of that Christ Whom we have to the last misused, and grieved, and disgraced!

But God grant it, this Easter night shall not have been given us in vain. What that order for each shall be—that, each has it in him to make sure, here and now. We can make sure of it, just because Christ, Who is exalted in strength over all thrones, dominations, and powers, is in each of us, feeding us with His own triumphant Life.

Blessed, ah blessed indeed, if, penitent and forgiven,

then, when the end is come, and death and hell give up their dead, we be found with our names written in the Book of Life!

But blessed, thrice blessed, beyond all desires, beyond all dreams, if we could but be found among the one hundred and forty-four thousand who have part in the first Resurrection, and follow the Lamb whithersoever He goeth; because in them is found no blemish, nor any lie. Blessed are the dead that so die in the Lord. Blessed are they that are called to the Marriage of the Lamb. Into which blessing we, too, even we, may pass. Thanks be to God!

THE FREEDOM OF SALVATION.

" Sir, we would see Jesus."—St. John xii. 21.

OUR Lord spent His days upon earth on that narrow edge of broken hill that stood strangely separate and aloof from the vast and teeming empires which divided off from it to the east and to the west. From His hills round the home at Nazareth He could look to the great ridge of Moab, behind which lay the memories of Nineveh and Babylon. Far, far away, beyond that barrier of cliffs, the highways ran through that wilderness, to the old scenes and cities of the mighty river, with its immense populations, and its strange wisdom. And then, with one turn of the head, He would catch the flashing glory of the Greek Mediterranean waters, in the far bosom of which lay all the isles of the Gentiles, the crowded homes of seafaring folk. And right across his own village lands the caravans trooped past, of alien faces, and unknown tongues, bearing through the markets of Damascus the wealth both of the Eastern Indies and of the Western seas.

So He stood, cut off from the east by the roaring cleft of Jordan, and from the west by the foam of a harbourless and untravelled sea. So He stood, Who was the Desire of all nations; and on either side of Him lay the millions, who wandered astray, bewildered and forlorn, wearied and unclean—the dim sad prisoners of the powers of the air, fast bound in trespasses and sin—scattered loose and astray, without hope, and without God. The very winds that walked under the stars on those green hills where the Lord prayed alone all night, would come to Him ever laden and thick with sighs out of the heart of that tired multitude, who sought and found not, who hungered and were not filled. They had sent to Him out of the East, asking, at His Birth, "Where is He? We have seen His star. Where is He that is born King of the Jews?" They had come from the West with pressing plaintive plea, "Sir, we would see Jesus."

So they craved, and He—had He no strong and masterful desire to answer their cravings? Surely we know how His Eyes looked out far and away beyond the narrow Jewish pastures, and saw, already, those who were far off, those other sheep, not of this small fold, whom also He yearned to bring home, that they all might be one flock under one Shepherd. Yes; and we know how, for a moment, at Samaria, His Heart was saddened with the sorrow of the weeping Sower, as He looked out upon fields already, to His Heart's eye, white with the glory of harvest, which others would be then reaping so gladly. Oh! let them remember on that day, in the glow and splendour of that autumn reaping, let them remember the joyless Sower, Who crept along the dark furrows, in the dim and cloudy spring. For that joy of the Reaper, He was never to know on earth.

That joy of the mighty mystery, which burned like a furnace in the soul of St. Paul,—that joy which over-mastered the Apostle's utterance as he stammered and staggered under its weight and wealth of glory—the joy of knowing that God regarded not the person of any; that God had broken down all walls of partition, so that there is no longer Jew divided from Greek, nor free from slave, nor male from female,—that joy, that enkindling mystery of joy, might never, on earth, be His, Who was Himself its Spring and its Giver. It was there, within Him, the great secret of a world's gladness, the secret which has ever since made the wilderness to blossom as a rose, and has brought springing waters again in all waste places, and has crowned with joy and gladness the heads of those once so sick and so weary, from whom their sorrow and their sighing have now all fled away. This was all within Him, but repressed, cabined, cribbed, con-fined. He must hold it down under bolt and bar; He must never taste of its blessed savour.

Nay; for He Himself has given the law, "Except a corn of wheat die, it abideth alone." Alone! Its forces all there, yet shut up to themselves, unused, unexercised, unfreed. Alone! the Heart of the Lord, charged with love that could redeem and feed and satisfy the whole world, must abide alone. Its sym-pathies, its gifts, its desires, its tenderness, its fount of tears, all this must be held under, curbed, fettered. And how hard was the strain to keep it under! For they were so ready for Him, those far Gentiles; and He knew it. Now and again, by their very violence of faith, they forced themselves under His Eye and into His pity. Though He drove them from Him—though He fled on before them, as they cried after Him—though He built up against them the barrier of His mission to none but the lost sheep of the House of Israel, yet still a poor woman here and there would continue urging with a persistence that outwearied the patience of the Twelve, and He was compelled to turn and bless with the wonderful sanction, " O woman, great is thy faith ! " or, perhaps, some centurion made even the Lord to wonder at a faith which He could not find in Israel. In these He foresaw the day which was forbidden Him: " Yea! many should come from the East and from the West " in that day. Many should come; but not now—not for Him on earth. Till death He is cut off from all this royalty of love, from all this wide range of compassion, from all this gladness of welcome, this rapture of loyalty. All His days on earth He abideth alone.

And why? Because our Lord took our flesh, not in pity, not in any fanciful licence, but in all sober earnest. He did not take it up as a dress, to do what He chose with. Nay, He took it, took it as it stood, as it really was; as St. John says, " the Word became flesh." He became that which His Birth from His Mother's womb made necessary and essential. That Mother was a Jewess, of a certain lineage, with a certain fixed body of natural and historic conditions about her; and all these are His; all this He undertakes. He pushes nothing of it aside; He uses no freedom of peculiar privileges; He will not pick out and choose.

What His flesh is, that He assumes. He is, therefore, a Jew; circumcised the eighth day, He is made subject to the Covenant of the Law. "Born of a woman, born under the Law," He fulfils all the righteousness which such a parentage makes human and obligatory. He is a Jew; and the Law still binds; none of its obligation is yet cancelled. Its Temple is still undestroyed; every jot and tittle of the old Law holds good, and demands fulfilment. To the day of His Death He is a Jew; He is cut off from broad human intercourse; He is circumscribed by the rigid demands of the Mosaic Covenant. He keeps the feasts, He defends His actions on the Sabbath days by examples drawn from cases of compassion permitted to every Jew, or by instances of special emergency that allowed freedom from rule to David or to the Temple priests. "I am not sent but to the lost sheep of the house of Israel." No! not till the last appeal has been made to those who had beaten and stoned the servants of the King; not till they had killed and cast out the only Son and Heir,—not till then will the vineyard be taken from those murderers, and given unto others, who will bring forth the fruits. So the Lord bound Himself down by taking our flesh. So He bowed His neck to the yoke —to the patient, hindering, humbling burden—to the drear and bitter rejection by those who were His own, and yet who would not, for all that, receive Him.

He lived a Jew. The Law did not end at our Lord's Birth, but only at His Death. The New Covenant was not established until it was branded by His Blood. It was death which freed Him, death which liberated His fulness of activity. He became Lord of all flesh on the day that He rose from the dead and ascended to the right hand of God. And hence a difficulty encompassed the Twelve Apostles, which the Apostle of the Gentiles, whose conversion opened so mighty a door of faith, wholly escaped. It was difficult for those faithful friends, who had walked behind the Feet of the Lord, to face the fact that the Resurrection involved a complete reconsideration, an entirely novel estimate of His Life during His days on earth. That Life could not be taken just as it stood for a model, or a rule, by which to guide the Resurrection Church. For all the conditions had suffered reversal. The obligations which bound the Lord are now broken; a new interpretation of life and its duties must be brought into play. That which Christ after the flesh might do was no rule to determine what the risen Lord, in His own fulness of freedom, might now require of His Church. That repressed secret, which abode alone, unused, inoperative, breaking upward only in rare flashes of Epiphany glory—that has now burst all its tangling enwrapments and is imprisoned no longer, and works its will out in power; and therefore very, very difficult it becomes to foresee to what lengths it may carry its spontaneity. Amid the terrible stress of this uncertainty, the companionship with Jesus, so dear to the Twelve—oh! so tenderly, so unutterably dear,— becomes almost a temptation, almost a snare. It was so possible, so easy for the Resurrection to appear only as a splendid ratification of the Life so sweetly lived among them. That Life had ended in a horror of shame; and now God's own Hand had blotted out the shame, and raised Him from the disgrace of death; and lo! all the old beautiful days rose again with Him, in dear familiar beauty. All that they had believed of Him was now sanctioned and sealed; He was declared to be what they had thought: and they might live out their days in the clinging memories of all He had said and done; in the unending delight of repeating to ever-eager converts, "So He spoke, so He looked, so He commanded, when we were with Him." So they might wait until, some day, they too should rejoin Him, and renew their old companionship in the places which He is preparing for them in the house of many mansions. So it must have been so natural, so tempting to think. And, so thinking, they would cling to the habits learned under Him: they would haunt the Temple services; they would have all things in common, as He and they had had, when Judas bore the purse; they would sit round one table in the old upper chamber, where they had sat with Him.

Yes! all this would inevitably work upon them: they would be instinctively satisfied with recording the old days. And, yet, there was this terrible fact to face, that, on the one vital question in front of that Church of Jerusalem, the Lord's practical Life afforded no help, and gave no direction. For the mystery now revealed was His lordship over the Gentiles; and this lordship lay dormant and inoperative all the days of the flesh. Its urgencies, its issues, its necessities, its width, its demands could not become visible until He had ascended up into Heaven. It was the Spirit that alone could make them felt, and not any tender imitation of the customs and manners of the Lord, as they had known and loved Him.

The Twelve were faithful to the new vision as it slowly made itself known; but oh! with what searchings of heart, with what bitter uprootings, with what violent shocks, with what agony of abandonment! To them it was a rending, not only of the most deepseated traditions of infancy, but also of the tenderest associations that knit them to their Master.

And here was the power of St. Paul. Nothing of this pathetic attachment hindered or entangled his direct apprehension of the majestic event. Once convinced of the reality of the Resurrection, he knows all that it involves. Nothing holds him back. The very rapidity of his own conversion lays open to him the secret of the convulsion which has shattered the old into fragments, and made all things new. The Resurrection, as he sees in a flash, is no mere act of justification by which God sets His seal to the mission of His Son to Israel. Nay; that mission had failed—"His own received Him not." They crucified Him, and by that Crucifixion wrecked their own reformation, and destroyed their own Temple. The Resurrection is no glorious end sealing a work done; it is itself the beginning, not the end. The full work had not really begun until Jesus rose from the dead. He is no dead hero, who has passed into his last rest; but a Lord of life, Who has by this inaugurating act begun to frame for Himself a Kingdom here on earth. It is by His risen Body that He sets to work to build a

New Temple, raised in three days out of the ruins of the old.

And, if so, then, St. Paul argues out the full and magnificent conclusion. If Christ be, indeed, risen, not to depart, but to live and work; if He can show Himself alive and at work on earth after He has risen from the dead; then, that work must be of a wholly new order to all that exists on this side of the tomb. Work done from beyond death cannot fuse or inter-mingle itself with anything that belongs to the present condition of things. It cannot be merely a new patch to an old garment. It is new wine that no old bottles can hold in.

And here a fresh question starts : what of the Mosaic covenant? To which side of the grave does it belong? It stands altogether on this side of death. It deals with this life that we now live; it teaches us how, as creatures of earth, we can serve God ; it has nothing but dim dreams of the possibilities beyond. Death ends its regulation, its system, its circle of duties, as a blind wall. But the Resurrection of Christ carries us over the dividing line of death; it plants us down altogether amid the vital energies of the region beyond. We have left death, and the life which closes in death, behind us. And, therefore, most assuredly, in making that passage, we dropped behind us all the obligations of Judaism. Judaism! Why, its primal principle turns on fleshly distinctions between Jew and Gentile, a distinction of blood, local, earthly, temporal. We can only conceive such distinctions holding among those born after the flesh ; among those who are shaped and directed by the narrow restrictions stamped upon them by their earthly origin and story. But, in Christ, we have escaped all that, if He be risen from the dead; our earthly birth and story have been left behind; yes! left behind, with all its age-long shame, with all its imprisoning curse, with all its ancient heritage of overmastering wrong.

And, now, we can understand, perhaps, the strong and fervent passion of St. Paul against all that even minutely obscured this cardinal principle. To St. Paul, as he casts his eye back out of his new security, out of his refuge in Jesus—to St. Paul, that Cross of Christ stands as a great stake set up between the things that lie on this side death, and the world that lies beyond it. Up to that dark Cross the grim earthly past, the old fleshly life, crowded with its memories of sin and weariness, presses and beats; but at that stake it all ends—ends as it all must end in the dissolution of death. And it cannot touch him, cannot reach him now,—those old hungers, those old infamies, those old miseries, those old heart-burnings. Look at them there! He sees them, as a soul would see them from out of the high towers of Heaven. Look at them, far far back! Ah, thank God, he knows them now no more!

And among those beggarly rudiments of the fleshly world stands, as he sees, the Mosaic Covenant. For all the honour of its Law, it remained over on that side of death. It clung to the things that go down into the grave; it dealt with man as a thing of earth, as of a particular seed, as he was through his birth in the flesh.

No; there was no mistaking it. It had no more direct dealings with the new life of the Resurrection, in which St. Paul now stood, than had the heathen rituals themselves. To fall back to it, was to fall back under "the rudiments of the world." Christ has died in vain. So to fall back, is to suppose ourselves still living that old life, which was ours through the flesh; and that life must be conditioned by the long human history of Adam's generation: and we therefore lie still under the bondage of that bad old past that had begotten us; we have never been delivered out of that bitter body of death. This is the conviction under which he burned: and it was because the sundering line between Judaism and Christianity was to him as absolute and as unyielding as the line drawn by death between life here and life hereafter, that he flamed out against the compromises that tended to blur and confuse the absoluteness of the distinction. Any such compromise that tended to represent our Lord as merely a Reformer and Purifier of Judaism, was to him the deadly denial of Christ. It was to commit the blunder of omitting the Resurrection. If Christ has died and risen, then that old life has perished for those who are in Christ; and, with it, have wholly perished the conditions which build up Judaism. They are gone; they are dead. Christianity cannot go hand in hand with them. It is not one system among others; it has no competitor. It is the only religion which starts with a vital and operative hold on the life beyond death. It offers us now and here, the life that shall be ours after the final resurrection. No other religion, not even the Law, ever dreams of making such a claim, of taking such a position. If this claim of Christianity be verified, the promises of the Law, and of all other systems, fall to the ground and cease. "I am dead to the Law," so he cries; "I took the Law at its own word: it killed me: so I died to it." And now he is free, for the Law had dominion over a man only so long as he liveth. He is free—as free as a wife from a dead husband. He has wholly ceased out of those conditions to which the Law applies; and now the life that he lives is no life of his own as he was,—Saul, of the tribe of Benjamin, a man ready to perish,—but the risen Christ lives in him; and he lives in Christ the resurrection life. His one prayer now is to know the power of Christ's Resurrection, and to become conformable to His Death; and so clear is this to him, and so decisive, that it is wholly separable and distinct in kind even from that companionship with Jesus when on earth, which had been enjoyed by the other Apostles, and which had been denied him. " Yea! even if I had known Christ after the flesh, yet now henceforth I know him so no more."

My brothers, " ye are dead. Your life is hid with Christ in God." This was " conversion " as St. Paul knew it, and meant it; and that conversion must be yours. " Ye are dead." What is it to be dead ? We all know what it is to turn away from the grave-side, in which we have laid to its last rest the cold body of a friend. All is done and over now. Something has been in the world which will never be again. A story, a presence with its good and its evil, with its joys and sorrows, is wiped out. Everything is ended. The great silence closes over it, as the waters close over a sunken ship, and leave no sign. It is all dead and over! We have said the last word; we have taken the last look. Now, let it go! Come away! Leave it to lie hidden! For you must go your way without it.

That is death: and we are dead, if we are in Christ. We have buried our old manhood. That old natural self of ours—the man in us that is born, and lives its little day, and dies—the self, as it is by human laws, as a creature of this earth,—that is with us no longer. It has had its day. It has done its business. We have wrapped it in its white shroud. We have carried it out to its burial; down in the dark grave we have laid it: it is buried with Christ's Burial. All that old past, so onerous, so tangled, so burdened, so sick,—it is all gone and over, as completely as a life that is dead. Never, never can it be again. The blood of Christ's Death lies between us and it; and it cannot touch us. Its sorrows, its sins are remote and alien, as the voice of a torrent, that we have crossed in the night, whose dull and smothered roar comes to our ears only in faint gusts of wind. The old is dead and buried. Was it dear to us? Had it its goodness and its gladness? Yes; and so St. Paul had everything that could have made life glad and good to him. A Hebrew of the Hebrews, cultivated, zealous, honoured, religious, blameless in moral excellence; yet all this he counted as well worth losing, as dung, as fit for burial, for the worms, if only he could lose himself, and his own pride, and his own impotence, and his own narrowness, and his own self-content,—lose all that made him only Saul of Benjamin, and gain that which would make him Christ's and God's.

Sirs, would you see Jesus? Then you must die with Him. For He, Who is as a corn of wheat, has died that He may bring forth the fruit of eternal life in you. Jesus, Whom you would find, stands risen on the far side of death, and thither you must pass to see Him! To gain that sight let all go; strip it off! All that you seek for yourself only; all that finds its end in you, in your pleasure, in your gain; all that ministers to your own ease, and vanity, and happiness, and success; all that merely feeds your own passions at others' cost; all that urges you to push yourself, to think about yourself, to caress yourself; all that will end with you here, and will be given over to corruption when you cease, and has no issue, and no hope beyond the grave;—oh! strip all that off! Drag yourself out of it; cast it off. In spite of all its fairness (and it may have much), it is yet weighted with a curse that will smite, and sicken, and sadden all its fairest promise. To fall back under its fascination is to fall back to the beggarly rudiments of this world, to fall back under the old miserable bondage, to build up again the shame which Christ died to destroy. Do not be afraid lest you lose the use of anything good and beautiful here. The materials which belonged to you, the gifts which you possessed, in body, soul, or spirit, will not, indeed, be lost. Christ will lay hold of them all, and build them up into His own new Temple. But the spirit that

animated them, the self that used and worked them—
leave that behind in its quiet grave. Do not wake it.
It is buried and done with. Its weariness cannot
overtake you. Its disease cannot reach or hurt you
any more. For between it and you stands the great
stake of the Cross: and you, with all your new life,
are hid with Him Who was dead and is alive again,
and is risen to the right hand of God.

> " Look, Father, look on His anointed Face,
>   And only look on us as found in Him ;
> Look not on our misusings of Thy grace,
>   Our prayer so languid, and our faith so dim ;
> For lo ! between our sins and their reward
> We set the Passion of Thy Son, our Lord."

THE GIFT OF GRACE.

(ADDRESS ON EPISTLE TO EPHESIANS.)

THE soul of the believer, as it works its way with prayer and meditation along the sequence of the Holy Books, has already, before it reaches the Epistle to the Ephesians, laid hold, with all the power of its faithful memory, on the fourfold image of its Redeemer, there to abide and work continually, the heart and force and life of all its spiritual effort; and then it has passed on to watch and re-enact the momentous movement by which that redemptive action embodied itself in an historic Church of world-wide and catholic capacities; and it has entered with fear and trembling into that tremendous strife, waged from within and from without, by which, and through which, the personal soul of the great Apostle forced its victorious way out of the prison-house of sin, out of the black dungeons of separate death, in spite of lies, and malice, and ignorance, and offence, into the clear and glorious light of that sufficing pardon which had been sealed to him by God in the Atoning Blood of His dear Son. There, in that long struggle against the fierce fetters of inward lusts, and the barriers built to bar the way

N

by the blind ignorance of foes who had zeal without knowledge, the soul reads out, in letters of flaming fire, the inner history of that *Judaic* Dispensation which, once for all enacted and recorded in the order of facts, yet again and again, within the secret world that lies shut up in each man's separate self, repeats its ancient story, renews its awful issues, rehearses its eternal paradox, travels along its old paths, sends up once more its cry of bewilderment, "O wretched man that I am!" breaks out yet again into its shout of recovered joy, "I thank God, through Jesus Christ our Lord."

This dispensation of the Jew reveals to our meditations that way of salvation along which God leads the soul which hungers after righteousness. That hunger, roused by especial stirrings which the hope and promise of God's peculiar favour have set in motion, is the starting-point of this road to life. The Jew in us—that obstinate and irresistible sense of a summons to intimate familiarity with an Eternal and All-Holy God—rouses within us the imperishable need of attaining the satisfaction, of winning the promise which such a summons holds out as our acceptable prize. We push forward, we reach out, we press and strain towards our impossible goal; and ever the formal necessities of such a prize grow sharper and more distinct, ever the difficulties increase, ever the demands rise sterner and more unrelenting, ever our failure deepens, ever our helplessness grows more manifest, more incurable, more radical, more deep-seated. Beaten, baffled, bruised, and shattered, our knees fail, our hearts sink, our soul sickens, our spirit despairs: until, over our fallen and prostrate weakness, God Himself uplifts the Cross of His Christ, and pours out the Holy Blood of perfect pardon, and drives the nails home into the flesh that sin had claimed to master and possess, until the very seat of sin's dominion is torn asunder and destroyed, and the peace of Christ's own eternal and living righteousness moves down for our acceptance, from the arms of that prevailing Tree.

Such is Redemption brought home to our aspiring self by the way of Judaism—such is the Cross of Jesus as the key and clue to all our righteousness, as the vindication of God's everlasting promise.

But there is another dispensation, another road by which our souls travel to the City of Salvation—the way of Gentilism: and it is this other way which offers itself to our contemplation, as we turn from the warring strife of the Epistle to the Galatians to the splendid peace of the Epistle to the holy, the beloved Ephesians. St. Paul, the prisoner of Rome, the captive of Christ, bound in chains at the very heart and centre of the vast Gentile Dominion, has turned away his eyes from the perils and problems that had encumbered the progress of God's chosen seed from law to grace, and gazes now, with the awe of an overwhelming admiration, upon the means which God had found to recall His banished—upon the work which God, by Paul's own mouth and hand, had achieved for the recovery unto holiness of those huge millions of lost and seemingly forgotten Gentiles. Here, as he looked back along the centuries, his eyes fell on no

sign of God's favouring presence, no sign of the Great
Shepherd making Himself a household; of the Good
Husbandman shaping out His vineyard, digging
Himself a wine-press, planting His vine; of the King
fashioning for Himself a peculiar people; of the God
Who makes for Himself a tabernacle, and Who chooses
a dwelling-place, and has a delight in holy habitations.
No; here rises up no household of Saints; no call stirs,
no promise excites, no hope impassions; no sense
of Almighty favour and help gather together com-
panies of faithful and obedient spirits. Nothing moves
in that grim and enshrouding night which has settled
down, fold upon fold, upon those sightless and forlorn
populations; no quiver of light shakes that black
solitude, no stir of spiritual emotion shoots through
that numbed and powerless mass. It is Death, the
very kingdom of dumb Death: such life as seemed to
stir in those heathen peoples was indeed no life at all;
it was not their own life, but the senseless impulses of
lust that dragged them along by chains and fetters.
Such lights as broke the impenetrable darkness only
deepened its black gloom; lurid flashes from the eyes
of prowling fiends, sparks set on fire in hell.

Yes; this is no imagination, no far-off fancy, no
unreal picture: they themselves, his converts in dear
Ephesus, had known and felt and endured its terrors.
"Ah! remember it, my people!" he cries to them.
"Remember it! recall all that horrible past from which
you have so marvellously escaped! Do not forget its
fearful reality, its dire and dreadful oppression. 'Remember that ye, being in times past Gentiles in the

flesh, were at that time without Christ, aliens from the commonwealth of Israel, strangers from all covenant of promise, having no hope, without God in the world; walking as other Gentiles walk, in the emptiness of their mind, having the understanding darkened, alienated from the life of God through ignorance, through blindness of heart; past feeling, giving themselves up unto lasciviousness to work all uncleanness, corrupt according to the deceitful lusts, partakers of those things whereby the wrath of God cometh upon the children of disobedience, dead in trespasses and sin, fulfilling the desires of the flesh, by nature the children of wrath, dead in sin according to the course of this world, according to the prince of the power of the air: yes, remember it, ye too were afar off, ye were strangers and aliens, ye were sometimes darkness, ye were in bondage to that evil spirit that even now worketh in the children of disobedience!"

Such have they been: let them never forget it! For only according to the measure of their recognition of this, their old doom of death, will they know and approve that immeasurable joy, which pours, like a strong flood, out of the heart of the Apostle, as he recalls, with boundless fervour, with rolling abundance of word and phrase, the surprise of the mighty change.

God has done it, He and no other. All along that dark night of dismay, He had been hidden, but His Mind had formed its counsel: He had a secret which only waited to be revealed. That Gentile world was indeed not forgotten or abandoned, though to the eye of the onlooker its fate appeared so desperate. God had from eternity schemed its redemption. He was only biding His time, He was but waiting for the hour of destined action; and now, behold ! God's passionate desire can restrain itself no longer; His abundant mercy can no more withhold its secret; the mystery, the hidden counsel, so long delayed, has leapt out from its secret place into discovered life. He, St. Paul, has himself been caught up by its sudden energy, and has found himself turned to be its tool. And, if the long hiding of God, if His prolonged and unbroken repression of Himself, had amazed by its utter desolation, by its impenetrable severity, all the more astounding is the overflowing splendour, the surpassing fulness, the glorious outburst of strength, with which God throws His whole Heart into the work of this disclosure. The blaze of light dazzles as completely as the profoundness of the dark abandonment had blinded. If before, God had been utterly absent, utterly withdrawn, utterly inactive, now He is Himself become wholly and entirely present, wholly and entirely revealed, wholly and entirely active. Before He did nothing; now He does everything. He Himself has entered on the scene in the fuller reality of His Being; He has Himself taken the entire work into His own Hands : God is the actor, and we have no eyes or ears but for Him; God is Himself the agent, and, lo ! there is no one who can stand beside Him. "See now that I, even I, am He: there is none other; I kill or I make alive; I wound and I heal."

Our spirits watch with solemn awe as St. Paul lifts the veil and discloses the uncovered and naked activity of the Most High. There it is, behind the screening glamour of history; there it is, the mighty life, the manifest energy of the Very God; we see it at its awful and tremendous work. There is a breach opened in that profound night of death; and that breach is filled by what St. Paul calls "the wealth of God's personal glory." If, before, God seemèd niggard of His presence, now there is no limit to the wealth of His self-manifestation; πλοῦτος, again and again St. Paul calls it: all His treasures are brought out, all His riches are outspread, outpoured, without stint, or scruple, or jealousy, or fear—the riches of His grace wherewith " God, Who is rich in mercy, hath abounded towards us, for His great love wherewith He loved us, that He might show the exceeding riches of His grace"—riches which no present happiness can exhaust, but which it will occupy all the coming ages to consider, and admire, and enjoy—riches which have no limit, since they are to continue their outpouring until we are filled with that fulness which belongs to the inexhaustible God Himself.

In the wealth of God's abundant love, then, lies the clue to this disclosed secret; by it the breach is made in the night's blackness. God discloses His very Heart of love, the springs of all His innermost Being. And out of this abounding, and inbreaking fulness of love, St. Paul sees a Will issue—a Will, strong, active, energetic, alive, that sets to work upon the black or hideous mass of corruption, and makes its operation felt within that womb of night. This Will does not remain a counsel in high Heaven, a plan, an intention, a scheme, formed by God to Himself, which He waits for others to use and to profit by. No; that Will is no mere design of God's reason: it is itself impelled by vivid and urgent desire, it leaves its hidden home within the Mind of the Father; it comes down, if we may so speak, from out of its silent seclusion, it inserts itself into the dark world of man, it presses its way in, it puts forth force, it acts, it moves, it empowers, it quickens, it makes alive. This is the wonderful sight that St. Paul contemplates with such adoring joy. God the Father, He Himself in His own masterful reality, has done the deed, has made known upon us the right hand of His power: He has worked the mighty work Himself: He, in St. Paul's own strong language, has "*wrought,*" He has shown us "the exceeding greatness of His power according to the working of His mighty power, which He wrought in Christ, when He raised Him from the dead, and set Him with His own right hand in the heavenly places."

"God wrought." If there is one thought that the Apostle dwells on more delightedly even than on that first thought of the wealth of God's self-disclosure, it is the thought of the power of that disclosure. It is a power, "δύναμις," a living force, exerted, operating, entering in, lifting, carrying, stirring, animating, penetrating, inhabiting, transforming. It wrought its work within the world of death, first by its action upon, and within, the perfect Son, Whom it begat through the Spirit, Whom it possessed, and bore into the wilderness of temptation, and clothed with transfiguration on the Mount, and upheld under the olives of the Agony, and lifted up upon the Cross of shame, and carried into the gates of the Grave, and thence, by its own inherent energy, in its supreme efficacy as the Will of the almighty and creative Father, upbore out of His tomb, breaking asunder the hard and sealed stones, and raised Him by its impulsion from out of the solid and rigid mass of the burdened dead, who lay weighed down, as by bands of iron, into the clogging mire of sin—raised Him, and set Him on high, and surrendered to Him infinite and irresistible supremacy over all principalities, and powers, and might, and dominion, and every name that is named.

This God did, according to the good pleasure of that Will, according to the mystery of His Will—God Who worketh all things after the counsel of His Will. Nor did He stay His right hand there. On us, too, in and with Christ, that Will has wrought; on us it lays its hand and puts out its force; on us it works its living work. The love which drove it, by sweet compulsion, to pour out its strength upon the Son whom it begot, drives it, impels it, to exert the same activity upon us whom it has included within the attraction of the Son; on us, whom it has made acceptable in the Beloved. In leaping out to enclose, and quicken, and upraise the dying Son, it leapt out too, by one and the same impulse, towards us, whom it saw lying dead in the Death of the Son, and whom it identified with the flesh of that Holy Body with undivided love, when it lifted It, and endowed It with recovered and eternal life, endowing our dead souls and bodies, at that one fiat, at that masterful stroke, by that one rush of power, by that one act of gift, with a right to all the life, and force, and grace with which it filled full the risen Body of the Lord. Dead once with His Death, we are now held tight and fast by the hand of God's encompassing love within the folds of the Son's requickened Life. Like a magnet, that strong love of God for the Son draws us, sucks us within the currents of its uplifting energy; we are caught up with Christ, we are, under that omnipotent attraction, enfolded within its heat, we quiver with its very life, we feel ourselves taken in within its mastery, within the pressure of its upward force. As the blood rushes homeward under the suction of the central heart, so we are dragged upwards towards that home whence God's efficacious love carries forward its work of regeneration through Christ, the Beloved Son, the Heart and Centre of the Church, which is His Body. Yes, "Blessed be the God and the Father of our Lord Jesus Christ, Who hath blessed us with all spiritual blessings in heavenly places in Christ: hath chosen us in Him, that we should be holy and without blame before Him in love: hath predestinated us unto the adoption of children: hath made us accepted in the Beloved: hath abounded towards us in all wisdom, having made known to us His Will, that we should obtain an inheritance in Christ; and hath made us, yes, us men, sinners, dead in trespasses and sins, to be for the praise of His glory: hath sealed us with His Holy Spirit, unto the praise of His own glory: hath loved us with His great love: hath quickened us with the quickening of Christ: hath raised us up with the raising of Christ, made us sit with the sitting of Christ Himself in heavenly places, in Christ Jesus." There is no limit, no reserve: that Living Will has laid hold of us to make us all that it desires, all that it sees us capable of being in union with Christ, to remake us into the form and fashion of Christ: "We are God's workmanship, created into Christ Jesus unto good works, which God has ordained for us to walk in." God foresees a good purpose in us, a positive use which we can be to Him, a means of gratification, a source of delight to Him: even this His might can effect in us, the might of Him Who can "suck honey out of the flinty rock, and make water-springs out of the dry ground." "We are brought nigh; we have access unto the Father with boldness and confidence, we are become fellow-citizens with the Saints; and of the household of God; we are builded together into Christ, fitly framed to be made an habitation of God; we are, according to the riches of God's own glory, strengthened with might by His Spirit in the inner man, so that Christ dwells in our hearts; we are rooted and grounded in love; we know the love of Christ; we may be filled with all the fulness of God, Who can do exceedingly abundantly for us, above all that we ask or think, according to the power that worketh in us;" so that "we be holy and blameless even now, before the eyes of God in love," and can, even now, "grow up into Christ in all things, grow up into the perfect man, unto the measure of the stature of the fulness of Christ, from Whom, as from the Head, the sap and force of the body streams down, to make active the entire and compact mass, so that it be fitly joined and held together by bond of joint and ligament, making increase into the edifying of itself in love." So gathered up into Christ, in the undivided unity of a single organic frame, which is the Church, we are verily preserved in the spirit of our minds; we possess within ourselves the new manhood of Christ, "created after God in righteousness and true holiness; we can forgive as God forgives; we follow God as dear children; we walk in the love wherewith Christ loved us; we walk in the light, as children of the light; we prove what is acceptable; we understand the Will of the Lord: we have no fellowship at all with the unfruitful works of darkness, we do not so much as name them, as becometh saints; we are filled with the Spirit; we are strong in the Lord, and in the power of His might."

Where, and how, can we stop? O my soul, how is it that thy faith quails, or thy tongue falters? How is it that thou canst not understand "the exceeding greatness of God's power towards us, nor what is the riches of the glory of His inheritance in the Saints?" How is it that such high language sits so ill and so uneasily upon thy lips? Is it not because thou hast never sounded all the height, and length, and depth, and breadth of that all-sufficing word of the Apostle of Grace; "not of yourselves, not of works, are ye saved, but of grace; yea, it is the gift of God."

The gift of God! The whole life and work, from end to end, is His and His only; who, then, can limit His wealth of overflowing goodness; who can doubt the exceeding value of His mighty power? Nay, rather, "unto Him that is able to do above all we dare ask, or think, be glory in the Church by Christ Jesus throughout all ages, world without end."

This, then, is the history of Gentilism.

The soul is bidden to look back, not on the old desperate moral struggles, by which it wrestled and strove all night with the great Angel of God's covenant, and yet never saw God's Face, or knew His Name, nor even was changed in itself from Jacob, the deceiver, into Israel, the Prince of God; not on its memory of baffled aspirations, and unfed hunger, and deplorable disappointment, as it fell, and strove to rise, and fell again, without advance, without improvement,—not on this is it bid look, but on its natural state of utter and irretrievable ruin. True, God never wholly abandoned the Gentile world, nor ever has wholly abandoned the soul of the believer; but there was enough in Gentilism to reveal what it would become 'if once it were left to itself, if once God had entirely withdrawn; there was enough to make clear what it was of itself, in its own tendencies, what it would inevitably sink into being, if the word of God had not ceaselessly worked to check and restrain the collapse. So, too, with the soul: it can see enough of its own wickedness to know what it would have become of its own nature if ever the power of God could be conceived to be withdrawn; it can contemplate the condition to which it would fall, if God once suffered it to work out the sin of Adam to its logical, its consistent conclusion. It would be death, complete, unmitigated death; not a mixed struggle of good against bad, but a sheer loss of hold on the good, absolute revelling in wickedness; the very heart made alien to holiness by a darkened understanding, so that the good ceased to be known to be good, and the evil would be loved as evil, without repulsion, without a sense of offence, without the warning of a conscience. We should be children of disobedience, to whom disobedience had grown to be the very nature, so that we followed its inspirations blindly, and felt no better stirrings, and looked for no higher aim, without hope and without God. This is the kingdom of that darkness, which we are only held back from becoming, because God has never yet left us to ourselves.

This, then, is the condition out of which God saves us, this and nothing less. So far as we ourselves went, we had given ourselves indeed over to this; and, if so, then from such a domination of utter darkness and death nothing could deliver but the sheer violence of God's Will, which could, without help from us within, shatter, by the strong impulse of its inherent love, our horrible imprisonment, and could seize us, and lay fast hold, and force us into new shape, and remake us from head to foot, and change us into another thing, by the mighty working of its own vivifying efficacy; and this it is which was done in Christ, blessed be God!

SERMON XIII.

THE LAW OF FORGIVENESS.—I.

"We preach Christ crucified, unto the Jews a stumblingblock, and unto the Greeks foolishness; but unto them which are called, both Jews and Greeks, Christ, the Power of God, and the Wisdom of God."— I COR. i. 23, 24.

THE Cross of Christ is, at once, the close of our shame, and the beginning of our glory. In one and the same act, the penalty is paid for our sin, and the medicine is applied which heals unto salvation.

Therefore it is that the Cross is no scene, merely, of a tragedy under the darkness of which we cower; but it is for us the hope that enlightens, the light that saves; and, far and wide, most lovely are the feet of them that bring us its good tidings, of them who preach Christ Crucified.

Christ Crucified is not only a pathetic Atonement for the Fall, not only the Victim of Good Friday; He reigns from the Tree, with an Easter glory, as " the Wisdom of God, and the Power of God." For the Cross is a remedy as well as an expiation: it is the application of Divine skill to the solution of an ancient wrong: it rectifies, it heals. And this it can only do if it acts by method, and by rule. If the Cross is to be a remedy, which cures, then it cannot be a carnal boon, dropped as a solace or a compensation out of a rich man's abundance.

For what is a remedy? It is force scientifically applied; it is power directed by wisdom. It is that which applies itself to some definite conditions: it places itself in exact and definite relations to that which it would heal. It proposes to heal some particular sickness—that and no other: it meets a distinct case—that and not another. Removed out of its context, and circumstances, and antecedents, any remedy would become wholly unintelligible, needless, foolish.

And the Cross is a scientific remedy for sin, directed against a particular and definite set of conditions, according to the purpose and direction of God; it is the application of His Power and Mind, by careful method, by intelligent discretion, to a disease which He alone could measure and appraise.

Christ Crucified is the Wisdom and the Power of God, as directed against definite evil. And everything therefore depends on our right estimation of the evil. Isolate the Cross from its conditions—look at it alone, and out of context—and it is bound to appear to you as meaningless and as foolish as would any other remedy which you divided from its definite relations. " Sacrifice, Atonement, the Sprinkling of Blood, Mediation ! " here is indeed a strange, an unintelligible language to those who have no gauge and no appreciation of the corruption from which these words receive their purpose and their application.

Ah yes! no wonder that to the Greeks the Cross should appear foolishness. To the Greeks !—to the young, the buoyant, the cheery-hearted; to all those, who have not yet tasted the bitterness of death; to all who have shut their eyes and closed their hearts against the inevitable, and have put off the thought of the evil day; and have covered themselves with flowers, and have hidden themselves behind pleasant screens, and have hugged the sweet gifts of mother earth;—to these, to such as these, what else could it possibly appear—that Bloody Cross, that Broken Body—but a blunder, a disaster, a folly?

To the Greeks—foolishness.

And to the Jews; to the respectable and the self-contented; to the worldly, the unalarmed; to those fortified in the plump complacencies of middle age; to the smooth crowd of the successful, swathed in self-importance and fed with comfortable flatteries; to those who, from the vantage-ground of assured self-righteousness, can so easily see the failings of others, and are convinced of their own peculiar value, as guides to the blind, as instructors of the foolish, teachers among babes; to those who cannot but feel themselves too important, too precious, too good, too worthy, for God ever to condemn;—to those among us who are Jews, that white Body nailed to the bitter Tree, smitten with the curse of the outcast, hung out to infamous shame—to the Jews, no doubt, it is a stumbling-block.

Yes; to the whole and to the sound, the Physician seems very needless and absurd; and his elaborate prescriptions look most tiresome and pedantic.

But to those who are sick. Ah! they know what it

means; they know to whom to look. They understand that serious eye of the doctor, that rigid discipline, that ordered apparatus, those intricate instruments. To them, who have the key, it is a very different matter; everything is intelligible, everything is expected, everything is justified. To them, it is just what they most urgently need, and most thankfully receive; "to them it is, indeed, the Wisdom of God and the Power of God."

It is the sickness that determines the remedy. Out of the conditions of the sickness which it cures, the remedy must receive its interpretation. Let us consider, then, the conditions of this our sickness of sin, and the mode in which they would affect the character of the cure.

Sickness and sin—the words run together. And, yet, there is a most vital distinction that must be drawn. Of the two, it is the *sickness*, to which we are most sensitive; for sickness pains us, and we all can feel this. But in the case of sin, each sin dulls us to the sense of sinning; the more we sin, the less it pains us to sin; we grow insensible, undistressed. The sin disappears out of our range of sensitive experience; we lose the capacity to feel, or to perceive it. But, while the misery of sinning vanishes, the misery of the sickness remains; it remains, as sharp and bitter as ever, though its cause is no longer experienced. The sickness remains; and it is the sickness which we so repudiate and abhor. The sin? That may seem to us a very light affair, that could easily be wiped out by a little regret, by a rapid confession. But we are weak, diseased, impotent: and that is miserable; and we loathe it; and it seems a violation of our being, an offence against God's creation, a breach in His intention and laws; and we cry to Him, in our wretchedness, the one cry to be healed—"Take it away, this misery, O God! Sickness, impotence, death are hated, surely, of Thee! Give me back sight! Heal my boy whom I love—he is very ill! Oh, bid me rise up and walk! Lord, if Thou hadst been here, my brother had not died."

Sickness, impotence, death — these appear to us unnatural and abnormal evils, which God is bound to sweep from us, if He is a merciful Father, Who forgives; and, so feeling, it startles us to discover that the Cross of Christ, our sovereign remedy, has taken away so little of our misery; has left us still, as of old, in a world crowded with ancient wrongs, and woes, and death,—in a world still swept by pestilence and scoured by war.

But have we not been making a perilous mistake? Let us be very clear about it. Sickness, as sickness, is not itself a violation of nature, a breach in the normal rules and laws of life. The sin which caused it—this, indeed, violates the order of nature; but not the sickness. Nay! sickness belongs to the same natural order as health; it proceeds by the same rules; it issues out of the same conditions; it manifests the same system. It is not one set of laws that make sickness, and another health; but the same set of laws which, under one set of circumstances, make health, make disease under another.

How did the circumstances change? Ah, that is another question. A wrong direction has been taken; the equilibrium of forces has been changed: that, indeed, was unnatural, and wrong, and lawless. But, given the new direction, given the changed conditions, then sickness exhibits the working of law as exquisitely, as flawlessly, as the most beautiful health.

It is as when a smooth and sliding river meets some sudden shallows down which its deep waters sweep over barring rocks and jagged edges. How all is changed in a moment! Up above, is the sweet and quiet peace of silent waters, gliding in massive stillness, with only a dreaming eddy here and there to mark the unbroken motion; and, below, is the wild chaos of the rapids, a mob of waters, shaken into seething foam, tumbling floods that roar and screech as they hurl themselves along to join the fury of the fall. Yes, a change indeed! And yet every flying drop of those crashing waters is shot hissing into the abyss, by the steady undeviating action of those very laws which held them silent and repressed, as they slid, without a sound, down the grooved channels between the even banks.

So with sickness: it works by law, by nature; and if so, then by a law which is God's own—by a nature which still, in its sickness, exhibits Divine workmanship and Divine Will. The advance of a cancer is, in itself, as regular and as perfect as the growth of a plant; and the outbreak of a fever is, to the eye of the physician, as delicate and as beautiful a process as the blossoming of flowers.

Nay, more: a great part of sickness is the protest of

nature against the wrong, that it has brought about the misdirection. Through these miseries, these struggles of ours, nature is seeking to liberate herself from distorted conditions, to throw out the poison, to break up the thwarting obstructions. The release from the internal wrong is to be won by giving the violence of the disease full play; and the aim of the wise physician is, not to check or repress the sickness, for that would be to shut the door against relief; but to work with the sickness, to co-operate with the protest of nature.

What can he do? He has three modes by which he can render assistance.

First, he may devote himself to preventing a recurrence or a continuance of the wrong which has brought about the misdirection of forces. Nature is making her struggle against the wrong already done: that she must be left to do; the misery incident to that struggle cannot be helped when once the wrong has been done. But if we can count on nature setting herself to undo the wrong, nature must count on our seeing to it that the wrong is not incessantly reproduced.

This first; and, secondly, the physician aims at supporting and succouring the vital forces, that they may not give way under the violence of the fight. In sickness, nature is battling for life; but the effort at recovery may be too severe, too terrible, for the patient to endure or to survive. The physician can aid in replenishing the inner forces, that they may be enabled to endure the agony of the relieving process.

And, thirdly, he is bound to detect, within the very heart of the disease, the elements and the conditions of a complete renewal. There is a vitality shut up within the sickness, which is struggling, not merely to survive, but to recover its footing, to renew its dominion over the diseased flesh, to regain its normal action and functions, to purge out all poisonous matter. The physician assumes this power of renewal; and, indeed, without it he could do nothing. If it is once there, he can co-operate from without; he can remove obstructions, he can untwist all the tangles, uproot all that clogs. He works from without to liberate an original principle of vitality and health, that can respond from within to this co-operation; but the vitality must be there.

Forgive me if this has seemed long and remote; for the interpretation of Christ's cure depends on our understanding these, the conditions of all remedy.

Christ, to our surprise, instead of sweeping away the suffering and the death which to us seemed the supreme evils, adopted them for His own portion, and left them, in their violence and their shame, for us to endure. Well, we now may ask, what else should He do? A remedy must co-operate with the disease; it must lay itself alongside of the sickness; it must make the sickness its ally. For the sickness is, as a mere consequence of certain conditions, perfectly natural, perfectly lawful, perfectly justifiable. Its actual working manifests God's laws, and, therefore, God's Will, as faultlessly as the working of those same laws in health.

If the wrong has been done, there is bound to be sickness. If the sickness were swept away, without the wrong that produced it being wiped out, or cancelled, God's world would be thrown intd confusion; God would have broken His own creation to pieces.

But how can the wrong done be cancelled, or blotted out? The sin has been sinned; human life has been misdirected, perverted, obstructed, distorted. That is done. Nothing can gainsay that. Nothing can make it not have been done—nothing except the annihilation of creation.

And if it has been done, then human nature is necessarily sick and suffering. Nothing can save it from that.

What, then, is possible? One way, and one way only. The way of the Physician; which we call, theologically, the way of sacrifice—the way of the Cross.

God Himself will co-operate with the sickness: will enter Himself under its miserable conditions. Is there anything offensive to Him in this—degrading, defaming? Nay! the laws of sickness are His own laws: He does but put Himself under Himself. There is nothing in sickness, or in pain, which is essentially abhorrent, as such, to God, except the misdirection which produced it. There is nothing evil in itself, except an evil will. And this is why Christ, the Blessed Son, in laying Himself down under the black scourge of death, finds no hand laid upon Him but the Hand of His Father. The cup of pain which He drinks comes from no devil. Not even in the darkest hour, has the Prince of this World anything in Him. The cup, the bitter cup, the cup so bitter and so fierce that He Himself shrinks from tasting its terrible wine—that cup is given Him of no one but the Father. Hung, then, on His Cross, He has never fallen one hair's-breadth outside the Father's Will. The laws, that make His affliction, are themselves expressive of the Father's purpose: He is still, in His Agony, " One with the Father."

Christ co-operates with the sickness; He is made one with our sick flesh and blood. How that task is accomplished will be considered in the two following sermons. But, before closing, let me illustrate the distinction that has been drawn between the cause and the effects of sin, in a matter that is just now very near to us. Perhaps one practical instance may make the distinction clear, and real, and living to us. The thrill and the terror of war are shaking the hearts of the people,[1] and once again we wake to the strange and perplexing distinction between the faith we hold and the scene in which it displays itself. What does it mean, this our Gospel of peace and of goodwill, with its fearless acceptance of the savage horrors of war? It comes with its sweet, Angel-song, breaking out of Heaven over shepherds 'mid their sleeping flocks ; and lo ! it thrusts and plunges itself down into the thick press ¦of this wild earth, where swords are smiting and the hot blood flies. How is this?

And we can answer—It sets itself, first, with all the

---

[1] Preached at time of excitement against Russia over affairs at Penjdeh, on Afghan frontier.

wisdom and the power of the Cross, against the motives and the temper that are the causes of war. It cannot tolerate, it loathes, it uproots, not only the fierce greeds and ambitions, which we all are so ready to condemn and which we so easily detect in every nation but ourselves; but also that barbarian temper which is now so busy and so loud among us—that bad animal-blood, which rouses itself within us all at the rumour and the touch of a quarrel—that spirit of pugnacity, so clamorous to take offence, so apt and quick with taunt and challenge, as it kindles with the tingling heat of passion until its fingers itch for the fight. Ah! how we have felt it all about us of late, rising like a steam of vaporous irritation, which is ready, at any touch of provocation, to rush into a flame. How swiftly this temper lays hold of us! How soon we learn to disguise it under brave titles! Yet, for all its fine names, it is the beast within us which is stirring, alive still in spite of the discipline and the pressure of Christian centuries, untamed by the wisdom of the Cross, untouched by the meekness and gentleness of Jesus.

With this evil spirit of pugnacity the faith of Christ can make no terms at all. It bans it utterly; it purposes, not to moderate, but to expunge it, in the Name of Him Who never flung back taunt against taunt; Who, "when He was reviled, reviled not again;" Who never sank to the level of those who attacked Him; Who gave Himself over to unprotesting death rather than permit personal honour, His personal "prestige," to assert itself by one syllable of retort; "Who was led as a lamb to the slaughter," and Whom no insult and no blow could persuade "to open His mouth."

This is the Lamb of God; Who, if we but believe Him, would take away out of the world the sins that make our wars. But then, that is only half the task set before Him. The causes are condemned: there remain the effects, the facts. War is there, the product of old wrong; war exists, it occurs, it recurs, it is part and parcel of the state of things: and Christianity closes with this world as it finds; it sets itself to possess the facts just as they are; it lays itself to them, face to face, to refashion them from within; and the courage with which it coalesces with the facts, in all their repugnant horror, is the measure of its spiritual potency, of its prophetic mission. And how freely, with what gallant abandonment, does the Spirit of Christ knit itself to the facts of war! Down into the very thick, into the very core of its wild tumult, it throws itself, it dives, it burrows, it buries itself. It winds itself in: it pierces into the innermost soul of this savage passion. It possesses itself of its deepest secrets—the secret of duty, of patriotism, of self-surrender. It seizes on these, it purges them, it refashions, it transfigures them; and lo, there emerges out of the noise and the agony, out of the blood, and fire, and vapour of smoke, a new and lovely vision—the vision of a Christian hero—of a soldier saint. Faith in the meekness of Jesus wins material for itself out of the heart of war: it finds, amid the mad cruelties of slaughter, new reasons for gentleness, new motives for

peace; and slowly it builds up the character of the
happy warrior, of him—

> " Who doomed to go in company with pain,
> And fear, and bloodshed, miserable train—
> Turns this necessity to glorious gain:
> Controls them, and subdues, transmutes, bereaves
> Of their bad influence, and their good receives;
> By objects, which might force the soul abate
> Her feeling, rendered more compassionate;
> As more exposed to suffering and distress,
> Thence also more alive to tenderness."

My brethren, courage is not of this fashion in its
natural condition. The rough native audacity, which
flung the Arabs against our squares at Abu Klea, is a
temper which, in its unchastened force, falls as a
tyrannous curse upon all the weak—upon the women
whom it degrades, and the boys whom it sells and
enslaves. But the Christian Gordon, with a courage at
least as stubborn and at least as reckless as theirs, wrings
out of the heart of battle a chivalry for the weak, which
is delicate as a woman's, and a pity for the fallen,
which is tender as a child's. Yea! out of the strong
our faith sucks sweetness; out of the eater it can win
meat; even as Samson found, within the grim and
horrid carcase of the lion, the happy homely noise of
buzzing bees.

Faith can do it—faith in the Wisdom of God, and the
Power of God. And that faith is ours. We may not
be asked to learn its wisdom and its power in the hot
agonies of war. But the same secret is at work under
all clouds of suffering, and misery. Will you believe
its wisdom—will you trust its power — when you lie
smitten, paralysed, tortured, impotent, battling for

life with some sore sickness, beaten, bruised, blinded?
Will you then make no wild protest, and send out no
complaining cry? Will you lie still, shut up within
the pain, wrapped round with folds of miserable sickness? Will you be content to commit yourself only
to the name of Christ crucified? Will you ask no
question at all, but simply let its power work upon
you in and through the sickness itself—seeing nothing,
knowing nothing—only committed, only resigned to
the Lord Jesus,—lying under His Eye, under His Hand,
as under a good Physician, Who knows all, and is
doing all, though the sickness still tarries, though the
fever does not abate? You may feel no change—bitter
the disappointment!—hour after hour; but oh! He
knows, with those quiet, strong eyes of His. He bides
His time; He is measuring the emergency; He is
anticipating the crisis; He is following the sickness
step by step; He is ready, unsurprised, unalarmed.
Oh, let Him do what He will! Doubt Him not.
Trouble Him not. Lie there until the change comes—
until the new secret begins to work, as work it will;
and you, at last, will feel its power, and it will be
to you as if you heard, within the dead carcase of your
distress, the soft sweet humming of the bees.

THE LAW OF FORGIVENESS.—II.

"And, behold, they brought to Him a man sick of the palsy, lying on a bed: and Jesus, seeing their faith, said unto the sick of the palsy, Son, be of good cheer; thy sins be forgiven thee."—Matt. ix. 2.

To our uninstructed eyes, when we are brought face to face with a disease, the scene is one of unqualified misery. There lies the sick man, restless, shaken by terrors, his brow wet with the sweat of his agony, his eyes staring, or closed with the weariness of pain. It is a horrible thing to watch: a horrible thing for a father to stand by while the devil shaketh his child, throwing him on the ground and rending him so that he gnasheth his teeth and pineth away; a miserable and a terrible sight for us to watch, and kneel, while we are helpless, and can bring no relief and can win no succour out of any pitying heaven, and have only to pray and cry, and yet can find no man who can cast out this devil from the child. Who is there that will make it all end? "Lord, come down ere my boy die."

And no doubt we are right to be terrified, to cry out to God.

This dismay is the evidence and proof of some tremendous wrong that has been done upon the earth.

It is an evidence that God's order has been broken; God's honour outraged; God's oath violated. Sickness brings it all out to the light. It is made visible, in order to convince us of all that which we have so easily passed over. God, Whom we, with a light heart, offend every hour, every minute, without a scruple, without a fear, may well bring us to book by this stern discipline. He may well shake us, as men are shaken to save them from sinking to some fatal slumber under numbing snows. Anything to be kept awake! A wrong has been done to God, and if we cannot see it in one shape, let us, in God's holy Name, have it forced upon us in another. If our sin leaves us unalarmed and unabashed, then let our misery, our unrest, bring us back in penitence to God's breast. We may be driven to seek God through wretchedness, as those poor ignorant Galileans who followed the Lord, seeking, pursuing, never letting Him rest, if only they might drag their sores and their sickness to His blessed and merciful feet.

And yet this is but the first, rude, ignorant movement of the fallen spirit. It cries to God to cancel its wretchedness—that first: but the wretchedness is not itself the wrong that has been done to God; it is but the proof and the witness of wrong. The wrong lies beyond, far behind, in some perverted motives, in some misdirected life. Sickness, whether it be sickness of body or sickness of soul, only makes it unmistakable that some secret disturbance has taken place, out of which disturbance, by perfect, and orderly, and natural rule, in obedience to the entire harmony of God's creation, the changed condition follows which causes us so much pain. It is this *spiritual* wrong that we discover in its horror, through the sharp evidence of God's goad as we kick against the pricks. If we bruise ourselves against the wall in the dark, it is not the bruise that we complain of; the blow itself is but the notice that we have missed our way. And the cry that we should send up to God in hours when the world's woe smites us heavily is not, "O God, I ask Thee this one thing, that Thou shouldest sweep away this sickness," but, "O God, I see, I know, I feel now, the hideous wrong that in the ages have been done against Thy name; that old recklessness in lust, that old, bad excess wherein the human race, Thy child, has wasted its substance in riotous living; I know it now, my God, more as it is in Thy Eyes; nor am *I* guiltless. I have been a partaker of that guilt; I, too, have added to the sins of my forefathers; oh, leave me sick, if it be Thy Will; but at least have mercy on my sin!"

That is what our Lord desired to win from those Galileans who crowded behind Him, like wounded animals, driven to Him only by their blind desire to escape from feeling wretched. This is what He desired, and this is what He could not win, and because He could not win it He made Himself strange to them; He fled far from them over the lake into the desolate wilderness, to escape their importunity. He hid Himself, and He cried out against them when they came pursuing Him with their sickness, "Oh, faithless and perverse generation, how long shall I bear with thee; how long shall I suffer you?" They were meant to

learn a nobler lesson—the lesson which was first opened
to the paralytic man, let down with so much trouble
from the roof, who, in response to his anxious pursuit
of deliverance and health, heard, for his reward, not,
"Rise and walk," but only, "Son, be of cheer; thy
sins be forgiven thee." For if the Pharisees had never
jeered or disputed at the forgiveness of sin, would our
Lord have ever added His healing word? Would not
the man have been left there, lying impotent as ever,
with no release from that disease until the day of his
death? If so, that would have been his moral probation. Would he, or would he not, have been bravely
satisfied to have heard as his reward for all his following after the Lord. "Son, lie thou on thy bed, and fear
not; let thy four faithful bearers carry thee away by
the way whereby they came. Let no sweet and secret
change pass over thy withered limbs; but, for all
that, be of good cheer, go in peace; great is thy
faith, and great is thy reward; for thy sins are
forgiven thee "?

Sickness is the witness to us of wrong that has been
done. It is the handwriting on the wall, wherewith a
man's hand writes the word that tells that we have been
weighed in the balances and found wanting. And in
this sense it is a judgment; it makes known the curse
of sin. But that is not all. The misery of sickness
witnesses not only to the wrong done, but also to the
right that has been lost. Sickness is the protest made
by nature against the misdirection of her forces. And
in this sense it does not dower as with a curse, but cries
out against the sin: "I have sinned, and lo, I am

sick. I have left God's Will, and lo, I am miserable. Yes, blessed be the Name of the Lord for that sickness, for it proclaims that I was never meant to take that road. Thanks to His mercy for this misery, for it burns into me the good news that I was never made for sinning. If by sinning I grow sick, then I must be made for obedience, for purity, for self-control, for God. It is by dropping away from God that I have grown disordered and corrupt. Oh, let me lift up my voice in prayer and praise to Him Whom, now first, I know to be my life and my health. I was made good, for evil slays me; it is alien, horrible, unnatural. Lord, this house of sin is no home for me. I will return to Him from Whom I fled—to my own Father in the house at home, Whose son I still discover myself to be, unworthy as I am to be called by His Name, here among swine in a far country."

Sickness is to the eyes of the physician the revelation of the laws of health. In the violence of the outbreak he recognises the determination with which the organic structure battles against the mischief done to it. He watches it all with a sympathetic care as it writhes and pants under the pressure of hostile forces, and his task is to co-operate with the sickness for the recovery at which it resolutely aims. But, first, before he begins the remedy, he has to cut off the secret sources of wrong. Until these are stopped, all his handling of the sickness can only be an idle palliation. How, then, is our wrong to be cut off by God our Good Physician? This spiritual sickness from which we suffer, this poverty of love, this impotence of will, this corruption of desire, how is its great source unseen to be stanched?

For this is the terror that has fallen upon us. We thought we could sin and repent and be free from our sin; we turned back from our wrong-doing so soon as we found its taste was as bitter as gall and its virtue to be dust. We loathe it now we have done it. Would that it were undone. We would hurry back now to our old place in Eden, shut in by the fourfold waters of the quiet garden. But lo! our sin has made us sick, and our sickness holds us fast bound, bound by our sin. Our knees are weak, we cannot rise and run, our heart fails us with its poverty of blood; we cannot desire God as we once did, and we have tasted the fruit and we cannot but remember how sweet it felt in the mouth before it turned to dust. That sweetness returns to us again and again; oh that we could forget it! Alas! alas! we remember it too well, and, remembering it, we long to repeat its pleasure. Nor can all the sure experiences of its secret bitterness banish the horrid appetite for yet another taste of its terrible juice. We were so confident, at first, that we would never do it again. So we think while repentance bites and while temptation is out of the way. And then—who can believe it even of himself?—somehow that fountain of regret has gone; its waters run dry; and we cannot sustain ourselves at the level of our repentance, and our forces flag. We had wrought ourselves up, and now it has all slackened, and we feel stale and flat and demoralised; and back with a sudden rush the old wrong streams in like a flood; our footing is shaken. One effort, and then we are gone whither the strong currents carry us! Our imagination is swept into captivity; we are borne down the stream, and the banks on which we were once securely standing, the banks of a secure and well-ordered life, with the busy cities, the patient fields, where men still plough, and sow, and gather into barns, they all pass us by. Faster and faster we go down the rough currents, unresistingly, knowing only that at last we shall hear the angry moaning of some dark and dreadful sea.

We know so well, so frightfully well, that the recovery of our sickness depends upon the stoppage of the secret wrong. And yet we find ourselves again and again doing the wrong that we purpose to stop. In discovering the misery of our sin, we discover also our powerlessness to cease from sinning. It may seem hard, but surely it is natural enough? The sickness that has come upon us deadens these very powers of desire and will by which alone sin can be resisted and beaten. And with weak will and meagre love, who can hold out against a sin made stronger by the very act which has impoverished the resistance?

The wrong cannot be cut off; this is the terror of the sickness that comes by sinning. And God, the Physician, may lay down for us His rules, His advices, His prescriptions; by this and by that we are clearly told the evil can be shunned. There they stand in black and white; all the statutes, commandments, and judgments which are the laws of spiritual health; and there, too, are recorded all the palliatives, the sacrifices and offerings by which we may be made clean and sound again from our defilement—and yet all is useless! We remain what we were. We faint under the burden of the Law. We cannot do the things that we would; and the blood of bulls and goats cannot take away our inherent and eradicable will to sin. There is but one hope. If only a new fire could be shot into our chilled and flagging heart; if only a fresh jet of force could infuse itself into our jaded and diminished will; if only a spring of living waters could be opened within that naked stone which we once called our heart—that, and that only, can save us, for that, and that only, can cut off the supplies of sin which continually reinforce our habitual disease.

And it can be done—it has been done—by that beautiful law, so natural, so rational, so intelligible, so normal, of vicarious atonement.

By that law, which is already and always at the very root of our human life; the secret of all its advance, of all its hope, of all its virtue, of all its honour, of all its pathos, of all its loveliness, of all its fascination, and of all its glory;—by that law which knits families into the blessedness of home, and friends into the beauty of companionship, and armies into the grace of chivalry, and nations into the splendour of patriotism;—by that very law, which is always the breath we breathe, the light of all our seeing, the core of all our story—by that law it is possible for God, without disturbing or traversing one atom of that natural order which He has Himself sanctioned by creating,—possible for Him to intervene, to break off the fearful entail, to shatter the chain that our sins have forged. God, the Physician, can defeat disease by Himself becoming the suffering patient! He may lawfully do it; for physically and actually such substitution is the daily and hourly incident of our corporate life. And, if it is physically possible, can it be questioned for a moment whether it be morally justifiable? Not morally justifiable? How can anything be more morally natural, more morally intelligible, than for the stronger to give his strength to the weak —than for the innocent to surrender his life blood to shield and aid the fallen? Why, this is the very instinct of all passion, the joy of all love; this is exactly what every human heart understands, and every conscience justifies. There is no imagination so dull that it cannot welcome this, and no spirit so laggard that it will not kindle at it. It is the very seed from which virtue springs. Love would not be moral if it were not vicarious. It is just because we are socially responsible for each other's fate that we are capable of virtue. We begin to be moral as soon as we put ourselves into the place of another. This is the starting-point of the very first ethical law, to do unto others as we would have them do unto us. And the growth of ethical force comes with the growth of love—love which fulfils the whole body of the Law out of the one motive of self-sacrifice for others; love which crowns itself in that highest act, by which a man will joyfully lay down his life for his friends. Atonement by the innocent for the guilty not morally justifiable? Rather without atonement no morality.

The spirit of sacrifice is the creator of ethics, and God sanctioned and sealed the entire body of ethical verities by which human society is bonded and fed, when He sent His Son, Who knew no sin, to be made a curse for us, and to bear on His shoulders the iniquities of the world.

The wrong, then, can be, and has been, undone by the intervention between the sin and the sickness of a stainless Will, of an untainted Desire. A divorce has been effected; God has driven in His wedge, by which He shuts off the sickness from the sin.

And now we can afford to turn and consider the sickness itself. Until the fertile evil could be stayed it was useless to work a cure. Every remedy would be baffled by a renewal of the wrong, but now hope has become at least possible. The disease smites us no longer with the sense of a curse, for we are no longer identified with corruption, no longer implicated in its meshes. Just as from within the human soul we can look out on our bodily affections as if they were foreign and remote, so now our spirit has been snatched by the spirit of Christ out of its spiritual distress, and lifted up and carried back within the shelter of His endless love; we are drawn into the vantage-ground behind and beyond our spiritual disease. We have a sure footing in Christ. We can stand in safety, as on the rock, above the roaring tide as it lashes about our feet. We are safe, held in His arms, plucked by Him out of the night. We have a recess, a refuge, from which we can now look out upon our own sickness at its worst period. It is outside our innermost life. This is the peace of the forgiven: the pain may be all there still; the sickness may burn, and sting, and fight; the misery may sweep over us unappeased; we can lie on the bitter bed of our palsy of old; and yet, miserable as we may feel at our own moral corruption, we are free from its condemnation, free from it in the same sense as our human spirit holds itself free from the physical tortures of its body. The spirit may long for relief, for cure, but it knows itself apart from its bodily pains. It has an existence within which they do not enter. It hears what the doctor may say about them, as if they were some strange matters of which it was hearing the news for the first time; it still can retain its spiritual fortress which they never occupied, and within which it is in peace and self-possession.

And so with the forgiven soul. All its deliverance, all its cure, has indeed yet to be achieved. It has not been spared, as yet, any wretchedness, any more than the world in which Christ rose felt any abatement on Easter Day of its wars and cruelties. But within itself, in the hand of the Lord Jesus, the soul possesses the secret of peace—peace that no storm can alarm, nor even its own sinfulness can wholly break; for it is the peace of those who, although in this world they have tribulation, yet are of good cheer, secure in Him, Who has long ago overcome the world—the peace as of those timid and sinning companions of Jesus, who straitened still in the narrow, upper chamber, with fright and peril outside, and the doors still closed fast for fear of the Jews—yet can be glad as they see the

Lord; can be glad as they feel yet once again upon them the breath of His salvation, the blessing of peace —peace, wrung out of the very heart of Him Who, rather than pray, "Father, save me out of this hour," cried, "Father, in and by this hour, wherewith my soul is shaken, this hour so bitter and so black—Father, through this hour, though it be unremoved, glorify Thy Son." His peace we have, which He left with us, His own peace which He giveth unto us; "The peace of God which passeth all understanding."

There yet remains for us to consider the slow and patient process of our cure, the carrying out of our forgiveness over the surface of our disordered lives. To-day, let it be enough to remember that the cure must begin with forgiveness, with stanching the springs of our wrong-doing. We are forgiven first, in order that cure may now begin, and go forward; for it is forgiveness that makes our healing possible. Forgiveness of God—that must come first; the heritage of sin must be broken off, the past no longer hold dominion over us. We must be forgiven. And we are forgiven because a stainless Will and an untainted Love have intervened within the lines of our sad story; have broken us off from the corrupt stem, and have ingrafted us into themselves. This is the first step of our deliverance. Much may yet be before us, but all has become possible now that we have been transplanted into Jesus. We can lie now on our bed, and wait for Him to say, "Rise up and walk."

My brethren, we all know by a hundred wretched experiences the impotence of an unnerved will, the poverty of a corrupt love. Our resolutions are so brave until the moment comes for keeping them; our intentions are so excellent until the pressure of facts confuses us; our desires are so eager for purity, if only they would not so strangely languish just as the passions awake in a storm. All would be well if we did not just slip and fall where it was vital to stand. Most miserable this incessant collapse! How it disheartens; how it disgusts! We are netted as a bird. We flutter up, but the meshes once again entangle us, and down we come to the ground, and the sky is as far off as ever. And what if, around and about this poor, this impoverished will, there was wrapped the irresistible might of a will that had not been broken, a will, new, fresh, undaunted, tough as steel, endurable as stone, firm as adamant?—what if the warmth of a love were laid about it to which the emotions of impure appetites are impossible?—what if we were given up to this love, so that it abode within us and possessed us, and held us fast, untroubled by our disasters, unhurt by our sins?—what if, after all our sinning, we still can turn back again and again to find this loving will there still, pure and strong as ever within us, still pressing, with unwearied patience, on towards the beauty of holiness, with its unwavering eyes ever fixed on the face of God? Would not this be enough? would not this be salvation? would not this be peace? "Ye shall mount on eagles' wings." That is our splendid assurance. No longer that fluttering tumult of the poor captives, tangled in the snare! Nay! but "on eagles' wings"—the wings of God under us, kingly and unconquerable, as they beat their strong way upwards, let the winds blow as they may: "on eagles' wings"—the wings of a holy will, the wings of a clean desire laid under us to bear us upwards. This may be yours, you who are in sickness, infirm, or palsied, or dead. This uplifting power may be made your own, if you will but forsake your own mode of cure, your own medicines, your own wisdom, and come and lay yourself at the feet of Him Who alone can make a breach in your sad captivity; Who, through His very Manhood has, alone, the power here on earth to forgive the sins of His fellows.

THE LAW OF FORGIVENESS.—III.

"Thy faith hath saved thee."—St. Luke vii. 50.

THE act of Divine forgiveness is an act of re-creation. We are new-begotten by the Father, through the waters of regeneration. In Christ, Who is our forgiveness, we are born again; we receive a new manhood, we are made new creatures. From first to last this is the language in which the New Testament expresses the nature of our pardon; and all its language is an echo of the words with which the Lord opened His mission in Jerusalem: "Verily, verily, I say unto you, ye must be born again. Unless ye be born of water and of the Spirit, ye cannot enter the Kingdom of Heaven."

What does this imply?

It means, that all our forgiven life dates itself from an act of God—an act originative, antecedent, fertile. God begins the work. The sickness of sin had made us powerless to begin the recovery. This was our confusion, our paralysis, our misery, our despair, that, sorry as we might be, sick as we might feel, nevertheless not all our sorrow nor all our sickliness could persuade us to love righteousness as once we loved it, nor to hate iniquity as only the unfallen spirit can hate it. Do what we would, it remained sadly clear that we were not at our old level; our standards had sunk, and we could not restore them to their former force; the influences in us that made after holiness were impoverished; and we, out of ourselves, had no means of replenishing them. No; we cannot begin. We cannot beget ourselves. That is the prime and fatal difficulty. It is the new start that has become so impossible; and yet it is the new start which is so vital a necessity for us.

God must begin, if we are ever to be rescued. Here is the very key of Christian theology, and the very core of Christian faith. Until we have laid hold of this interpretation, the language of the Epistles and the fabric of the Church remain hopelessly unintelligible.

God must begin. This is the secret that burns through all the strong appeals of St. Paul and St. John, as they reiterate their conviction that nothing of our own enters into the primary movement of our justification. No goodness at all of ours drew out a response from the co-operating favour of God. It was our badness, not our goodness, that drew it from Heaven. It was pity for our perishing that moved the Father to send His Son to save the world. While we were yet sinners, Christ died for the ungodly. Not because we loved God, but because we could not love Him, did His love for us break out over us in His Son. God first loved us while still we loved sin rather than holiness, in order that, by loving us, He might restore to us the lost power of loving Him. The heat of His love alone it is which wakes up in our cold hearts the forgotten love for Him.

We cannot begin until God has begun. To doubt this is to be "under the Law." It was, in St. Paul's language, "the Law," which said, "Return ye, My people, and then I will return to you." This is the law of works—the law of work and wages: it said, "If only you will prove our repentance, if only you will turn again into the old ways, God will forgive, God will be merciful!" The despair of the law of works lay in the discovery that this preliminary effort on our part was just the last effort that it was possible for us to make. Nay; if we are to be recovered and recalled, we must wait for a stronger Hand than ours. We have no part in it. God must anticipate our beginning. He must take the first step; He must do something to relieve the dilemma. He must arrive to succour, before we deserve anything; He must forgive, before we have ceased to sin; He must justify, while still we lie guilty.

You recognise the language I am using. It recalls a theology which has isolated the particular truth conveyed by these terms until, in its isolation, it has become grotesque, unreal, deceptive,—yes, and morally perilous. But it is here, as in so many other cases, the isolation of the terms, not the terms themselves, which are at fault. Justification by faith, itself a paradoxical expression, which can never hold itself together against the analysis of a solvent and penetrating logic, has yet a most valid signification in that deep region where the secret of life runs back, behind logic, into paradox. It is the assertion of our absolute exclusion from the creative act by which God acquits us; in that act we have no more part or lot than in the act of our first begetting. God forgives us without our helping Him. We are justified, we are acquitted for and by nothing at all of our own, not even by our faith.

But how, then, is it rational? How is it intelligible? Forgiveness is hope. How can God have hope of men who have proved themselves hopeless? Forgiveness is favour. How can holiness show favour to that which has proved itself irredeemably corrupt? Forgiveness is love. How can purity love the impure? Impossible! Yet that is what forgiveness must mean. If God has forgiven sin, then God's repugnance has been changed into attraction. What can so change Him?

Not anything, again we say, of ours. We, in ourselves, are as yet unchanged. No! But the act by which God forgives, carries with it, out of Heaven, the power to work the change in us, which will justify God in forgiving. God's forgiveness goes out from Him in such a form that it makes us, it enables us, it obliges us, to become that which we should be if we deserved to be forgiven. God the Father forgives us by anticipating that which will follow on His forgiveness.

How is this done? What is this strange, this miraculous forgiveness?

Christ, the Wisdom of God, the Power of God.

God, the Father, forgives us by sending us His Son. And, in saying this, we dispose of a swarm of questions with which people besiege us. How is it, they ask, that the Father requires this bloody scene on Calvary? Has He no forgiveness for us without shedding of blood? Is He not ready to forgive us of His own Will, of His own mercy?

Yes, indeed! He is ever ready; He has never ceased to be willing to forgive. How else, but as longing to forgive, does He cry to us, all through the Old Testament, the cries of a Father Whose Heart still yearns over His lost children, "O My people, what have I done unto thee?" "O that Israel would have hearkened unto Me!" "Is not Ephraim a pleasant child?" "Turn ye, turn ye; why will ye die, O house of Israel?" "Hath the Lord any pleasure in the death of the wicked, but that the wicked turn from his ways and live?" "Why, why will ye die?"

The Father has never slackened in His readiness to forgive; but how is He to forgive? Forgiveness means restored favour. What is there in us on which His favour can rest?

Forgiveness means renewed hope; what is there in us on which Divine hope can fasten?

Forgiveness is a renewal of love; what is there He finds within us with which His love can fuse its force and its fires?

It is not that the Father is unready to forgive; but that His ready forgiveness is shut up, of melancholy necessity, within Himself. It can discover no way by which to enter, no point of attachment by which to lay hold. The love of God wanders round this bitter, inhospitable world, and can find no haven that is not barred.

And therefore it is that He sends His Son in Whom His forgiveness can find a road into the repellent earth, into this repugnant humanity. God's expelled forgiveness, as all other doors are bolted, will open a way for itself; as no man will admit it, it will itself become a man, that it may find admittance. God will forgive man in spite of man. God's forgiveness issues out of Heaven in the shape of a Man, wearing human flesh. Jesus Christ is the Forgiveness of the Father. The Father had already forgiven the world when He sent His Son to be born of the Virgin Mary, to be crucified under Pontius Pilate. He arrives, bringing with Him the pardon of the Father; and this pardon is effectual. For there is now in man one spot, at least, clean from defilement, on which the eyes of God's purity can afford to rest. There is now, amid the loveless herds of sinners, one Heart, at any rate, upon which the Father can risk the outpouring of His love; one Body, amid the hopeless and the faithless and the diseased, which can admit the rushing power of the transfiguring Spirit. The love, hope, purity, of God— long homeless and unhoused—have found at last a footing within our flesh, a resting-place, a habitation, a temple. They had looked, and there had been no man—not one that doeth good, no, not one!—not one that could respond to their appeal—not one that could surrender himself to their intimacy,—no, not one; and, therefore, not one whom God could forgive.

But now there is one Son of man in and through Whom God's forgiveness can begin to work. Christ, the Forgiveness, becomes the one forgiven Man; the one Son, Who has sanctified Himself to do the Father's Will. "Lo; this is my beloved Son, in Whom I am well pleased."

God begins to forgive before we deserve it; and He does so by and through His Son. This is His forgiveness, which comes speaking peace to those that are near, and to those that are far off.

God has forgiven us before we begin to find it out; and all our reconciliation to God is just our discovery that we have long ago been forgiven in Christ Jesus.

Just as a secret act of God's original energy underlies all our natural life—one act, prevenient, enduring, hidden,—so a secret act of forgiveness, original, enduring, prevenient, underlies all our regenerate life. God spoke once, "Let Us make man;" and lo, in the unending force of that fiat, we all are, we have our being. God spoke once in Christ, "Let Us work out man's forgiveness;" and in the everlasting power of that one word, so spoken and done, the new race of the forgiven finds itself existing, the Church of the redeemed rises, grows, gathers, swarming upward out of some hidden will, as clouds that make and build themselves out of the very vacancy of air under the strong eye of the risen sun.

This is the secret of Baptism. Baptism is no seal of a life already restored; it is the act by which restoration is first made possible. The diseased life has to be brought under the regenerating Will, for its

cure to begin. Yes, God must begin. He has origi-
nated a way of pardon, of healing—Christ, the
Wisdom of God, and the Power of God; and the
first thing of all to be done, is for us to be brought
under the influence, under the pressure, under the
heat, of this regenerative Wisdom.

Our cure must begin in an act by which, far back
in the dim and secret recesses of our life—there, where
God's congenial act of creation still works beneath
our incumbent corruption—far, far back, in the silent
secrecies, impenetrable, invisible, God reverses the
distorted directions of our life-power, God cuts off
the supplies of wrong that feed the mischief, dams
up the current of our shame, imbeds the germinal
seed of our new humanity. This restorative action,
first lodged in His Christ, is by Him deposited
within the bosom of the Church, His Bride; there
(as we at any rate believe) it works in its fulness, in
its freedom, with the least amount of check or
hindrance, with the least risk of loss or impoverish-
ment.

And, under this action, we place our babes; that
it may effect its lodgment within them. Once forgiven
of God, the redeemed life can begin. It does not
start to win its forgiveness—the old, sad, wearisome
impossibility! Nay, it starts forgiven. It begins
with forgiveness, with Atonement, and, in the power
of that pardon, it works out its own salvation: with
fear, indeed, and trembling; but with a hope that can
never fail.

Never fail! No; for the enduring forgiveness

is not in doubt; it is not a prize for which it painfully toils, or pitifully and brokenly prays. It abides behind and beneath, a possession, untouched by its own shifting feelings, deeper than its own yet irresolute desires and wavering will. The Will of God in Christ, pledged to it, certified to it, by Baptism——endures on and on through all. I fall, I faint, I fail? Yes; but under me lie the Everlasting Arms. Until I myself repudiate my Baptism, and kill out my baptismal grace, I am still a forgiven man. I have not lost my Gift. It is in me still. It is under me. And, again and again, I may have sinned, but under the covering wings of the Church, through the Absolution of God's Priest, I can assure myself of my full renewal, of my perfect pardon. Through Absolution, the enduring efficiency of that baptismal grace, not yet all lost, finds once more its road unhindered, its channels unchoked. As God began by forgiving me, so it is He, not I, Who begins again and again, by Absolution, each stage of my renewal. His grace goes before; it makes my healing possible. He sends me out forgiven, with a forgiveness that is independent of my mischance; for it stands, not in my worth, but in Christ's merits. And, therefore, I will not fear; for the Rock is under my feet. No! "I will not fear, though the earth be removed, or though the hills be carried into the midst of the sea. Though the waters thereof rage and swell, and the mountains shake at the tempest of the same; yet still, deep within the keep and citadel of Zion, there is a river, whose streams run on untainted, making glad the city of God, the holy place of the tabernacle of the Most High."

Here is the great *background* of our restoration. God, alone, with His own Arm, brings us salvation. His own force sustains Him. God acts; we are powerless. God staunches the ancient wrong. God cuts us out of our evil past, running His holy Will, like a knife, through the strong cords of necessity which bound us to our dreadful past. God, out of His sole compassion, introduces His Forgiveness, in Christ Jesus, into the world; and only by the force of that antecedent forgiveness is our recovery possible.

And now the scene changes! In the *foreground* we lie, sick, diseased, " the maimed, the halt, the blind, the dumb." There we lie, one by one, each laid out on his lone and miserable bed, and separately, slowly, that world-wide pardon, sealed in Christ, draws near, and reaches each single sufferer. It is our individual recovery that is now in hand. And lo! now, at this stage, it is God Who holds back, Who waits, Who cannot begin. It is we who must make the start. On us the whole burden of movement lies. If we will but move, God will co-operate; but we must make the first effort. God waits upon our initiation.

Remember the old scenes in Galilee. They repeat themselves in us. Jesus is so withdrawn, repressed, silent. The sick must seek, pursue, catch Him, as He passes; they must press in, through thronging crowds, as the woman with the issue of blood. They must take up the roof, and be let down by ropes. They must follow, and cry, until the Apostles are weary. They must go on crying their "Jesus, Son of David" with relentless persistence, against the rebuke of the multitudes.

And, then, when they have reached Him, the effort is still all thrown upon them. "Lord, if Thou canst?" said the poor father at the foot of the hill. "If I can? Nay! Not if I can; but if thou canst! It is all a question of thine energy, thy courage, thy faith! If *thou* canst believe, all things are possible."

And when it is done, it is as if our Lord had done nothing, as if the man had done all. "Thy faith hath made thee sound!" That, and nothing else. From within the man the power came—a spring was opened, a force set free, a key turned, a bolt flew back, and lo! it is all done in a moment. As if by the mere upward pressure of the human will, strength streams into his palsied limbs, health pours itself through his dried veins. He stretches out his hand, long withered; he rises from his bed, and lo, he walks! It is done, and by the man himself, under the eye of the Master. "Yes; thy faith—that, and nothing else—thy faith hath saved thee, hath made thee sound. All things are possible to him that believeth."

In the *foreground*, it is we that begin. Everything turns on us. Grace is near at hand; but we must find it for ourselves. And grace, when found, still demands something of us; it is we who must summon up our energy to use it, to touch it, to discover its secret, to put out its power. Jesus calls upon us to act, as if we had ourselves the capacity to obey.

But how, and why can He ask this? Only because that which happens in the foreground is the fruit of His own antecedent action, in the secret background.

We are forgiven, already, in Him. He has already stemmed, for us, the current of our sin. He has already bound the strong man, who held us so fast, and has robbed him of his authority, and has stripped him of his armour. The victory is won, long ago. The cords are cut. The Power of this world has been judged, mastered, cast out. The Lord has ascended, to take His great power, and reign. He holds already all the keys of Heaven and Hell. He sits at the right Hand of God. All power is given unto Him. All things move under His sway. He opens, and no man shuts: He alone shuts so that no man can open. It is done. It is won. He is exalted far above all principalities and powers. He has stripped naked all the forces of sin, and has triumphed over them openly. He is ascended up on high. And therefore the road of escape for us is open. We are already released, before we know it; forgiven, before we have begun. The past is fallen away from us. God's mercy looks out upon us. We are already made free. And, therefore, because of this one perfect and sufficient Sacrifice long ago offered and accepted for the sins of the whole world—therefore, because God has long ago begun on our behalf—therefore it is that Christ can expect great things of us; can look to us to obey; can just stand, there, and bid us "stretch out our hand," or " rise and walk " !

In the Name of the ascended Lord—all things are possible to them that believe. All things are possible, just because we have not got to win, or to deserve our pardon, but only to exert the forgiveness already established at the right Hand of God. We have not got to be forgiven ;—we were forgiven eighteen hundred years ago. Now we have got to discover it for ourselves ; to use the promise sealed to us ; to put out the powers that are in us from God.

You are forgiven. Now, try what it means to be forgiven. "Stretch out your hand!" Rise from your sick sins! "Rise, and walk!" Try it! Begin! Believe that it is done, and make a start!

" Oh! but I have so long forgotten," you say, "those ways of spiritual living! This old world of faith has all become dim, remote, unreal to me. I have lost the taste. My love for holiness is withered. I have no instinct after purity. I have no spiritual organ: it is diseased, palsied. I do not see the things you speak of. I do not hear those voices you promise me. I am weak, thin, paralysed, how can I rise and walk, in this heavenly kingdom of yours! It is years and years since I really felt at home in it, or moved amid its mysteries, and understood its language, and fed on its sweet secrets,—years and years ago! Now it is all gone from out of me ; and lusts are strong, and habits are rooted, and all is bent one way. I cannot do it ! "

You cannot ; but Jesus is gone up on high, above

every name that is named. He has broken off your cords. The past is dead—He has killed it. The ropes lie still tied round your arms; but they are cut. You are loose; for He has redeemed you. You can start afresh, to-day, from the beginning; for He has bound the strong man. Your organs, your spiritual faculties, were withered and maimed; but a new creative action is at work within you; you have been taken into the forgiveness of Christ, and that forgiveness is a force that re-creates.

It has all been done for you.

Try. Believe. Look up at Jesus. Do just what He tells you. With eyes rooted on His, begin. Stretch out that withered hand of yours. You can do it; for He orders it, Who has already Himself made it possible. Leave that weary, weary bed of miserable sinning. Rise; rise and walk. Forget the long years behind you, the sad dreary sickness, the terrible memories. Look at the Master, and lo! it comes; it is done. You rise under His magic. You are doing what He bids. You are doing the impossible. Before you know how, the weakness has dropped away from you; you are carrying your bed.

God, the Father, of His good mercy, grant that all those who so lie sick, may press, and touch the hem of His garment, that they may know in themselves that they are healed of their plagues!

THE COMING OF THE SPIRIT.

"And hath made us able ministers of the New Testament; not of the letter, but of the spirit: for the letter killeth, but the spirit giveth life. For if the ministration of death, written and engraven in stones, was glorious, so that the children of Israel could not stedfastly behold the face of Moses for the glory of his countenance, which glory was to be done away; how shall not the ministration of the spirit be rather glorious?"—2 COR. iii. 6, 7.

WHAT is this contrast that starts into such sharp outlines before the eyes of St. Paul—the contrast of the letter and of the spirit? We may well set ourselves to answer this question, for the words have passed into a proverbial familiarity, which has succeeded, as proverbs so often succeed, in bandying them to and fro until the original significance, once emphatically precise, has dissolved into a cloud of vague misunderstanding. It is supposed, perhaps, that St. Paul is contrasting the outer expression of a principle with its inner meaning—the letter of the Law with its spirit, and hence that he is opposing the wrong use of the Law, as illustrated by pharisaic pedantry, with its right spiritual use, as interpreted by the Mind of Christ. Or, again, the letter is taken to represent the ceremonial details of the earlier covenant, while, by the spirit, is supposed to be intended that inner moral law of the heart which lay burdened under the wearisome ritual of the Pentateuch until it was set free in Christ. And here, again, it is the unfortunate Pharisee who figures as the representative of externalism, while we are glad to identify ourselves with that inward spiritual service which the prophets of old asserted, and which is independent of exact conformity with all the precision of a narrow ceremonialism.

And some of all this may possibly be half true; but yet is it at all what is meant here in this passage of St. Paul?   Let us look at it a little closer.

"The letter killeth; the spirit giveth life."   It is evident, first, that the phrases do not express any general principle, but have for him a perfectly exact, and definite determination. The contrast he has before him is that between the old and the new covenant, between Moses and Christ; and to appreciate the vividness of his antithesis we must begin by throwing our imaginations back into the days when as yet the Church of Christ held no Christian book in its hands. Its faith was not as yet rooted in a written word. It was Judaism that was based on a book, and it stood in broad contrast on this very point with Christianity, which held its Gospel in the shape of the spoken word, made present and energetic, though the mouth of a preacher, by the force of the Spirit of God, upon the hearts of a believing body. A living story housed within a living society, vitalized by a present Spirit, witnessing to a present and living Christ:—that is the word of God administered under the new dispensation; and what need, St. Paul is asking, what need of written authorities to qualify for such a mission as this? What need of certificates and testimonials, such as his opponents require him to show, or upon which they rested their own claims? "Need we, as some others, epistles of commendation?" Nay: his own people are sealed to him by spiritual evidence; they are his living certificates. "You are our epistle ministered by us, written not with ink, but with the Spirit of the living God." And this clinging to documents, so characteristic of his own foes, stamps them, he thinks, with the brand of that older covenant which had always been a matter of letters, of writings, of communications, of things graven with a pen on the face of a stone, rigid, motionless, external, menacing. But the Apostles of Christ carry with them no written message, no mere book of the covenant. They have a more glorious ministry, not of the letter, not of any writing, but of the Spirit.

The letter is first, then, that revelation of God which had been effected through a writing, through a communication, through a fixed and durable proclamation, through a record, through a statute, through a rule—in a word, through a Law. The letter is the written Law of God. And this Law, which is the letter, is no ceremonial rule. St. Paul has in his mind that moment when Moses bore down from the summit of Sinai the Ten Commandments which are the Law, for it was then that his face shone with the glory that was under the veil, "the glory that was to be done away." The letter, then, of which St. Paul speaks, is definitely those God-given letters graven upon the tables of stone. It is essentially the moral, and not the ceremonial, Law; and the letter is that Law, then, which our Master summed up for the lawyer in the great commandment, "Thou shalt love thy God with all thy heart, and with all thy soul, and with all thy strength, and thy neighbour as thyself."

By the letter is meant the moral Law; and we know therefore at once how and why the letter kills. For St. Paul has analysed for us the three stages of death to which the Law dooms. It kills us, first, by its manifestation of that disruption which lay concealed under the happy outflow of young and brimming life. That strong and fearless energy, which is the core of our human nature, is brought up short and sharp by a relentless voice that refuses it its unhindered joy. It clashes against the obstinate resistance, the sudden obstruction which bars its road with its terrible negative, "Thou shalt not covet;" and, in the recoil from that clashing, it knows itself to be subject to a divided mastery. It knows itself to be capable of violent variance with God. It knows itself to be somehow spoilt, disordered, corrupt. The unity of sound organic health has suffered rupture. It has in it the evidences of a disorganization and a dissolution, which is death. "I was alive without the Law once; but when the commandment came, sin revived, and I died."

And the Law not only declared sin to be there, but it also, so St. Paul is not afraid to assert, provoked and irritated the sin, which fretted at its checks, into a more abundant and domineering extravagance. "Sin, taking occasion by the commandment, wrought in me all manner of concupiscence." Man's primary revolt reacted from this first recoil into a fiercer onset. Curiosity, imagination, vanity, impulsiveness—all are set astir to overleap the barrier, to defeat the obstacle that so sharply traverses its instinctive inclinations. "The Law entered that offence might abound," and where offence abounded, death reigned, for the end of sin is death.

And the letter therefore which provoked sin into extravagance, that letter killed; and it killed not only by manifesting sin, not only by aggravating evil, but also by convicting. Over against the very men whom it irritated into revolt it stood as a judgment which could not be gainsaid nor denied. It fastened men down under the bolts of a conviction from out of which there was no escape. And they knew it. They knew the sting of its terrible truth. Its wrath unnerved them, and its presence confounded. Every mouth was stopped, for the handwriting was against them. They were shut up within the prison-house of a criminal doom, and that justly. They lay there tormented in that flame, waiting the just judgment of God; for the letter convicted, and therefore it killed. It killed; and this by God's own intention. It was given that it might kill: It was no written pharisaic literalism that so relentlessly slew out the soul of man; it was God's own written word, engraven with His Finger on tables of stone. "Yea, sin, that it might appear sin, worked death by that which is good, that sin by the commandment might become exceeding sinful." Better far that the secret poison should be brought out into

violent action. Its sickness, its pain, its agony—these
are, after all, proofs of capacity to struggle ; these are
methods of liberation. The body is releasing itself
from disease through these bitter experiences ; and let,
then, the letter kill. Let death dig in its fangs. Let
the doom deepen and darken. So only shall at the
last the spirit of the resurrection quicken ; so only
shall those that sleep in the dust at the last awaken.

Through sin the letter slew, and slew according to
the intention of God ; and, what is more, there was
no hope of relief or escape through man's spiritual
advance, for the higher the Law the sharper its sword
of judgment. As man's apprehension grew more spiritual, the discovery of his fall became more desperate.
Each fresh insight into God was a fresh insight
into sin, and the path into fuller life was therefore
a pathway of despair. The Law slew because it was
just and pure and holy, and the quickened spiritual
instincts would but learn the touch of a more biting
terror ; so that when at the last hour of that old
covenant there stood upon the earth a Jew greater
than Moses and Abraham, Who accepted the hereditary
Law and promulgated it anew, asserting it in all its
rigour and width, enlarged in range, intensified in
power, interpreted with all the infinite and delicate
subtlety which the Mind of One Who was One with the
Giver of the Law could convey into its edicts, so that it
comprehended the entire man in its grip, and penetrated his innermost recesses, and carried its searching
inquiry into his backmost corners, and made its claims
good over the very springs of conduct, and suffered no

minutest motive to escape revision, and demanded of his most secret will a perfection of intention such as belonged to the moral heart of the all-holy Father;— why, such a Gospel, if that Sermon of the Mount had been all, would have struck the very chill of the last death into the despairing soul, who listened and learned that not one jot or tittle of that Law could fail. Alas for men! The sermon that some lightly affect to be the whole Gospel of Christ would be by itself but a message of doom. This moral Law, so high and pure and holy, this belongs, taken by itself, to the older covenant; this is the very letter that kills, this is the Law that convicts,—kills, interpreted by Christ, as it had never killed before, dooms more witheringly than of old it ever had doomed; and the cry that would close the message of that sermon, the cry of any honest soul brought face to face with that tremendous manifestation of the Mind of God, would be the cry of the broken and terrified sinner: "O miserable man that I am! who can deliver me from the body of this death?"

The letter kills, and yet the letter hath a glory to St. Paul, the glory that shone from the face of Moses descending from the mount. The letter has a glory, for it is the manifestation of the very mind and being of God. The moral Law graven on the tables of stone was the primary and absolute establishment of these essential relations which determine all possible communion between man and his Maker. Without the Ten Commandments no communications are possible; for purity, truth and goodness,—these are what God is; these are what God must be in all His actions; through them He exhibits Himself; in the form of them He communicates Himself. Verily the letter hath a glory. It is the revelation of the Divine Will in action, the revelation of God. For this, men had looked and yearned through weary years; to discover this they had toiled, and sighed, and prayed. Many kings and many prophets had desired to see these things; for this they had ransacked nature, searching for that which lay always hidden behind the dumb silence of that breathing earth, that which seemed always suggested yet was never disclosed. "Oh that I knew where I might find Him!" So man cried in the bitterness of his search. And now, listen: there is a revelation; the dumbness breaks, the silence yields, those flying footsteps of God pause, the air opens, the heavens are sundered. There is a presence: there is a voice; there is an utterance; there is a vision; there is a glory—and it kills!

Consider the surprise and the seriousness of such a situation. God stands over against man in glory, the glory of the proclaimed intention, of the manifested Name, the glory of the letter. God stands there in the Law, inviting, appealing: "Come; My oxen and My fatlings are killed, and all things are ready; come to the wedding." God stands there in that Law, pleading and beseeching: "Oh that My people would but hearken unto Me! O My people, what have I done to thee?" God, face to face with man; God hoping, asking, desiring, loving, calling, electing, promising, tending: and man lies there before Him dead—dead in the face of the glory, killed by the glory—dead, even though within his very deadness he can hear with the ears of some inner manhood, a manhood now dark and imprisoned, yet a manhood that still delights in the Law of God—can hear the blessed salutation, and the thrilling news, and the splendid promise, and the tender pleas. Deep within the deeps of his soul there is the blind stir of some unutterable response, and yet that response cannot come to the surface, and the will of the mind cannot carry itself out to act. It is fast bound in misery and iron; and he, the man, lies there, therefore, dumb and dark and dead, praying only that the hills might cover him, that the mountains might bury his shame; praying only that he might be hidden in some deep gulf from out of the burning Eyes of that God Whom, in his earlier confidence, he had so longed that he might find and behold.

"God showeth His Face and the earth shall melt away." God shows His Face in the Law and the letter kills. Man lies there dead before his God—dead, until —what is it, this sweet and secret change? What is it, this breaking and stirring within his bones, as when the force of the spring pricks and works within the wintry trunks of dry and naked trees? To what shall we liken it? Have we known the first wonderful pause that comes to those who have lain through long dull hours, with closed eyes, with stunned senses, with sightless soul, under some weight of pain that bruises and benumbs and crushes and breaks—have lain there choked under the tyranny of weary hours, upgathered into the mere effort to endure, hardly asking that the agony should ever have an end, and then have sud-denly known that the pain has for a moment paused, has slackened, has ebbed?   The throbs have lost their violence; there is a softening, a relenting, a touch of peace, and hardly yet they dare to believe it, hardly dare they whisper to themselves that the worst is over, that the pulses of sharp pain have really grown weaker. Yet the sweet peace increases and soothes and con-soles; and lo, at last they are lying there quiet and calm and happy, possessed with a blessed stillness and a mighty thanksgiving.

Who can tell the wonder of such hours?   And it is an hour like that which comes to the man whom the letter of God had smitten and slain.   As he lies stung and despairing, there is a change, there is an arrival. Far, far within, deeper than his deepest sin, behind the most secret workings of his bad and broken will, there is a breaking and a stir, there is a motion and a quiver and a gleam, there is a check and a pause in his decay, a quickening is felt as of live flame.   What is it? He cannot tell; he cannot measure; he cannot con-ceive; only he knows that something is there and at work, strong and fresh and young; and as it pushes and presses and makes way, a sense of blessing steals into his veins, and peace is upon his harried and hunted soul, and the sweet soundness of health creeps over his bruises and his sores: and he who has faith, just suffers all the strange change to pass over him and to work its good will, as he lies there, feeding on its blessedness, wondering at its goodness, sending up his heart in silent breaths of unutterable thanks.

So it is come; it has happened. St. Paul felt and watched it, this transformation that was begun over the earth. He saw those lame and impotent men rise and leap and sing at the coming of the new force, under the handlings of the new ministry; and, so seeing, he knew the full meaning of the Lord's promise that the Spirit should come, and that every one born of the Spirit should be even as the Spirit. Its coming heralds a change, absolute and final, from all that had been before until John: and the essence of the change is this—that God, Who in His manifestation of the letter stood there over against man, calling, inviting, appealing, has now passed over on to the side of the men whom His appeal has overwhelmed. He, the good Father, is bending over the sinner, and into his wounds is pouring the oil of pardon and the rich wine of grace, and entering within his human spirit by the power of His own Holy Spirit; He, God, is lifting him up, is carrying him, is enabling him, is recovering him, is filling him with His own fulness, is inspiring him with His own breath. God is on our side; God is with us; God, Who invited, now undertakes for us who receives the invitation; God, who calls, draws to Him now those whom He has called. Not only does He send out His messengers to those whom He can gather among the highways and hedges, but Himself also turns the hearts and moves the feet of those whom His messengers discover; and they who by themselves would fear, and refuse, find themselves strangely stirred to accept, and are lifted by fresh hope, and are gifted with new courage, and are carried wondering along the paths that they despaired of travelling into the halls of light which they had not hoped ever to see.

God Himself in us fulfils His own demands on us. God Himself moves over to our side to satisfy the urgency of His own Will and Word. In Him we do what we do, and we are not afraid, though the Son of God has come "not to destroy that Law, but to fulfil it"—yea, even though from us is required a righteousness exceeding that of Scribe and Pharisee. We are not afraid, for "the Spirit giveth life"—here is the blessed gospel of eternal glory. If "the ministry of the letter had a glory, how shall not the ministry of the Spirit exceed in glory?" The Spirit giveth life, but still "the letter kills." God has come over to our side, but He has not ceased to stand over there against us. By His power we can afford to face His Presence, but it is the same God as ever Whom we face. There He still stands as of old, and His demands are the same, and His modes of communication are the same; and still it is true as ever that without holiness no man shall see the Lord; and His purity is as white and unstained as ever, and His righteousness burns with as hot a flame,—the same Eternal God with Whom is no variableness, neither shadow of turning, and His being is holiness, and in holiness we hold communion. No jot or tittle of that ancient requirement, then, is removed or diminished. The revelation of the letter of the moral Law holds good for us as much as for the Jew; and it is because that letter inevitably holds good, that God has Himself entered within us, and striven for its fulfilment.

And therefore I would ask you to-day: Have we that

letter that kills? Do we know its sharp death? Have we at all the sense of an imperious moral Law, obligatory and absolute, which rigorously searches our souls, and sifts our motives, and tests our every act, and penetrates within the tissue of our will, and pierces like a sword between joint and marrow? Do we live as if we always had in face of us a demand, a requirement, as urgent, as insistent, as incessant as that voice of a trumpet exceeding loud, which broke out of the terrors of Sinai? Are earth and sky full of a great voice to us, that thunders out its " Thou shalt," and its " Thou shalt not "? " Thou shalt love thy God ; " " Thou shalt love thy neighbour : " they are strong and unbending words. Do we with our whole being desire holiness and love God ? Do we know this pressure of a law as of a burden, of a necessity under which we faint or quail? Have we any rules that hold us like iron, and cut us, when we strain against them, like cords? Is there any perception within us of a law which it is the misery of death to fail or to disobey, and which, nevertheless, we have obstinately and constantly broken? For the Law ought still to kill, and we ought to have moral standards, which of ourselves we should despair to satisfy. Have we such moral standards? We ought now to be feeling a moral light thrown upon our souls such as it would devour us with shame to have to meet alone. Have we tasted that light? Do we bring these rules of God to bear on our practical lives day by day, and hour by hour? Do we know the alarms and the anxieties of a severe conscience? Have we wrestled with that law of duty—which is the Name of God,—

wrestled through long nights until the morning broke,
—wrestled until even though we won, yet in the morning we halted on our thighs?　Are we at war with any
one sin—at war even at the cost of plucking out an
eye or cutting off a foot?　Have we resisted unto
blood?　Some such sin every single soul here to-day
holds within him.　Have we taken, then, the pains to
discover it?

Oh, that we might taste of this austere judgment,
that we might know ourselves, that we might be
serious with ourselves, and drag up our life into the
light of God's law,—that we might face the full
rigour of this letter; for only those whom the letter
slays will be quickened by the Spirit of God.　Lying
dead there—dead before the eternal Eyes, in penitence
and in confession, killed by the letter—we may then
receive this new gift, this boon of price, and be quickened by the Spirit of Him Who raised Jesus our Master
from the dead.

Newness of Life

THE BEAUTY OF HOLINESS—THE ENERGY OF UNSELFISHNESS — THE FRUIT OF THE SPIRIT—THANKSGIVING.

THE BEAUTY OF HOLINESS.

"**Wherefore remember, that ye being in time past Gentiles in the flesh, that at that time ye were without Christ, being aliens from the commonwealth of Israel, and strangers from the covenants of promise, having no hope, and without God in the world.**—EPH. ii. 11, 12.

OF one thing, at least, those early Gentile Churches of St. Paul had entire assurance—the abject misery of sinning. The Apostle is never weary of recalling, nor they of remembering, the bitterness of their old experience. It is on them like a nightmare—odious, horrible, and profound; and the Apostle himself had drawn so near to it in the person of his converts, that he seems to identify himself with their story, and to have tasted of their misery.

For it had not been his own experience—that was bitter enough, but it was of a wholly different cast and type. His, as we know, had been the agony of a soul that had, from its earliest hours, known the sweet call of righteousness, and the blamelessness of a clean service of God; and his sorrow had been the sorrow of a divided self, the sorrow of losing hold of that which he had loved, the sorrow of the man who loves purity, and loves it only to discover his powerlessness to attain it. This had been his discipline, to be perfected by the chastisement that scourges moral pride into the humility of the Saint; and his conversion had been a conversion from seeking holiness in one way to seeking it in another.

But, since then, he had thrown himself into the thick of these crowded and burdened commercial cities from Antioch to Rome. He had learned their life; and how vividly he lets us feel what he has found in that old Pagan world which we know only through the partial and remote evidence of its books and its arts! These—what are they, but as shells strewn on the shore of a great deep, the rare evidence of a life that has gone from them, fragments torn out of some world strange and immense, which lies hidden far within the silence of untrodden and impenetrable seas? Their books, their art, so lovely and so high—these tell us what a few rare souls had dreamed, what one single tiny people had the wonderful power to produce and to admire during the brief flight of a few generations.

But here, in St. Paul's Epistles, we go down below the fairy ring of artist and philosopher and poet; we travel far from the pleasant spaces and still retreats of beautiful Athenian culture. We are taken in the track of one who is pushing his way along in the press and stress of those unheard and disorganised populations that throng the streets of Syrian and Asiatic cities. He is himself part and parcel of this de-nationalised mass, and he gives us touch and trace of their living temper. He rubs shoulders with the crowd. He pushes and jostles with porters and grooms.

He mixes in with the common habits of vulgar and unhistorical people. He knows the ways of shop-keepers, and of tradesmen, and of artisans, and of slaves. He works by their side in the shop; he sleeps in their lodgings. He comes across aldermen, and justices of the peace, and town clerks. He is acquainted with police and gaolers. He can make us see and feel what a Christian, what one of the same habit and belief as ourselves, would see and feel as he moved up and down that world which lay covered by the wings of imperial Rome.

And as he contrasts this foreign life that has become to him now so familiar, with the old home life in the midst of Jewish traditions, what he seems to feel most strange and most terrible is the absolute dominance of sin. The Jew writhed under the radiance of a holiness which he passionately pursued, but over the Gentile, as St. Paul knew him, the cloud of sin had so thickly settled that he seemed to have lost the sense of righteousness. There seemed to be no struggle left in him, no impulse to resist. Sin held him; sin mastered him; sin possessed him; sin lorded over him. It had attacked him in every function. It had impregnated his reason, so that its very capacity to distinguish good and evil had been obscured and confounded. It had poisoned his heart, so that no stirrings of conscience any longer might protest or warn. It had unnerved his will, so that he cowered, dragged captive by evil principalities and powers, led dumb and slavish behind dumb and slavish idols. It had befouled and besmirched and besotted his appetites, until they had ceased to spring out of the purities of nature, and had become twisted and thwarted into monstrous deformities and unnatural horrors.

Of course it was wholly true that there were Gentiles who were a law unto themselves, who knew the anxieties of moral scruple both accusing and excusing; but these little exceptions hardly hindered for a moment the sweep of the Apostle's vision. The massive reality, in its most typical and most normal form, was a condition in which all sense of moral distinction was hopelessly blurred, and all touches of remorse or regret or penitence or confession had vanished and been lost; and there is a positive welcome of sin, a welcome of it, as the Apostle says, even when others do it, and when, therefore, there is no glamour of temptation thrown over it. Their whole tone was polluted; and their minds so unhinged, and their desires so poisoned, and their tendencies so distorted, that they not only do the foul and extravagant wickedness, but, without a scruple and without a sigh, they take pleasure also in them that do it.

Sin, as the Apostle keeps asserting, sin tyrannised. And then, secondly, he notices the misery of this captivity. They were most miserable, these people, and miserable not through agony of conscience, not with the misery of their own cry, the cry of an imprisoned and defeated manhood. No sense of a lost ideal tortured them,—of a darkened future, of an insulted God, of an outraged Spirit, of a defiled temple. These were the familiar consequences of sin to the

Jew who had sinned against the Most High. None of these affected them. They sinned on—so it seemed to the Apostle—without disturbance and without fear, and no sword of God seemed to be uplifted to smite, no conscience pricked or stung. And yet they were miserable—miserable as with the misery of a dull and melancholy disease, miserable with the dejection of disorder, miserable as those are miserable whom some unknown secret in the past has laid under a heritage of woe so that they cannot prosper, but are marked down by sorrow, and are haunted by a dark fate, and fade and mope and fail and weaken, heavy and oppressed as sodden woods that drop their dead leaves slowly, one by one, through the thick darkness of autumn evenings, until all the air is gross with the odours of decay. So sad, so darkened, were the days of these miserable multitudes; and three or four points the Apostle specially notes that give character to the misery.

It was, first, the misery of blindness. They saw no road through the world. They followed no tracks. No goal lay before them. They groped their way along day after day, and made no advance. They were living, as the Apostle said, "in the night." They were "children of the night." They belonged to it. They prayed for no dawn. Why should it end? They had been born into it, they and their fathers before them, and into its gloom they would again beget their children. It was their heritage, their nature, to be in the cloud of that night. "Children of the night," the night was their home.

They were blind, and the blindness was miserable; and, being in the night, they had the misery, too, of hopelessness. They felt nothing in them that was prophetic. They heard no promise of a better day. They never even listened for news of some deliverance. They were there without hope in the world. Hopeless and also loveless; for they found nothing under the cover of the present dismay that told them of a Father ever caring, and tending, and watching, Who Himself behind the night never slumbered nor slept. No hand was felt upon their heads in blessing; no touches of love covered their troubled hearts; no Divine friendliness breathed over them its peace. They were without God in the world; aliens from the covenant. Through life they went untended, unregarded; and into death they passed "unhouseled, unaneled." No blessing went before them. No voice in the morning and in the evening spake to them of the kindness of the God, who was a shield, and a refuge, and a home.

Blind, hopeless, loveless, and also fruitless. "What fruit had ye then in those things whereof ye are now ashamed, for the end of these things was death?" What they did came to nothing. They walked after their passions, and found themselves somehow in the pit. They did what they liked, and lo, they found themselves beguiled. They obtained nothing. They achieved nothing. They profited nothing. Their pleasant things were as vanity. If their affections fastened on anything, it perished. If they gave their heart to any joy, it all closed in mockery, and tears, and shame. Everything that they cared for came to an end, an end dishonourable and degrading as the end of the beasts that perish. All died together. The same end came to all. Joyless, heartless, empty, cruel; " their vines were the vines of Sodom and the grapes of Gomorrah." They were miserable.

And again, being miserable, they hated themselves; and hating themselves, they hated also each other. Discontent is always irritable, and nothing so surely or so sharply irritates it as the discontent of others. The look of a depressed face is full of annoyance and provocation, and the companionship of the depressed is always charged with smouldering passions that break out in hate and malice. They lived therefore at enmity one with another, and their social life was ill-humoured, fretful, and angry—the joyless life of disappointed men. Joyless and also powerless. These men whom St. Paul watched had no will of their own, no purpose towards which they pressed, no choice, no deliberation. They seemed to surrender themselves to impulses; and so surrendered, they were carried hither and thither, as dried leaves in a storm, tossed to and fro, he tells them, by every wind that blew, swayed by every new temptation, dragged at the heel of the bad whims of principalities and powers, the captives of lusts, the slaves of tempestuous and gusty passion, given over in the despair of self-abandonment to the prince of the power of the air, carried about by dumb idols, even as they were led. So they lived and walked, these Gentiles, in " the vanity of their minds, in the lust of concupiscence, fulfilling only the desires of the flesh, with their understanding darkened, alienated from the life of God, in the blindness of their heart, in filthy conversation, past feeling, given over to lasciviousness." So they walked, according to the challenge of the Apostle, and his converts confirmed him by the memory of their experience : "For such were some of you, but ye are washed, but ye are sanctified, but ye are justified."

Sin, as the Apostle knew it, is a depressed and a depressing thing, blind and hopeless, and joyless, and fruitless, and powerless. Why is it, then, that so much of our popular language is at variance with this estimate of the Apostle, and with this experience of his converts? We have rid ourselves, it is true, of that familiar assumption in old plots and plays, in which vice wins all the honours, and virtue appears only as imposture. We do not believe now in the scapegrace, popular and kindly, who carries all the applause by some crowning act of reckless generosity. We have learnt too well the shallowness and the insincerity of this thin ideal of old dramas and novels. We know how fatiguing Charles Surface is when we come across him in private life. We look at life more deeply and more earnestly, and a great deal of our higher fiction has spent all its strength in exhibiting the unwithering beauty of goodness. And the very poets, who have adopted the passions as their theme, have thrown all their force with almost Biblical seriousness into denunciation of the weariness and the cruelty of unnatural hungers. And yet still, there is so much abroad in our talk that reveals how little we have yet got hold of St. Paul's meaning or measure—so much that lets out our secret belief that sin is somehow more interesting than holiness,—that it has in it a fuller fund of life, a more varied and vigorous abundance, which attracts the imagination and wins the affections more than the poorer, and thinner, and staler round of virtuous and beautiful living. And I would not now refer to the habitual falsity of minds which still struggle to sustain the wicked pretence that drunkenness is amusing, or that a fast life is brilliant and merry. Any one who has got past the ignorance of a mere boy has been astonished to find, I suppose, how ugly and how disgusting is the life of the coarser passions which he has been taught so diligently to fancy comic or fascinating. People tell us of the insincerities of preachers in our pulpits who disregard the practical experience to which men of the world are at least faithful. But in the matter of drink, which is faithful, and which is sincere—the man of the world or the preacher,—the man of the world who persists in continuing in story and joke the absurd illusion that drunkenness is amusing, or the preacher who asserts that it is one of the most sickening, and hideous, and stupid things that our eyes can shrink from, or our souls abhor? It would be at least something if those of us who know the ugliness would set ourselves to break up a superstition which is as degrading as it is false.

But I would chiefly think of a subtler falsity than this—the falsity of temper which considers that people who do wrong are more interesting and more attractive than those that do right. We are often prone to think so, even when we do not in the least propose to follow their example, and become more popular by freer sinning. And yet, whenever we think so, we may turn round and ask ourselves, " How is it, then, that I am so far from the estimate and the experience of St. Paul ? " For to him sin is certainly not a matter that would win popular attention. He finds it a very dull, depressed affair, a poor and miserable blunder; and this quite apart, you will remember, from all question about the tortures of conscience or the judgment to come; quite apart from all that makes it not only inexpedient, but wrong. In itself, he says, as plain sin, undisturbed by after thoughts or after reckonings, it is a thing which does not attract but irritates; does not fascinate but disgusts; does not charm but horrifies.

And if we will but be honest and sincere, does not our own experience tally wholly with his ? Day by day we are more and more struck, surely, with the dulness and deadness of sin, with the fascination of goodness.

In the first place, what we find is that sin is so stagnant. When we sin we never grow. We decline, or at the best we stop where we were, and our character seems to have no longer any movement in it. It is stuck fast in the deep mire. We know that we are not developing, and so knowing, we grow weary with ourselves. But goodness is full of change, of suddenness, of surprise. The more you see and know of a man whose life is bad, the less you find to discover in him, and the less you like him. He is at his best the first time you come across him; but if you meet him again after an interval, obviously he has not got on. He has worsened ; his youthfulness has gone a little out of him ; and his badness is more prominent, and he looks a duller and a less agreeable man, and you begin to fear what the advancing years will do with him, as his early animal spirits sicken, and the gaiety which gave him at first a certain charm, dies out, as die it must, and nothing is preparing to take its place but the morose ill-humour of a disappointed life. And how different with the other, who has committed himself to the ways of goodness ! He is always growing, advancing ; he is full of new discoveries for us. As we watch him, as we know him, as we live with him, we learn more and more of the gifts that spring up in him. His character has ever new lights and shades. His very dulness grows luminous as we keep company with him, for, even where we least look for it, we find in him some kindliness, some sympathy. Again and again we see the most delightful boyish characters darkening down into depressing men under the influence of a bad life ; and, at the same time, quite common and unattractive characters gradually winning a power and a grace and an interest which startle us, as the growing years carry forward in their souls the work of spiritual holiness. Their companionship wears so much better ; they so much more repay knowing ; and, as the lighter loves and joys of youth die down, and as the stress of stronger and sterner cares begin to press upon us more heavily, and there start out on the edge of the cup of life "scull-things in order grim," ah, how the good man serves

us then! What help, what cheer he brings us! And
how hopeless and how inadequate is the man of loose
principle and of carnal life! He can do nothing for
us; he shrinks away; he shrivels up. Amidst sorrows,
and by beds of sickness and of death, he is profoundly
useless; he is utterly out of place. Goodness alone
lasts and gains by time, and is brighter and more
delightful and more interesting the longer we abide
in its company. The bad, as Plato nobly said, may
go off at the start of life's race with more promise
and hope than the good; but then they come in so
badly, they are so sadly outrun before the close.

And all this is so obviously true that we cannot but
stop to ask how it is sometimes that the opposite
belief can hold its ground at all; and perhaps one
or two reasons may be briefly touched. Very often, of
course, some person thoroughly attracts and charms us,
who is full of faults, and sins; and, often, there is
something in the faults which seems to belong to the
attraction. But, then, does that mean that we are
charmed by his faults? Surely what we always mean,
when we look a little closer, is that the faults issue out
of a character which, by its very failings, gives evidence
of the excellence of which it is capable. And this
we do by virtue of that deep law which Plato first
asserted, that the great capacities for crime are the
same as the capacities for great virtues; that the
materials of the two characters are identical; that all
magnificent criminals are made of the same stuff as
the most holy Saints. It is only high natures that
are capable of great sins, and great sinners have

therefore, this wonderful attraction to us, that we feel ourselves in the presence of the qualities that are at once most precious and most perilous. And this lends pathetic interest to sinners of a high type. In them we are conscious of the pathos which belongs to a splendid wreck, a pathos which it delights us to follow in a book or on the stage—the pathos of a tragic failure. But here, again, in real life, let us say in our own family circle, vice is apt to lose all this dramatic interest, and show itself in practical plainness as exceedingly painful and unpleasant.

Or again, grant that the primal forces that go to make good and evil are alike, and naturally the story of the process by which such characters determine the anxious and alternating issue is full of incident and attraction. We can watch such a drama with a living interest which we cannot give, it is true, to the tale of an habitual and humdrum goodness; and, moreover, this drama contains the material for such strange surprises,—for the same powers which are now displaying themselves in such a doubtful and distorted fashion, since they are themselves susceptible of the other alternative, and are as capable of holiness as of sin, may therefore throw themselves out in strange reversals and startling reforms,—conversions we call them; and it is these surprises that so enchant us. But it is the surprise of the change which makes the former sin interesting. The sin is exciting, because it comes to an end. These publicans and sinners to whom we are drawn in the Gospels are publicans and sinners no longer when we are drawn to them; and the beautiful fame of the Magdalene derives its beauty not from the seven devils, but from their expulsion; and all this confuses in us our power to say what it is that makes sinners so interesting, for, in following out their fortunes, we are so often tracking the very qualities which will at last throw off their false nature, and show themselves to be virtues.

And there is yet another point to remember—that it is unfair, in estimating our level of interest, to contrast splendid sin with the dulness of commonplace virtues. Nay; with commonplace goodness compare, if you will, commonplace sinning, and I have little doubt which you will choose; for if commonplace goodness is dull, commonplace sin is ridiculous and repulsive. But brilliant and exceptional sin can only be measured by comparison with exceptional and brilliant holiness. If we are charmed, in spite of ourselves, by the bewitchment of this or that enticing wickedness, let us remember to compare that character as it stands with what it would be, if all those beautiful gifts and exquisite capacities had been given over to the handling of the Spirit and to the transfiguration of Grace. If that fine nature, now so strangely disordered and thwarted, had allowed itself to win its perfect stature, it would have lived in the heart and in the memory of grateful generations with the sweetness of a St. Francis, or the glory of a St. John.

St. Francis and St. John! How the very names recall us back from our dreams of the fascination of evil to our assurance of the enthronement of good! Dear names, at the very sound of which our heartstrings thrill as with sweet music! Dear blessed Saints of the Most High, to whom we turn always with such undying interest and with such untroubled love; who hold our eyes fastened and our souls bound by all that is most fragrant, most persuasive, and most fair! Ah! we have forgotten, as we look up at these soldier-saints, we have forgotten the dim and shadowy histories of sin, which now and again so sadly touch us. We know only "how lovely are the messengers and how beautiful the feet of those who bring us good tidings, the sweet news of peace."

And let us press it home to ourselves: how is it we suffer people to imagine that goodness is not interesting, nor holiness attractive? How is it that we have not moving about us those saints who would so lightly shatter those fond imaginations? Is it that our type of excellence is so meagre and petty and repressed? Goodness, if it be true goodness, must mean an exhibition of heightened energy. Sin is always sickness, and sickness cannot but be depressing, uncomfortable, impotent, and poor; and whenever it is not this it is only because some goodness is at work within it stronger than the sin. It is not, it is true, sin because it is unpleasant—God forbid!—but it cannot but be unpleasant if it be sin. Goodness is always soundness, and we must not endure to be contented with any standard of goodness which does not give proof of its health; and this it does only when it is cheerful, vigorous, elastic, free, hearty, hopeful, springing, gracious, delightful, beautiful, and strong.

True, that we are under the discipline of a recovery

from wrong. It may be impossible for our moral efforts
to feel or look other than painful or hard. But this
must only be true through the penitential stage. Still,
the tendency of our life must be towards health, and
therefore towards a more energetic and exhilarating
existence. Holiness, in the sense of St. Paul, is always
a freeing of the soul from impotence, the setting loose
of spiritual energies, of vitalised activities. Is that
what it means to us? Have we found it—that is the
question—have we found it to be a way of increase, of
enrichment, of growth, of vigour, of exultation? If
not, then we have not yet understood it as St. Paul
understood it—not yet understood it according to the
power of the new Spirit Whose working worked in him
so mightily; and if so, we need not be surprised if it
has not in us the same power of charming others which
it had in him.

THE ENERGY OF UNSELFISHNESS.

"Let all bitterness, and wrath, and anger, and clamour, and evil speaking, be put away from you, with all malice: and be ye kind one to another, tender-hearted, forgiving one another, even as God for Christ's sake hath forgiven you."—EPH. iv. 31, 32.

WHAT a strange change it had been for St. Paul's converts, as they passed out of the old into the new—the old so rough, so angry, so violent and venomous, so loud and so brutal—that life woven out of such bitter threads and melancholy hues—"debates, envyings, wraths, strifes, backbitings, whisperings, swellings, tumults"—that life of the flesh, "hatred, variance, emulations, wrath, strife, envyings, murders." That is what has been banished and crucified by those who had found themselves, amid the heat and tumult of that loud quarrelling, suddenly mastered by the vision of Him Who won them by His meekness and His gentleness—the Man of human kindness, the Priest of compassion, the King of Peace, the Lamb of God "Who, when He was reviled, reviled not again." This was the message that had reached and held and possessed them, the message of the preacher who besought them "by the meekness and the gentleness of Jesus." Who can measure the sweetness with which such words would fall upon a world hot with angry feuds and bitter revenges—"the meekness and the gentleness of Jesus?" As cool water to fevered lips, as wet grasses amid arid sands, as the sound of soft rains falling on barren fields, so the kind words stole in as a blessing and a boon upon hearts worn and heavy laden, upon those who crept out of the tumult to hide their wounds and weariness within the comfortable fold of that Good Shepherd Who led them into such rich pastures, and by such quiet waters.

And yet we all of us are subject to a suspicion, a criticism that may be silent in church, but which will yet rejoin us at the church door, and before we reach home will have had its say—a suspicion very old and very familiar, but, for all that, one which it may be well worth while to consider again. It suggests that possibly something, after all, may have been lost in the passage from the old state to the new. Very rough, very uncomfortable that old condition of things may have been; but was there not a vigour in its vivacities and a robustness in its violence that we miss in the kindly new? Is there no loss of manliness in passing to this new temper? and is it fitted for the actual world? For rough work needs rough methods; and our work here is rough, and cannot be pushed through without a good deal of energetic emphasis. And, again, there is a hearty and muscular naturalness in that boisterous scramble of man against man which we like in books and in plays, even though in real life it is rather oppressive and unpleasant. And this humility, this gentleness,—they disturb us

as something unnatural, artificial, laboured. Are they
quite real? Are they not apt to be very full of provoking mannerisms and insincerities? So every one,
I suppose, has said to himself again and again; and
with this suspicion at work within him he easily
accepts the more formal and public criticism which is
familiar in our ears, pronouncing that these Christian
graces, beautiful as ideals, charming us as spiritual
excellencies with their choice flavour of exquisite
piety, do neverthless represent an unearthly and un-
social type of virtue; that we lose as citizens what
we gain as saints; that by walking in the Spirit we
cease to be equally effective forces for economic purposes; that the business of a State would prefer in its
factors the old character at the cost of its quarrelsomeness, to the new at the price of its passivity.

Now, this suspicion and this criticism are familiar
and strong because they have a great deal of plausible
evidence behind them. There is much in our religious
habit and temper which would tend to confirm what
they suggest; and certainly our religious thought has
failed to give us any logic which would displace the
suspicion or expose the criticism; and through this we
are easily led into three great disasters.

First, there have been bred up among us a public
mind and tone which have so deeply accepted these
assumptions of which I speak that it has been found
easy for science to persuade us that wherever the
root-instincts of men are allowed free play they are
necessarily selfish; that from this primal and cal-
culable motive all the vigorous and positive qualities of

industrious production issue; that the degree of vigour so displayed will be in proportion to the amount of selfishness in action; and that, however much this natural impulse may and ought, for ethical reasons, to be checked and limited, yet such checks and limitations will curtail the normal action of commercial industry according to the degree with which they repress the free play of self-interest. That is a well-known position which we have allowed to pass, and in which we have detected no flaw. Perhaps its careful abstention from the moral region succeeded in putting us off our guard.

But then there comes the second disaster, that when the parallel position is taken in that region of ethics we seem to have lost our power of protest. Who does not know how naturally, how obviously the argument meets us? Who can resist its patent evidence, its plain and plausible logic? Our eyes are taught to range over the turmoil of a swarming and warring life of nature; and everywhere we learn how all things push forward to self-preservation, towards fuller living —how upwards towards this richer existence everything presses, and thrusts, and aspires, and that in that vital vigour lies the secret of all type and growth and transformation. And when we pass from the lower level, without any perceptible break, into the long strife of human progress, surely it is the same law, that we cannot but detect, directing and ruling the advance—the law of preservation, the methods of self-interest. Men struggle to endure and to grow; and the principles which best serve that endurance and

that growth they call Ethics; and, if so, then, since
the forward movement derives its force from self-
interest, ethics have inevitably their justification in
a wise and skilful selfishness. This we hear, and
religious and serious people, though they do not like
the sound of it, practically abstain from denying it,
and at last doubt whether it can be denied.

And there follows a third disaster. They are driven
to suppose that heroes and saints, who use very
different language, have in reality, unknown to themselves, this very motive at work which they most
violently repudiate. The saints imagine that they
are losing their all for Christ, while in reality that
is impossible; no such vigorous action as they put
forth could be produced by anything short of self-
interest; they, too, must be, in the end, in pursuit
of their own happiness. They do not think so, because
they ask for no happiness on earth, but that is only
because they have caught sight of the richer blessing
to be theirs hereafter. It may be true that all ideal
ethical systems repudiate this self-interest, but they
can only mean to repudiate the lower and lesser in
view of the higher and the better; for all ethics must
be bound to assume that man, in acting, seeks his own
perfection and happiness, and is, therefore, in a high
sense selfish.

Now that, you will say, is philosophy, and none of
us here may be philosophers; we cannot therefore
travel into the discussion by which such a problem will
be finally solved. But one thing we all can do, and
it is very urgent that we should do it; and that is, that

we should try to make out what it is we mean by selfishness, and what by unselfishness; for it is this word "selfish" that, after all, is the difficulty.

Are we at all right or rational, let us ask ourselves, when we assume that all action which vigorously advances the fortunes of the agent is for that reason to be called selfish? We have made these theories, we have let ourselves assume this; but why? Why should we make such an assumption? What evidence is there that vigorous pursuit of personal good proceeds out of selfish motives? Surely St. Paul, the preacher of meekness and gentleness in Jesus—surely he is rather a hard instance to bring under our assumption. No one, I suppose, pretends to doubt the genuineness of the Apostle's self-surrender. Unselfishness, as we know, was with him a passion—the master-passion of his life. But is there, then, in him none of that vigorous vitality which works ever upward and onward? Is there, then, no assertion of the fullest personal energies? Were his cravings unliberated? were his forces unused? was his character typically one of repression, of curtailment, of subdual? Was his Self—that which lies at the heart of Self—that which is Paul—was that ineffectual and passive? Was there in him no burning curiosity, no pertinacious aspiration, no splendid ambition, no striving after perfection? Had he, then, no purpose, no chosen prize set before him for which he hungered, and in the hope of which he endured? How his own words leap to our memories to answer our questions! Always he ranks himself with those who stand as types of strenuous life. He was as an athlete bent on a prize; he was as a runner with his eyes set on a far goal, who, with muscles strung and fibres tried and trained, summons out all that is in him, puts out the gathered forces and bends all his issuing and springing energies upon the hope set before him, towards which he ever presses—presses towards the high mark of his calling, not regarding those things which are behind, "counting all as dung" that he may win Christ, that he may wear the crown laid up in Heaven for him who runs a good course here on earth. This eager, passionate, burning pursuit of the perfect manhood, of that excellency which is made open to him by Christ Jesus—this, looked at from without, is surely identical in appearance with that impetuous craving which pushes all men forward towards their highest interest, and which we have assumed to be selfish, wherever it appears. If, as spectators, we were asked to describe that vigorous assertion of a vital self which is the root-impulse of all natural life, what words should we choose, what words should we prefer to those which speak of "forgetting the things which are behind," of "reaching forward to the things which are before" us, of pressing towards a high mark—towards some secret perfection? And yet all this in the Apostle proceeds out of the very heart and heat of his *unselfishness.*

Evidently we have been too vague in our generalisations; we have classed with selfishness what may very well belong to unselfishness. How have we made the blunder? By assuming that all movement towards the better life has self-gratification for its final motive; that all vigorous assertion of personal life proceeds out of selfish greed. Christianity challenges that assumption all along the line; it denies that the pursuit of the higher life need be, in any sense or degree, necessarily selfish. It may be selfish; but it is just as possible that it is wholly the other. And, more than that, in all its most energetic and effectual types it is sure to be unselfish, for selfishness is never, as a practical fact, able to kindle into life the more fervent and daring forms of self-assertion. The selfish man seeks his own good very sluggishly; it is the unselfish Apostle who pursues it with the zeal of a Martyr and the passion of a Saint.

Let us attempt to make this clearer. What exactly does it mean, to say that one's own good is selfishly sought? It is selfishly sought only when it is desired for the sake of the gratification it brings, for the sake of the honour and pleasure and gain it may reflect upon its possessor—that is, when it is not sought for its own sake, but only for the sake of what it brings after it. Success is selfish, when it is craved not simply as successful action, successful attainment, but because of the feeling of pleasure, which is not success itself, but is that which accompanies success—that feeling that we know so well, of gratified importance, which glows and warms within us as we watch over our own success, as we reflect on it, as we recall it, as we retail it to others, as we pride ourselves upon it, as we crow over it. We may often hunger for success in order to feed this feeling, and then success, no doubt, is selfishly desired; but must it be for this for which we desire success? Have we always this after-feeling in view? Is there no such thing as desire for success simply as success, without a single momentary thought of its reflex action which will follow upon ourselves? Why, the whole history of man, the whole sum of experience is loud with the answer. Take any workman, take any artist—what is the secret of their inspiration? What is the key to all their highest work? Surely nothing but the work, the love of the work, the love of good work as such, the desire to see the effort of labour issue in the finest result. That is their end; that is their motive. Good work satisfies them as good work. It wields a continual fascination that draws them forward at all costs and at all risks to themselves—through austere discipline, through long hours of weary disappointment, through hunger, and cold, and nakedness; and they ask no question why; they would be wounded and stung as with a whip if you hinted that it was because of some after-pleasure to themselves. They are happy, no doubt, in their work—this they cannot help being; but to think much of that happiness is, they know well, to ruin their work, to sap their zeal, to undermine their skill.

And it cannot be that they are deceived, that they have beguiled themselves into a condition of self-deceit in which they cannot distinguish what is selfish from what is unselfish; for vanity, selfishness, self-love, the sucking of the grapes of gratification— these are all passions still in them which they know quite well by experience, since every day they feel them mingling with all their inspirations. But that which they so feel and know they know also to be utterly distinct from the inspiration which makes them artists, and they know also that the further such motives as those extend the less genuine is their artistic work, and that if those motives altogether prevailed they would cease altogether to be artists. No man has ever produced the highest artistic work for the sake of the pleasure it brought him; such an aim inevitably drains the life-blood out of his heart.

And in business and in all employments the same impulse tells. He is the best workman who works for the sake of the work;—the merchant, for instance, who has forgotten what he can gain by being richer, but who has the keen zest of a sportsman for following up a scheme, and the fascination of an artist in the handling of his funds. In everything work would be at a standstill if there were not in vigorous action something more than the motive of gain—the delight in the result being produced in the best possible way and on the best possible lines; and wherever, throughout a country, this artistic motive in work languishes, there the productions deteriorate and the trade must fall.

That is the verdict of a world-wide experience, and Christianity seizes on it in its primary truth. Did you lightly suppose that there was no motive but self-interest that roused men to the pursuit of their own good? Christianity frankly, yet firmly, says exactly the opposite. When has selfishness ever spurred men to heroic audacities or lifted them into splendid action? How often has selfishness won any ardent and eager disciple? A great mass of very commonplace and ordinary activity can be accounted for by it. When we have no strong motive working upon us, then it is that we fall back on self-interest; when we are indifferent, undetermined, idle, then it is that we set to work to calculate which course will please us most, or by which path we shall win most gain. Selfishness is the dull drudge that sweeps the house, that does a good deal of plain and obscure and plodding work for us; it has sufficient force to carry us along through commonplace matters where we need no special effort. But whenever we are really roused, or alive, or strenuous, or enkindled, then we throw the calculations of selfishness to the winds, we laugh at the question of our gains, and forget to ask what will come of it all—we feel only the keen craving, that at any cost, our cause should win; we throw ourselves into it, we give ourselves to it just as runners who yield themselves up to the passion of a race, and run as if there were nothing in all the wide world to be done but just to run and to win, without ever dreaming of asking the why or the wherefore.

Nor is it only the joy of the artist that is the seed of vigorous action; there is another motive, even more powerful, more universal, and more fruitful — the motive of love. A man will do far more for the love of others than he ever will do for himself; he will display a finer vigour, a nobler patience, a steadier courage, a fuller energy on behalf of mother, and home, and wife, and children, by the side of which the efforts he will make on behalf of his own interests will look but poor and thin. Nor is it only others that he helps by doing this; it is himself who is vitalised by the new hope; it is his own being that is enlarged and enriched—his own interest and good and perfection that he attains through this devotion to the other. He is made a better man by loving. We have all seen it. A young man without responsibilities, left to himself, with nothing but his own interest to serve, how idle, how profitless he is, how meagre, how sluggish! His powers lie all dulled through and through with indifference; he hangs about life listless, unquickened, bored, fatigued. Even though all his future prospects depend on his industry he cannot be got to put himself under pressure; no calls, no reproaches, no warnings, will induce him to put his energies out in action; he is selfish, and because he is selfish he is idle. But how he has surprised us when the touch of love has laid his hand upon him. For, lo! he is a new being, his manhood stirs, his will quickens, his senses are all alert. Night and day he schemes how he may win prosperity; he toils with perseverance, he endures with a valiant cheerfulness of which no one believed him capable; for the sake of that other he will slave as he never slaved for himself; and all through the long days that follow, as he thinks of her in the house with the children, he will set himself to the grim task of life with an ardour that would have died out and been beaten years before, if it had been but his own poor, pitiful self for which he was spending his strength.

And do you retort that such love is, after all, but a

piece of indirect selfishness, that it is for his own joy that he works when he works on behalf of his wife and his home? Then, if so, why is indirect selfishness so much more vigorous than selfishness when it is direct? A motive, if it is the animating motive, must surely be most effective when it is most visible, most distinctly present. How is it that selfishness is so far more powerful when it conceals itself in the love for another and pretends to be unselfish? Surely we are playing with words when we reduce life to such a game of pretence, to a mad charade in which motives only move by dressing themselves up in disguises of their opposites. Love, as a fact, moves by charming a man into self-forgetfulness, by absorbing him in devotion to another; and through this, and this alone, it obtains its motive power. If a man could persuade himself that in loving another he were really loving himself, why, his very love would perish at the discovery.

Self rouses itself, then, into vigorous activity only when it serves an aim other than its own gratification, and, above all, when it loves; and if love could be raised to the highest power, then the vigour and vitality of that personal self would be at the very height of their fulness; to be given the power of loving would be to be given the power of living. And therefore our creed woke a dying world into new life by bringing to bear upon its stiffening limbs and chilled heart the invocation of a God Whom it could love. It was dying, that old world, and dying of selfishness; but it woke under the presence of a Lord and Master to Whose graciousness and to Whose beauty it could offer the honour of an unselfish service and the glory of an unending self-surrender. It was aroused to do for Him what it had not the spirit to do for itself. The weariness of self-service, the daily melancholy of self-love—they fled away like a cloud before the hope of an eternal devotion to the Name of Jesus Christ; and, instead of the tired, dispirited Pharisee, sick to death of self-service under the law of works, you have the great Apostle of the Gentiles, illumined, radiant, transformed, endowed with power upon power, energy upon energy, gift upon gift, " in labours more abundant, in strifes above measure, in prisons more frequent, in death oft." Active, strong, inexhaustible, he now finds store upon store of treasure within his soul, once so dry and so bare. " Who is weak, and I am not weak? Who is offended, and I burn not?"

Selfishness is bound to flag. It brings upon us poverty of blood, loss of brain and heart, a sunken, tired, and burdened life. Is it not at the root of so much in us that is dispirited and disheartened, and fretful, and listless? You meet men and women who drag themselves along, who are dim with sheer indifference, who find no light and no joy in all that this world can bring them. My brethren, when this humour creeps over us, let us closely examine and see whether it be not some self-seeking that has brought it upon us. For life will look sordid and meagre and meaningless, after a time, to a man of selfishness. He feels it profoundly stale and unprofitable, he realises so little, and there is so little that is worth the cost of realising. The aim is mean, and it is impossible to be energetic for long in serving its claims; but love, love for others—this enriches, this enkindles, this evokes in us the desire to be better men; it sustains us in the effort of self-improvement. "Love fulfils the law." Everything becomes possible to those who love. The commands of the Lord are no longer grievous, for the soul that loves is gifted by that love with fresh energies; it discovers in itself unsuspected possibilities, and is supplied with ever-flowing currents of new vigour. The impossible becomes possible to all who look to another and love—the hard loses its hardness, and the grievous ceases from grieving. Love enlightens, and warms, and cheers, and renews, and again and again the self within us presses forward under its sweet breath toward the hope set before us.

Unselfishness is the only salt that preserves our soundness; unselfishness is the only fire that purifies, and refines, and betters, and makes perfect. We shall be enabled to do so much if only we love. We live by loving, and the more we love the more we live; and therefore, when life feels dull and the spirits are low, turn and love God, love your neighbour, and you will be healed of your wound. Love Christ, the dear Master, look at His Face, listen to His words, and love will waken, and you will do all things through Christ Who strengtheneth you.

SERMON XIX.

THE FRUIT OF THE SPIRIT.

"The works of the flesh are manifest, which are these: hatred, variance, emulations, wrath, strife, seditions, heresies, envyings, murders. But the fruit of the Spirit is love, joy, peace, kindness, goodness, temperance."—GAL. v. 19–22.

As St. Paul looks back at that bad life out of which he had snatched the souls of his Gentile converts, it is its bitter brutality that he most vividly remembers and recalls. It was a jarring life, in which there was no tenderness, no courtesy, no kindliness, no peace. It was full of collisions, of friction, of wounds, of sores. It was a loud and violent life, in which men fought, and hit, and swore.

As he runs over his list of old habits once familiar to them, his picture is as of some back alley in our crowded towns, in which all is shrill, rough, boisterous, with women screaming, with children shrieking, a nest of noises, a swarm of jangling cries.

This is what they have left behind, this which had made life one long quarrel, pitiless and brutal. They had left it, mastered and enthralled by the sweet vision of Him, the Man of peace, and meekness, and lowliness, Who had been led, quiet and patient, as a lamb to the slaughter, and, as a sheep before its shearers, had never opened His mouth; Who, when He was reviled, reviled not again; and when He was threatened, threatened not; One Who never gave back railing for railing, but only blessing.

"You all remember it," he keeps crying to them,— "those old days, so merciless, so angry, so cruel; how you grated on one another, how you rasped one another, how you bit and devoured one another like snarling dogs." It had been one long quarrel, a life of wrath, "full of bitterness, clamour, evil-speaking:" they knew it all but too well what he meant, for "the works of the flesh" are manifest, "which are these—hatred, variance, emulation, wrath, strife, seditions, heresies, envyings, murders."

"Works of the flesh," St. Paul calls them. His keen eye sweeps over the whole range of this loud quarrelling; to him, it is no senseless storm that rages on without rhyme or reason. Nay! it has, all of it, a story and a cause: it is the witness, on the surface of life, to inner disorder. These rough oaths, these venomous taunts, this bitter tumult— these are the natural issues of the root from which they spring. They are "works"—normal, and antici- pated, and legitimate deeds, which appear in obedience to a law of rational production. They are "fruits "— results that grow out of certain creative activities, as accurately and inevitably as grapes from vines and figs from fig-trees.

And what is this root which so legitimately flowers into these uncomfortable blossoms? "The flesh," St. Paul names it; the flesh is as much the seat and home of this passionate violence as it is of those other passions and appetites with which we commonly identify it. This petulance, this savagery, this hail of malice, this outcry of rage, this havoc of revenge, this recklessness of cruelty,—all this finds its principle, its origin, its motive-cause in that same activity of the flesh. Set the law of the flesh in action, and you must have quarrels. Out of the flesh they fly, these oaths and screams, just as sparks out of a smitten flint. It would be a miracle if men who lived after the methods of the flesh failed to envy and to hate one another.

Now, can we see why this is so — why hatred, variance, emulation, strife are manifestly works of that same body of sin which has for its fruits those other vices, uncleanness and drunkenness, which we more easily connect with the motions of the flesh? To answer this, I will ask you to enter a little more deeply than usual into the solid and broad meaning which St. Paul attaches to this, his favourite term for the root-principle of human sin—"the flesh." Obviously, it is much more to him than the mere matter of animal passions. It expresses to him the typical nature, the essential form, of all that can be set in antithesis to spirit. "The flesh lusteth against the spirit." It includes the pride and the falsity of intellect. It embraces the disorder and stubbornness of the will. What, then, is this "flesh"? How can we describe and define it?

Let us try, in answer to this question, to conceive the mode in which sin arises. Man, when he begins to think and scheme, discovers himself looking out upon a world in which he has already been instinctively and spontaneously playing a busy part. He finds himself, before he takes the trouble to notice it, or to consider, already netted into a web of living relationships, within which he displays those gifts and energies with which he is endowed, and which he brings into use under the natural pressure of circumstance, under the dictation of emergencies. His family, his people, have ways and habits of securing their living, of asserting their business; and into these he falls, and acts under their unfelt direction. There he is—there he lives; he eats and drinks; he wakes, and works, and sleeps; he grows, marries, dies: and all this happens, so to speak, without asking him; his customs fix it; his nature prompts; his inner spontaneity issues in its normal actions. If this were all, his human life would all spring up as naturally, as obviously, as a forest grows and spreads with unfailing pertinacity; or as a river runs wherever the earth yields it readiest way.

Nor need this instinctive life of man stand still; it might be capable of advance, of growth. Its spontaneous reactions, in face of irritant circumstances, might move forward towards surer and more subtle adaptations. It might advance under the discipline of accumulated experiences, even as plants and birds perfect themselves, and yet, still, it would be without any interruption of that even and unsinning naturalness which belongs to the powers that are God-sown, God-planted, God-watered within him.

Now, see his temptation—how it arrives.

He looks up and sees the great arching heaven, and

the spreading surface of the teeming earth, and the dreamy woods, and the silent pastures, and the breathless hills, and the moving waters, and the hurrying swarms of fish, and bird, and beast; and in amid it all he sees men, his fellows, scattered in buried hamlets, or thick-pressed in gathering towns; his brothers, his mates, his sisters, his children, his own house and home—narrow, yet so dear. How near, how familiar it all is! And he can lie there, on the hillslope, and watch it—watch the thin smoke curling amid the trees; and the mother, within the shadowed house, with the babes; and the sister, with her bucket at the well: and can hear the far cry of his father to the ploughing oxen, at the turn of each furrow in the field. There it lies before him—human life as he knows it; he can watch, and note, and name it all.

And, then, in amongst it, there is one whom he also can observe and consider with peculiar fascination. He can see him amid the throng: he can follow him in and out; he can stand by him, and hear him speak; he can attend on him wherever he moves, can enter into all his occupations, can listen to his laughter, and sadden with his tears. There he goes— look at him! a man like other men, yet whom he knows as he knows no other. Who is it? Who is this man on whom his eyes fasten? It is himself. He watches himself, he notes himself. He can observe, and consider, and examine himself, as much as he can all the crowd of strange men who move about him. His own impulses, his thoughts, his feelings, his fears, his hopes, his loves, his hates, his secrets, his fancies, his wants, his passions; he looks upon them all, and learns to know and to name them. He learns; yes, for they are as wonderful, as surprising to him, as if they belonged to another man. Though they are his own, he cannot make them; nor tell whence they come, or whither it is they point; or why they crowd in one moment, and die away and leave him dry and empty at another. He has them, and feels them; but yet he stands outside them, as a spectator.

And he may rightly take this observant interest in himself. He has just as much right to wonder and pore over his own intricate and fascinating fabric, as he has to admire and love the symmetries of a flower or the mechanism of a bird. All are miracles of Divine skill, and he as much as any. He may love himself, just as he loves his neighbour. But then, this self-study, this self-admiration, this self-regard,—how crowded it is with moral risks!

First, he so quickly loses proportion between himself and others. This interest in observing himself is singularly fascinating.

His true interest, indeed, in himself, lies in his being a work of God's Hand; and all other men are equally God's work, and, by this scale, therefore, ought to be equally interesting. But are they so? Can he keep true to this scale? Can he resist the inclination to feel that his delight in himself is an altogether different affair from his delight in others? The moment he has distinctly singled his own personality out from the herd of men, how vividly it poses, how emphatically it asserts itself! Other men sink back into an obscure background; the one absorbing thought is, "There am I. That, then, is what I am." The divine proportion is already lost; and then, with this rise of self-interest, a wholly novel question inevitably opens. All other things which interest us as works of God, are accepted as they stand; their place, their fitness for their place, their allotted function—these all belong to the admiration they excite: we never feel inclined, unless in the case of the most violent exceptions, to question or to dispute their nature and situation, any more than we should ask why this flower was of one hue and kind, and that one of another. The fact is enough: a rose is a rose; it would be ridiculous to ask why it was not a lily. But as soon as we clearly conceive ourselves with sufficient interest, we compare ourselves with others, we distinguish all the differences, and the question starts instinctively to our lips, "Why am I exactly where I am in the world? Why should I be fixed to that spot, in that rank, with that particular work, office, opportunity? Oh, if only I had that other person's gifts! if I had only been given his chance! And why not? Why should I be cut down to this limited area, these narrow and rigid duties? Why should I be debarred from eating of the tree of knowledge of good and evil?" A serious question this, if once it has been started; it holds in it the germ of revolt, the seed of all sin. And the seed will grow and sprout; for self-study develops rapidly—once started it is ever on the increase; more and more absorbing becomes the interest. And with each increase of interest, comes an increasing sense of importance; self begins to fill the scenes up to the edge of the horizon; other men sink back and back into a less and less distinguishable crowd. And as self-importance swells, so inward greeds grow, and wake, and stir, and prick.

And now, too, there is yet another danger to be marked. Man observes himself, we say, just as he observes other men; he learns what he is, just as he learns what they are—by watching and noting his own spontaneous acts and words. But there is a difference. With himself, he not only notes his acts, but he notes down, too, how he feels as he acts; he takes notice of his own pleasures and pains, as they accompany and follow his activities. But, with others, he is very little apt to do this. Their actions he sees and hears, and, therefore, notes; but their feelings, with which they act, these are out of sight and hearing. He can calculate them from his own, but that is another matter. In themselves, they do not very obviously appear. He can watch what all men do, without necessarily observing what they feel as they do it. But, with himself, it is far otherwise. That glow of pleasure that kindles all over him as he does this or that; that sharp throb of pain that struck into him like a wild-beast's claw,—these are to him the most noticeable facts. They stamp themselves very forcibly upon his memory; they hold fast his imagination. The actions which brought them become interesting to him, not for what they did, not for their true aim, not for themselves, but because of the feelings they quickened in him, because of the taste they left behind in his mouth. The act that brought the pain had been done for some instinctive purpose ; but, now, he will set himself to avoid it, not necessarily because the purpose was wrong, but simply because the effort was painful. For good or for evil, that is, he has abandoned his old standard of action ; he is trying life by a wholly new and different scale.

And pleasure! Ah, here is a new possibility altogether, a new motive, a new end. Certain actions, done, at first, according to rules of natural instinct, in obedience to the upward growth of healthy life, have been discovered to possess this perquisite of pleasure ; and now, the fact of this pleasure is fastened upon with singular interest. Why not have it repeated? Why not recall it? Why not extend it? Why not make sure of having it always at hand? How can it be secured, and how enlarged? Ah, how easy, how natural are such questions! Yet, by them all the courses of human life are upset, reversed, entangled, disjointed. Before they were ever asked, man would act because the outward occasion demanded it ; he did what circumstances suggested or required. Now, he will do the acts which bring him pleasure, not because they are morally required, but because they bring him pleasure. He will not wait for the fixed occasion ; he will invent and create the occasions in order that he may repeat his sensitive experiences.

Note the completeness of the fatal change. He is no longer, by wise or advancing skill, adapting himself with richer fulness to the outward demands and methods of existence ; he is, rather, refashioning and reshaping outward existence according to the demands of his own inward, and arbitrary, and wilful desires. He has made his pleasures the canon, and is employed in forcing life unduly to repeat, and unnaturally to reproduce, those occasions which best suit his self-interested rule. Once let him begin to assort his days and his aims by such a measure, and the worst is but a matter of time. Step by step, the organisation of nature is disturbed and disarranged. There can be no correspondence preserved, according to this rule, between without and within, between his inner appetite and his outer environment : and without such correspondence there is no health ; the whole man sickens into decay, he corrupts, he falls to pieces; only his strong greeds remain, battening on the disorder that they produce.

We have it at last, St. Paul's typical sinner, his child of wrath. Is this not just what he intends by the mind of flesh? " The flesh " represents all that a man is, when he is his own aim, his own end. His power of self-observation, that Divine gift, in possessing which he is the image of his God, has about its use this terrible risk—that he may cease to observe himself as he is in God, as he is in God's ordered world, set to fulfil an office in combination with his fellows, the member of a vast body, pledged to a peculiar or disciplined service: he may forget all this, and only observe himself, himself just as he stands, with his own private appetites, likes, gifts, feelings.

And, so observing, he may separate himself off from all else, hold himself up before his own eyes, and fasten upon himself all his interest, and his thought, and his imagination, and his pains; and may spend his every effort in scheming how best to serve, in richness of pleasurable experience, this self, who has become his idol, and before which he bows himself to minister as to a god. This he may do; and that which a man has then in front of him as his aim or end—whether it be low and gross, or whether it be delicate and intellectual—that is "the flesh." And the life that he lives in obeying its behest, that is "the life after the flesh;" that is "minding the things of the flesh;" that is "walking after the flesh." And the end of that walk is Death.

And now, dear people, we can easily understand why life in the flesh is a life of jars and quarrels, as much as a life of passion and lust. The man who walks after the flesh is absorbed in self-interests. He has dropped his eyes from their outward gaze at that busy and social world which encompasses him. That world is calling to him with all its voices, but he hears them no longer; it is appealing to him to act, to hope, to aspire, to give, but he pays no heed to its invocations. He has forgotten its wants and its movements; he is dead to its touch and to its cry. His brothers look to him for help, but they have ceased to interest him; his sisters turn to him for tenderness, but he is chill as a blind stone. All this crowded scene of our human story has lost for him its charm, its colour, its warmth, its neighbourly friendliness. He has turned his eyes within; he has bent all his gaze in upon himself: it is his own feelings that alone have an interest to him, his own needs that alone entice. He is busy night and day in considering himself: he is picturing his own success; he is planning his own pleasures; he is brooding over his own possibilities; he is filled with his own imaginations. Round and round himself he is always weaving the everthickening web of his own fancies, and his own schemes; and fainter and more distant grows the sound of outward things.

This is the "man after the flesh:" and consider what he must become in his intercourse with men. He walks abroad, brimming with self-interests; and he is bent on things fulfilling themselves according to his fostered expectations; and, so walking, he must of necessity jar at once against a world that he has not taken the pains to study, or understand, or revere. He clashes against it, as against a wall; he is pushed and squeezed by the crowd of bustling men, who have no time to give to his broodings, and are at variance with his designs, and upset his favourite plans, and traverse his ambitions. He is disappointed, as he must be; for this earth demands of us a social temper, and he is hopelessly and helplessly individual; it asks us to give, and he is proposing only to take. He is wholly out of tune with a world that exists only through self-sacrifice, and is bonded together by the grace of humility; he must be repudiated by it, he must be disregarded, he is bound to be checked at every turn, and he gets cross, angry, bitter. And, then, the evil aggravates itself: for human life does, it must be confessed, turn a very cold shoulder to men of this temper; it becomes very merciless and rough in encountering downright selfishness. For it has duties of its own that press, it has work that hurries, and it cannot afford to deal gently with men who are out of harmony with its aims. It ignores them, it laughs at them, it brushes them aside, it bowls them over. And the man so treated grows more and more wounded, hurt, indignant; perhaps he rails and storms at the world that he finds so hard, at the men whom he thinks so unsympathetic and so cruel. Perhaps he retreats into sulky silence, and shuts himself up in clouds of vaporous passion, and fumes out his angry soul in secret broodings, and hugs himself the closer, and vents his grudge against life in spite, and scorn, and uncomfortable depression.

Ah! do we not know him, as he goes about the house like a shadow, like a threat? He is always out of gear, always difficult, always disappointed, always petulant. As he comes into the room he conveys a sense of chill, of weight, of effort : his temper is so unsteady, so incalculable; he asks so much of us, he brings us so little; no sunlight, no light, no fresh-ness go forth from his presence. He is never easy, never willing; he has to be pleased, to be attended to, to be enticed into good humour. His sisters, his mother, have all to slave for his contentment; his wife wins peace only by burying all her own confidences, her own fancies, her own longings in the depths of a sacri-ficial silence, and in suffering all to give way to his wilful temper and his tyrannous wants.

My brethren, is that so very rare a character amongst us? True, our surface life looks more sweet and more kindly than that ancient Pagan world of St. Paul.

The peace of Christ has breathed over it a touch of tender courtesies. But beneath—when we pierce the outward shell of gentle behaviour—beneath still stirs and seethes that old mob of quarrelsome passions —those " works of the flesh—envy, malice, wrath, anger, evil-speaking." The fairest Christian home, when once we win our way to its intimacy, is too often such a melancholy revelation ; it turns out, so sadly often, to be a very nest of fretful and angry annoyances. The life, that courtesy covers, is all jars and jangles, like sweet bells out of tune ; it is made sad with grievances, and rubs, and spites, and heats, and moods ; and all is bitter, angry, sour, ill-humoured, cross-grained.

Such a state of things, once ingrown, is hard to correct or cure. We see and feel the miserable discomfort of it all, and we long to escape out of the whole heritage of wrong which the fretful years have hanged upon us. But we cannot tell where to begin. We make resolutions ; but each day, somehow, renews the old uncomfortable jars. How shall we recover, or escape ? Not by struggling to correct it piece-meal ; but by going below the surface : by accepting St. Paul's analysis of its origin. This quarrelsomeness, this friction—this, the surface evil, has its roots much deeper. We often talk as if bad temper, or moodiness, or depression were accidental infirmities, which we catch, like a cold ; or which come and go with the weather : we treat them as the peculiar phenomena that accompany an east wind ; or as unlucky habits which we regret, but accept, and must allow for.

St. Paul pronounces them to be no accident at all; he does not regard them as incidental and unfortunate defects of constitution. Nay! they belong to the basal body of evil; they are the normal and natural products of an inward condition; they have a scientific origin, and an evitable cause; they are works of that same law of the flesh out of which all other sin sucks its strength.

Yes; they spring out of the flesh, and, to correct them, you must penetrate down to that flesh, and there cut off their supplies. Self-preoccupation, self-broodings, self-interest, self-love—these are the reasons why you go jarring against your fellows. Turn your eyes off yourself: forget your own pet schemes, the hopes you are always nursing to yourself, the self-importance that you hug. Forget them, throw them aside, push through them. Look up, and out! There is a larger world outside you, brimming over with far other hopes than yours, illumined by a vaster sun, travelling to some far historic goal. Look up, and out upon it! It has its interests, its purposes, its ends, which it is your glad privilege to learn, and, by learning, to obey and follow. Give it your heart, and it will show you its own. Take its road, and it will, then, take yours.

Look up, and out! There are men, your brothers, and women, your sisters; they have needs that you can aid. Listen for their confidences; keep your heart wide open to their calls, and your hands alert for their service. Learn to give, and not to take; to drown your own hungry wants in the happiness of lending yourself to fulfil the interests of those nearest or dearest. Break through your own moody musings, and run out abroad, from these closed and darkened chambers of self-consideration, — out into the wide and teeming earth, where, not your scheme, but God's great hope, is working out its world-wide triumph.

Look up and out, from this narrow, cabined self of yours, and you will jar no longer, you will fret no more, you will provoke no more, you will quarrel no more ; but you will, to your own glad surprise, find the secret of "the meekness and the gentleness of Jesus;" and "the peace of God, which passeth all understanding," will drop down like dew upon your happy-hearted days; and the fruits of the spirit will all bud and blossom from out of your life—"love, joy, peace, gentleness, meekness, goodness, long-suffering, faith, temperance."

THANKSGIVING.

"And it came to pass, that, as they went, they were cleansed. And one of them, when he saw that he was healed, turned back, and with a loud voice glorified God, and fell down on his face at His feet, giving Him thanks; and he was a Samaritan."—LUKE xvii. 14-16.

INGRATITUDE!—there is a fault we all of us easily recognise and heartily condemn. Other sins there may be which we are half inclined to pass over, we know too nearly their fascination; but ingratitude for kindness, for love, this never fails to shock us; we refuse it all apologies; we pronounce against it an unfaltering sentence. And this story, therefore, commends itself at once to all of us; our only difficulty lies in believing it possible that nine out of the ten men should have been so graceless. For we may notice that we are always startled by a display of ingratitude. It seems to us a thing incredible, a thing which our ordinary humanity repudiates, and repudiates with indignation; and yet it is very odd that we should, in the face of experience, retain our surprise; for surely there is no feeling so rare, so uncertain, so brief as gratitude. In politics it is a proverb that you can never count on a people's gratitude; and every one who has had any philanthropic experience has learned quickly enough the rapidity with which it will vanish under the slightest pressure. And yet kind people, engaged in good works, still creep up to us and pour into our ears their sad tale of disappointment, as if it would be to us a new revelation that those whom they had striven to benefit could actually be unthankful. They talk of it as if they were especially aggrieved ; as if all good work for our fellow-creatures must cease if this were to be its reward ; as if they were staggered by some abnormal display of human wickedness. And yet, why should there be all this melancholy astonishment at the unthankfulness of others ? Surely we need none of us go very far away to discover how easy constant gifts become assumed rights, nor how difficult and how rare it is to sustain a heart with thankfulness for mercies which we take for granted just because they renew themselves every morning. Have we ever, then, taken the trouble to examine the quantity and the quality of our own habitual thankfulness to God, for " our creation, preservation, and all the blessings of this life " ? Never, but from under the discipline, it would seem, of some bed of sickness or death, do we ever attempt to sound the abyss of our ingratitude for all that has been done, unnoticed, for our habitual use and comfort, by a God " in Whom we live, and move, and have our being."

And even in a matter where it would seem almost incredible, even in a matter such as that brought before us by the miracle of the ten lepers, even in the matter of recovered health, there is strange room for ingratitude. Who can believe it, even of himself, who

can believe the quickness with which the memory of
sickness, and of all its prayerful longings, can be wiped
out of our hearts when once the tide of returning
strength has swept up again into our veins? That
pitiful weakness in which we lay moaning and crying,
that dark anxiety which sucked us down under the
waters of fear, that miserable discomfort in which we
wearily tossed from side to side, crying, in the night,
" Would God it were morning!" and, in the morning,
" Would God it were night!"—all this, which seemed
to lie upon us heavy and impenetrable as some black
cloud, all this flies as a thin dream from off us, and is
gone in a moment. And even pain, pain that may
almost have maddened us, pain such as digs its claws
into spine or brain, pain such as rends and sears the
roots of our nerves—pain is wholly forgotten the
moment it is withdrawn. Nothing, indeed, can vanish
out of remembrance so rapidly as pain. It slips off as
a cloak; it disappears like a stone thrown into some
gulf. We shake ourselves, we pull ourselves together,
we look about, we rise, and walk, and talk, and read ;
we are back in the eager movement of affairs ; we can
hardly credit our own cheerfulness as our spirits return
with a rush, and we find ourselves released ; we laugh,
and hope, and scheme, and look forward just as if no
such suffering had ever been or could ever come again.
As health creeps over our limbs and renews our wasted
flesh, it is as if some sponge had been passed over the
sick days. And as health returns, confidence returns.
A sense of self-sufficiency is involved in the very
conditions of good health; for to be in health is

to find ourselves adapted to the purposes and conditions of life: we fit again into existence; we are once more in correspondence with all this living earth; we give and take freely, we use, we act, we move, we enjoy, and everything comes easy, and everywhere, therefore, there is food for satisfaction; we come and go lightly and successfully; motion and action have become so natural as to be again unnoticed efforts.

It is the *natural* that so beguiles us. Health is our natural condition, and there is a strange sway exercised over our imagination and our mind by all that is natural. The natural satisfies and calms us by its very regularity. Its response to our expectations seems to give it some rational validity. It is right, for it is customary; and its evenness and sequence smother all need of inquiry. It was this which bewildered us in sickness—that it had wrenched us out of our known and habitual environment; it had thrown us into uncertainty; we could not tell what the next minute might bring; we had lost standard, and measure, and cue; we had no custom on which to rely. And then, in our distress and in our impotence, we learned how our very life hung on the breath of the Most High, in Whose Hands it lay to kill or to make alive; then we knew it, in that awful hour of withdrawal. And as the inner man failed within us, so nature, too, then seemed to fall away from us without. How they crumble up—those deep foundations, those high ramparts, those strong walls of our life. To the sick man, the earth which seems, during health, so sturdy and so old, fades and faints into a shadow of vapour, a dream, succourless and insecure; our fingers seem to clutch nothing; our feet totter and our brain swims; we go down to the skirts of the grave. But, with health, the normal solidity returns to the fabric of life; the all-familiar walls range themselves around us; the all-familiar ways stretch themselves out in front of our feet; we can be sure of to-morrow, and can count and can calculate, not because the usual is the less wonderful, but simply because it is the usual. We move in it unalarmed, unsurprised, and God seems again to fade away. Though we may dimly acknowledge that all this solid earth must finally be dependent on His sustaining Will, yet this acknowledgment only takes place in the remote recesses of our abstract reason. It does not tell with any vivid emphasis on our will, on our imaginative desires. We are as those nine lepers who were healed "as they went"—imperceptibly, unaccountably. Lo! it has happened; it is all done. Somehow the evil thing has dropped away from off them; they find themselves as other men. No doubt it has all to do with that good word of Him Who bade them go and show themselves to the priests; and when they were standing before Him, when they waited for His Voice, how their whole souls hung on Him, their sole Helper! their eyes, their hearts, their passions, all bent themselves on Him. Would He do it? would He deliver them? Oh that He would speak! But now it is so different; it has happened "as they went;" they feel it in them, they know not whence, and that strange

Voice of His melts a little into the dim background. There are other matters which occupy their attention: the wonder of the feeling of new life; the sense of delicious surprise; the desire to see whether it is all true, and to experiment, and to test it. And, then, their friends are about them, their friends from whom they have been parted for so many bitter years; they are being welcomed back into the brotherhood of men, into the warmth and glow of companionship. "Oh, come with us," many voices are crying; "we are so glad to have you once more among us! Come, we may hold your hands now, and you may sit with us, and eat with us, as in the old days long ago. Let it all begin again—the sweet ways of human kindliness, in the sunlight, amid the works of men, your brothers, in the tender and pleasant places of home." So the happy earth closes up round them with friendly looks, with warm embraces. Very thankful they may be feeling to that great Healer Whose command had been so blessedly fulfilled. It is not said in the story that they did not feel grateful: grateful, no doubt, with that vague, general gratitude to God the good Father, with which we, too, pass out of the shadows of sickness into the recovered life, under the sun, among our fellows. They may well have felt genial, grateful: only they did nothing with their gratitude, only it laid no burden of duty upon them; it was not in them as a mastering compulsion which would suffer nothing to arrest its passionate will to get back to the Feet of Him before Whom it had once stood and cried, "Jesu, Master, for Thou alone canst,—do Thou have mercy on me."

"When He smote them they sought Him." It all happens, we know, over and over again with us. We are, most of us, eager to find God when we are sick, when the normal round of life deserts us, and by its desertion frightens and bewilders us; but so very few of us can retain any hold on God in health, in work, in the daily life of the natural and the constant.

And by this we bring our faith under some dangerous taunts. Who does not know them? The taunt of the young and the strong: "I feel the blood running free, and my heart leaps, and my brain is alive with hope; what have you to tell me, you Christians, with your message for the sick and for the dying? I have in me powers, capacities, gifts; and before me lies an earth God given and God blessed; and you bring me the religion of the maimed, and the halt, and the blind, a religion of the outcast and the disgraced, a religion of hospitals and gaols; what is all this to me?" And the taunt of the worker: "I have will, patience, endurance, vigour; by this I can win myself bread, can build myself a house, can make my way. This is my task; here and now lies my work, cut out for me,—a work which must be done before the night falls: and you bid me wait till failure has broken in, until disease has spoilt me, until death threatens me, and then, at last, you promise you will step in with your news of some far-off land of harps and white robes and golden cities. Here, on earth, where I stand, my task is set me; necessity is laid upon me. Woe is me if I cannot hold my own, and feed my wife and child. What have you to bring me here and now of force, of courage, and of help?" And there is the taunt of the scientific mind: "Why," it asks, "do you go creeping about in the dim corners of life, crying after God in all that is unusual, exceptional, unnatural, accidental? You are of those, surely, who peep and mutter, wandering to seek God in dark haunts, and terror, and disease, and infirmity, and corruption. You find God only in strange deliverances, in miracles, interventions, in magical healings, and abrupt breaches of custom. But order is more Divine than disorder, and uniformity than arbitrary miracles. We seek God in nature, not in the unnatural; in the sure, and not in the accidental; in health, and not in the failure of disease; in the high energies of splendid life, and not in the pains of death."

Those taunts are very real, and living, and pressing: how shall we face them?

First, we will be perfectly clear that for no taunts from the young, the successful, and the strong, and for no demands either from the workers or the wise, can we for one moment forget or forego the memory of Him Who was sent to heal the broken-hearted, and to comfort the weary and the heavy-laden; and Who laid His blessing upon the poor, and the hungry, and the unhappy; and Who came as the Good Physician, not to the whole, but to the sick; and Who would leave ninety and nine sheep in the wilderness to seek for but one that was lost in the cloudy and dark hills, and Who poured out more joy over one penitent sinner than over ninety and nine just men who needed no repentance; —of Him who found praises among babes and sucklings only, and sat at meat with publicans and harlots. No, nor can we cease to walk as exiles and pilgrims here on earth, looking for a heavenly "city, not made with hands, eternal in the heavens." We dare not lose one scrap of that high promise, we will hold it fast ; for God knows how little we can afford to forego this consolation, in a world so tangled with wrong, and so weary with sickness, and so smitten with sorrow, and so soiled with sin.

No, we will withdraw nothing. But have we no living message for the strong and the young, for the happy and the wise ? In what form, let us ask, ought religion to offer itself to these ? What should be their natural religious attitude towards God ? Surely we know it would be in the form of thanksgiving; they should stand before God holding in their hands the sacrifice of praise, the thank-offering of their entire being. Thanksgiving ! That is the note of faith by which it employs and sanctifies not only the poverty and the penitence of sinners, but also the gladness of work and the glory of wisdom.

And has our Christian faith, then, no voice of thanksgiving ? Nay, our faith is thanksgiving. Thanksgiving is its root, and its heart, and its life ; our faith begins and ends in thanksgiving, and all its scheme of redemption, its message of the Cross and the Passion, the Agony and the Bloody Sweat, is but ministerial to that supreme end of all prayer and of all reconciliation ; the office of thanksgiving, the act of adoration. Our faith begins and continues and ends with thanksgiving, for it has its roots deep laid in that song of thanksgiving which rose on the first dawn, "when the morning stars sang together, and all the saints of God shouted for joy;" and it looks forward for its flower of triumphant honour to the day when, before the great throne set on the crystal sea, there will go up, as the sound of many waters, the voice of the thousand times ten thousands of Angels and Archangels, singing for ever and ever the new song of the Lamb. And, between the gladness of the first creation and the gladness of the final redemption, there still abides with us, unbroken by our own sin, unwearied by our disasters, the secret of restored thanksgiving—that unceasing Eucharist which no despair can blacken or defeat, since the darkest day that the world can ever see, when, with foes about, and treachery within, in bitter loneliness of spirit, under the dreadful shadow of death, Jesus, our Master, held fast the red chord of praise and gladness, and in the very night of the Betrayal, though His Soul grew troubled and His Heart shuddered, "took bread, and lifted up His Eyes to Heaven, and gave thanks."

Thanksgiving!—this is our worship, and in the form of thanksgiving our religion embraces everything that life on earth can bring before it.

Here is the religion of youth, the religion of all the hope that is in us. Let it, in the Name of Christ, give thanks. Union with Christ empowers it to make a thank-offering of itself; to bring into its worship all its force, its hope, its youth, and its vigour. Hope unoffered will soon disappoint; youth unpresented will soon weary and grow stale; and happiness is only kept clean and untainted by the salt of thanksgiving. Youth and hope—they need religion just as much as weakness needs consolation, and as sin needs grace; they need it to forestall their own defeat, that they may be caught in their beauty and in their strength before they pass and perish, and so be offered as a living thank-offering; that they may be laid up as treasures, eternal in the Heaven, where "rust can never bite, nor moth corrupt, nor any thieves creep in to steal." How much might have been spared of that withering sadness, which embitters so many as their pulses slacken and their hearts grow cold, if only, while yet their grace was in them, they had laid it all, a happy offering, on the altar of their praise; or if they had brought to God, not the penitent remains of a wrecked and stained life, but souls still white with the radiancy of hope, and bodies still glad with the glory of living.

Thanksgiving! It is the religion for wealth, and for work, and for the present hour. It redeems wealth by ridding it of that terrible complacency which so stiffens and chokes the spiritual channels that, at last, it becomes easier for a camel to get through a needle's eye than for a rich man to find his way into the Kingdom of Heaven. And it redeems work by purging it of pride and of selfishness, and by rescuing it from dulness and harshness. For work, strong and successful work, has its own perils. Who does not know the hard Pharisaic temper of self-satisfaction, the contempt for the weak and thriftless which can come with the thought, "I have done pretty well; I have got ahead; I have stepped steadily up; by prudence, by skill, by patience, by pains, I am what I am. Thank God, I am not like those thriftless poor, like those who never make an honest penny, nor stick to a steady job, but beg, and drink, and go down to Hell: thank God, I am not like this publican"? Or, again, to many of us, how flat, and mean, and dull, and monotonous, and inglorious is the daily drudgery which we call our business! How our spirits shrivel under it; how our aspirations freeze.

We can save ourselves from all this, save ourselves from the harshness, and save ourselves from the withering, if we will come and give thanks. Give thanks, you that are strong, for your strength of hand and brain; give thanks, not to yourself, but to God; for what have you that you did not yourself receive? Give thanks, and so, by the glad surrender of your own glory to God, learn, through your very success, to widen your sympathies and your pity for the unsuccessful and weak. For how was it that you were given the gifts that they lack? As you learn the preciousness of your own privilege, pity them the more who have it not. And dulness and monotony!—what is too dull and too monotonous to lift up before God, and to offer in thanksgiving, even though it be the routine of the counting-house? We may lift it up, and lo, the light is on it, and glory embraces it, and there is joy among the Angels of God over the heart that gives thanks.

Thanksgiving fastens on the present hour. For thanksgiving you need not look, and wait, for some new heaven and some new earth in the groat hereafter. "Behold, now is the acceptable time;" now, as you are, in your work and in your play, you can lift up hallowed hands, you can sit in heavenly places, you can stand with Angel and Archangel, and give glory to God for His kindness and His mercy, which endure for ever.

And, again, it is by thanksgiving that religion closes with the natural and the normal, and the necessary. Thanksgiving asks for no change, it looks for no surprises, it takes the fact just as it stands, as law has fashioned it, and as custom has fixed it. That and no other offering is what it brings. And however fast the necessities of life may grip us, however irrevocable may be the decrees by which the strong years have laid their rough hands upon us, though we be snared with the cords which the sins of our fathers have bound about our limbs, yet by willing praise we bring our own freedom into play within the very web of destiny itself, we intermingle our voice with the commands of Nature, we insert our own free choice into the very heart of the decrees which fasten us, we identify our will with God's, we possess ourselves of the secret of our fate, and we become master of that which would master us. Are you fast bound in misery and iron? Give thanks to God and you are free. The very iron of necessity is transfigured by this strange alchemy of thanks into the gold of freedom and gladness. Nothing is impossible to the spirit of praise, nothing is so hard that Christ cannot uplift it for us before God, nothing so common that He will think it unworthy of His Glory.

Let us " in everything give thanks, whether we eat or drink, or whatsoever we do."   What holy whispers would pass to and fro between the Father and us if, at every heart's beat and at every pulse of breath, we could repeat our untiring hallelujah with them on high, who, again and again, at each pause, at each close of God's unceasing display are ever saying, again and yet again, " Hallelujah."   Here is the secret of Christian cheerfulness; and no power on earth can break it down when once we have discovered that there is absolutely nothing but sin itself which is not fitted to renew and to replenish the delight of giving thanks.   Why, then, are any Christian faces clouded and thick?   Why are there any Christian hearts that are sullen and tired?   Call upon your spirits to give thanks unto the Lord God.   That door of escape is ever open, that gateway into gladness can never be shut; and, day after day, you can " magnify the Lord, and worship His Name, ever world without end." " Lift up your hearts unto the Lord," for indeed " it is meet, right, and our bounden duty, that we should at all times, and in all places, give thanks" to God for His great glory.

The Christian Life here on Earth

THE ACTIVITY OF SERVICE—CHARACTER AND CIRCUMSTANCE.

SERMON XXI.

THE ACTIVITY OF SERVICE.

MATT. xxiv. 37–39.

THE text speaks of an experience which comes to all
of us in our turn, as life gradually builds us round.
At first, in our childhood, it is otherwise. This earth
seems, then, to have no fixed hardness; the spot on
which we stand melts off indefinitely into a dreamlike
distance, which is hazy and vague, and peopled with
we know not what possibilities, holding within its rays
strange fairy worlds which rumours may fill as they
will, and everything seems possible, and anything
might happen, and no relentless law of undeviating
existence has imprisoned our expectations and experience, and the world of our hopes mingles with the
world of our senses, and earth and Heaven are not
afraid of each other; their lines cross without a shock.
But, as we grow up, we know how solid and how hard
the whole thing becomes. The earth takes its stiff
limits and its exact rules; it is seen, and known, and
measured—a round ball, rolling in space, compact,

and massive, and blind, and entire,—a round, rolling ball, and we roll round with it. We are things in it, embedded in it; we belong to it; we have a fixed spot and lot on its surface. To it we are tied; we are bound to definite purposes which we never dream of disputing. So we travel with the moving earth; and our days are settled for us; occupations and holidays repeat themselves, year after year, with stolid regularity, against which gradually we give up protesting; we make up our minds to live out our own parts; and all the emotions that beat against this even tenour of uneventful days—dreams, impulses, alarms, hopes, aspirations—cease to be more than empty visions. The common day closes in upon us, settled and familiar; the common world is about us, with interests that ever increase, with work and play, with rule and habit; and the steady block of endless business fills in our allotted space of action, fills it in down to every cranny, thick and solid and unyielding. We are occupied with the routine of waking and sleeping, and the mere necessities of social contact. It takes us all our time to get through what must be done; pleasures, meetings, professions, these keep us busy; how can we stop the round world turning? We eat and drink, marry and are given in marriage, and it is to us as in the days of Noe, as if the world were going to last always. How firm it all is! how confident of its own solidity! Who can resist its supremacy? As we look out on the busy scene, at the ordinary movements of a large city, at the men of business as they hurry along with anxious countenances, or stop and talk with serious and important faces—at all the toiling carts slowly making for somewhere, and the ships that load and unload, and the turmoil and rush of the streets— everything conspires to build up an unbroken toil, the interruption of which it is impossible to fancy or credit. And it is idle work to consider what would best have to be done if a flood were to come and destroy it all. If we are to do anything here we must leave these things out of account. We must go on as the world asks of us, eating, drinking, marrying and giving in marriage. We must do it, for it is the natural and inevitable way of the flesh. We cannot remain young and romantic; we cannot pretend to be young when we are old. We are not permitted to indulge a pleasant, easy, and irresponsible imagination. Surely, we are intended to settle down, to confine ourselves to a very narrow hope, to a life of prose and work and business, very practical, very occupied, very pressing, very absorbing. To say we do all this, is simply to say we grow older and undertake responsibilities. Middle life is meant to be one of active and incessant occupation, and that cannot be wrong and unnatural.

But, if so, what are we to say? Has the faith of Christ no message to those who find themselves in the thick of the world's work? Is it only adapted for the aspirations of youth? Is it to fade out of our life like poetry, or are we to wait to pick it up in old age, when the busy world of service is at last done with and the strong years are dropping behind us, and we can at last afford to detach ourselves from the great business of marrying and giving in marriage, and eating and drinking? Must we wait till then before we can at last begin to heed the warnings of the Lord, Who cried as He left us, "Behold, I come quickly, watch and pray; let your lamps be ever lighted and your loins ever girt, and yourselves like unto men who wait for the Lord when He shall come back from the wedding."

Ah! those high words! how strangely they stir us, as now and again they speak to us out of some evening lesson! And how bitterly that familiar taunt smites us, "Do you, then, sitting in your churches, listening to those strong words in some brief pause of your swarming interests and pressing enterprises, do you call yourselves disciples of Christ Who spoke them? Why are you not praying with your eyes strained, on the watch for Him Who cometh? What have you to do with all this eating and drinking, and marrying and giving in marriage? Surely, if you had one jot of sincerity, you would be as those early Christians in Jerusalem who sold all they had, and were content to live waiting for the Lord, gazing into the dark, and crying, 'Even so: come, Lord Jesus!'" That taunt hits us hard; but what are we to do? How are we to alter this life of ours? It is practically impossible. And then some of us come to a conclusion which is sure to demoralise. We let the taunt stand, imagining it is true; and we suppose we cannot be all Christ meant us to be. We have no time to think it all out; we must make concessions to necessity; we must to some degree take the world as we find it; and so, without ever laying the ghost that has troubled us, we slide back into the regular round, and do it with an uncomfortable sense that it is not quite consistent with Christ to be so engaged with affairs, that all our life-work is something that we should not be doing if we were Saints. It is a concession which has never quite been reconciled to our Sunday conscience.

And yet this hesitating compromise only raises our old feeling in a new shape. For how is it possible to take a sensible part in life if it is done half-heartedly and condescendingly? The mass of civilisation is very difficult and very exciting, and you cannot enter it without throwing into it the full force of your zeal, and skill, and abilities, and eagerness. You cannot keep pace with the present life, if you would finger it timidly, and engage in it superficially, in a spirit of a compromise. You must believe in it, work in it, rely on it, bend all your powers upon it; and if Christ disallows that, if He cannot sanction the devotion o your full energies to the work of this life, faith in Him must require you to be but poor and ineffective citizens, who will be left far behind in the race—men afraid to give it their best.

Here, then, is the question: Did our Lord ignore these necessities of life? Is there anything in our circumstances to-day which forbids us entering the life to which He called us? The answer is in several divisions.

First, we can remember that He distinctly antici-pated that His disciples should find their general existence to be passed under a system of things totally unlike that associated with Him Himself. They were to live in the world just as He left it, undissolved, unchanged. In that they would be living, and, to the eyes of the flesh, all outward things would continue as they were from the beginning. And He would be gone and they would see Him no more, and the world would be one which would go on, as it were, without Him. They would not see Him in its ways and fields. Very far He would seem from their daily habits, and works, and interests. They would look for Him and not find Him. He would be "as a King gone into a country very far off." They would be wishing that their eyes might behold Him; they would be wondering whether they heard the rumour of His coming. "Nay, if any say unto you, Lo! here is Christ, or, lo! there, believe it not; or if one say, He is in the desert, go not forth." Many longings, many lookings, many hopes, many prayers would suffer delay, disappointment, despair. The Bridegroom would be withdrawn, and then "they would fast in those days." They will fast long; and there will be no trumpet call in the night, and no call of the Bride's approach, and no sudden shining of lights under the stars. The Bridegroom is taken from them, and the world will look as if it had wholly forgotten He was ever there or would come again. The world and the Bridegroom will seem completely divorced, utterly strange to one another. There will be no sign of Him anywhere; all will be stolid, silent, unmoved, dull, clouded, and blind, and no whisper from afar will shake the heavy folds of night. The Bridegroom will tarry long: and while He tarries, it is as if He would never come; and all those who belong to His Church, whether they be wise or whether they be foolish, will be alike—will appear the same to the outward eye; all will seem alike to slumber and sleep. All the ecstasy of devotion, all the glory of the marriage scene, will be inert and ineffectual as a dream. Those hidden hopes will fail to appear at all on the surface of life as we look over it; they will not colour it or transfigure it. The earth will hold on its way, undisturbed, as a system of things, by the existence of the risen Christ.

Secrets, indeed, there are; we know them: secrets that are felt and touched and taken beneath this cloud of night, beneath this veil of slumber; secrets from that far world where the Bridegroom waits for the dawn; secrets that carry with them His present peace and power, yea, His very Presence itself, in His transfigured Flesh and Blood. He has not left us comfortless; He comes to us. But He comes secretly, stealing silent and noiseless as a thief in the night, and no sound shivers the darkness, and no movement shakes the solid earth. Only the spiritual eye sees Him, and the spiritual ear catches the faithful whisper, "Take, eat, this is My Body; it is no ghost, it is I Myself, fear not." All this is most real, but it is hidden, and the great fixed order of things feels nothing of it, and still the natural fabric stands, the round earth turns and turns, and it is all as if nothing had been done. "Look at it," you will say; "surely, there is no Bridegroom coming, He is very far off; those who look for Him are much the same as those who have no such expectation."

So our Lord pictured the days in which we live; and we ought not to be surprised if what He foretold has come true, and we find ourselves living in a world out of which the light of His Presence seems to have faded—a world that, to the natural eye, seems utterly unmoved by Him; a world which, except to the eye of faith, is slumbering and asleep. As He foretold us, He is not seen to be visibly managing things; they appear to be managing themselves, just as they have been from the beginning. That sharp division which makes us feel, as youth dies down in us, the difference between Christ Whom we believe in and the world in which we actually live and eat and drink—that division He justifies and anticipates, and He prepares us to find it very long. He may say, "Behold, I come quickly:" for, to His prophetic eye, a thousand years is as one day; but the servants, what did He tell us of them? what would they be feeling? "How long, how wearily long it is before our Master cometh!" So He foresaw, as He pictured that wicked servant who would be tempted to say in his heart, "My Lord delayeth His coming; my Lord tarrieth long." That it is which will be the temptation, the temptation even of the master servants. So it is that He cries again and again, "Watch; take heed." Why that anxious, urgent, incessant warning, if not because the danger will be so great, lest they should grow weary, and doubt whether He ever would come, and fall into the snare of thinking that "My Lord delayeth His coming"? It will, as He well knew, seem to be so very remote and incredible, and the world will look so totally unprepared; and verily, as in the days of Noe, they will eat and drink, marry and give in marriage up to the last minute. It will be a thing impossible to credit, it will be felt when it comes like a trap, like a snare upon the face of the whole earth. Therefore, "watch;" you will need to force yourselves, to do violence lest your eyes should close and you should sleep. "What I say unto you I say unto all, watch."

What of this long withdrawal of the Bridegroom, how was it to be spent? In prayer and meditation only? Has His Church no part to play in the world of busy society, where they eat and drink and are marrying and giving in marriage? No: His going is no reason for His Church's inaction, but the source of her activity. "It is expedient for you that I go away." Expedient. Far from withdrawing His Church's interests from earth by His withdrawal, He endows it with more effective energies, larger capacities for action. She can do more on earth, and not less, now He is gone. He shows this by picture after picture. He tells us that we are to be a society carefully and shrewdly organised, and this organisation is to be formed with a view to work, production, fruit. We are to be organised with a view to our capacities, so to be arranged as to serve best for direct, present, practical usefulness here on earth; we are to be as a house which a householder has left, in which house every one is in his place, each according to his gift; and in this house there will be careful provision, that each shall have his food in due season—food brought him prepared through the hands of officers appointed for that one service, while at the door will ever sit the porter who will have the office of watching while the others work. How careful, how orderly it all is! No loose shiftiness to fill up an interval. No indifference as to what may be done in the long waiting time. His going does not destroy or diminish the seriousness or care with which the interval is to be organised. How busy it all is to be. What! did we fancy that the haste and urgency of worldly business would conflict with the solemnity of watching for the Lord? Why, this Kingdom of His is to be, during all the waiting time, like a house of business. It will be as a merchant house, in which everybody is bent on making all he can out of the money given him. He gives no picture of a Church ever on its knees at some silent shrine, praying for a far-off time. He foresees a body of men busy and intent, absorbed in the practical use of their gifts, bent on turning five talents into ten or two into four. Who are those whom He approves at the Judgment Seat? Those who had sought with deepest zeal to better the state of men here,—to feed the hungry, clothe the naked, visit the sick and the prisoners. He blesses an active Church, busy in present benefits, whose members have spent themselves in the service of human needs. It is such as these whom He will welcome, "Come, ye blessed of your Lord."

Here, then, is the character of the Christian life, in this lower world; and, if so, we can boldly face the taunt. The Master is gone, not that we might stand

and gaze after Him, but that we might turn to our work with doubled interest, because He has gone. It is His absence that intensifies our interest in the present world.

Let us recall, familiar as it is, how this will be.

First, earth is dearer for the sake of Him Who is gone, in the same way as the things of the dead are precious to us after they have been taken from us. Every little thing they touched, however mean, is sacred to us now; every spot that they once loved is the shrine of prayer to us. And Jesus, our Lord, He is gone from our eyes, yet once He was on earth among us, and left it dearer for being here. He has been with us. This sky, these hills, this sea, He saw and loved them; and everything here speaks to us of Him. The wind that is in our ears, He heard it as it rushed along the streets, and it spoke to Him of the Spirit of God. The flowers in our gardens, the grain in our fields, the birds that sing and fly, His love spoke of all these. And everywhere He went, and all of it is His house. The strength of the young man He looked upon and loved; for the misery of sin He had compassion and forgiveness. He looked upon a rebellious city—rebellious as we see cities still—and as He looked He wept over it, remembering how often He would have gathered its children together. He saw multitudes hungry, as we see them now, and had compassion for them, and gave thanks and broke bread. All was once His, and all still speaks of Him. The Word was made Flesh; He took compassion upon it, and made it His home. And we who are in the flesh, therefore, are invited to recall Him at every turn. What a new fount of love, if we would use it, for this poor forlorn earth of ours! Before this, we might have loved it because it was ours, but now, because it is His; and such love is more tender, more lasting, and more gracious; and yet tenderer is it, and yet more irresistible when it all tells of Him Whom the veil of death hides.

His absence makes us love earth more fervently.

Then the further reason. He is gone as a King to a far country; He is King and Master still. He is gone, but His house is still His own, and it is to us, His servants, that it is committed, committed to us because He is gone. Earth is thrown upon our hands and our care, because the Master is withdrawn. Our pleasures, our homes, our interests, our lives, our eating and drinking, marrying and giving in marriage, all these are talents intrusted to us, and our Lord looks for gain to Himself from them. Very urgently He desires that gain, and so urgently that, to any who hold to Him by anything short of eager love, He may seem as a hard man, gathering where He has not strawed, reaping where He has not sown. So eager a Master, He asks for patience, industry, and courage. —"Well done, thou faithful servant," He says to him who is ever on the alert to make the most of his time and chances. "Well done, thou hast been faithful in few things, thou shalt be ruler over many things. Enter thou into the joy of thy Lord." Here is a freshness of zeal thrown into our earthly occupations because our Lord is far away, and we are left responsible.

As simple a reason remains still. Not only is all His committed to our keeping, but He Who is so far out of our sight has left us in all souls that suffer, in all bodies that are sick, living pledges of Himself, sacraments of His Passion. Such as these are not only tokens of Him, or possessions of His: they are Himself, He makes Himself one with them, He places Himself under our eyes and hands, bidding us handle Him and see that it is He Himself. Earth, with its hunger and sickness, is still a place where we may find Christ. For in all we do to help and brighten, to succour and relieve our fellow-men, we hear His voice of salutation—"Blessed are ye of my Father; inasmuch as ye have done it unto the least of one of these, ye have done it unto Me."

Lastly, earth is made dearer to us because He Who is gone will visit it once more. We are to be as those that hold a house ready for a Master Who at any moment may be heard knocking at the door. How He will love to see it all kept as He would have it kept! How eagerly we should scheme to please Him, to picture His returning look, His eyes falling on this and on that which we had done for Him! Oh, if everywhere He might but find the signs of some loving forethought, of some tender loyalty to Him! Is all prepared? Is everything in its place? Shall we ever be tired, as it were, of running round the room once more to see if all is in order? He will look over all to see what we have done to make gain of His goods. He will come to see what fruit is come of the Cross. What have we been doing with the power of

the Precious Blood?   Will He find faith in the earth?
Ah! if we so judge and examine what has been done,
how pitiful, how meagre all that we have yet achieved
will appear!   Did He die only to attain so poor a
victory?   Did He die that He might find the earth
the place that, in our hands, it has become—the sad
prison-house which He would find, if He came back
to it to-day?   These hungry, why are they not fed?
These sick and prisoners, why are they not visited?
Had we not the power to do better than this?   He
committed to us all power.   Why have we not put
it to full use?   Oh, my God! what have we been
doing with Thy great work, committed to us?   Let
us remember that there is an austere tale told us by
the Lord, of a servant who grew idle as his Lord
delayed, and who began to neglect his office, and to
live carelessly, and to eat and drink with the drunken,
and to smite his fellow-servants; and his Lord came
in the day that he was not aware of, and cut him
asunder, and gave him his portion with the hypocrites;
" there shall be weeping and gnashing of teeth."

" Behold, I come quickly."   We had thought that
that news might paralyse our interest in things here,
might drag us out of active service into passive
watching for Christ.   Surely, it is just the message
which sends us back into the world, and sends us back
with ever anxious zeal.   He is coming, and coming so
quickly, and nothing is done and no room is ready.
There is no time to be lost.   Work at once; work
while it is day; work that His goods may not be found
so utterly wasted; work that He may not say, " Oh,

thou wicked and slothful servant, thou knewest I was a hard master." Work, for the sin that is so fatal at the last is the sin of sloth and carelessness. Work, for by your works ye shall be judged. Work as those who, with loins girded and ready feet, are ever listening for a knock at the door, and are ever asking one another, "Is He coming? Is it the Lord?" That is our watching; no idle aspiration: ours is the religion of practical action in among the hard, busy, urgent pressures of daily life. We watch for the Master, but His going does not impoverish, it endears the earth to us. It adds dignity, worth, and beauty to our daily life, to all our hands find to do, to all whom we can touch and love. For, in everything, we say, "He once did what I do to-day; and He gives it to me to do to-day in trust for Him; and one day He will come again and look around and see whether I have done it for Him." We watch, indeed, for Him, proving by our care and interest for earth our loyalty for the Master. We watch, but watch in our service as we give out the meat in due season; as we stand each in our place; as we work for the hungry and sick; as we lay out the talents. So the busiest man may be the most ready for the Lord, and he who is most useful watch best. "Blessed is that servant whom his Lord when He cometh shall find so watching."

CHARACTER AND CIRCUMSTANCE.

"I tell you, in that night there shall be two men in one bed; the one shall be taken, and the other shall be left. Two women shall be grinding together; the one shall be taken, and the other left. Two men shall be in the field; the one shall be taken, and the other left."—LUKE xvii. 34, 36.

THE Christian life, as we have been seeing, has two aspects which stand in the sharpest contrast one to the other. On the one hand, it has its seat and source far hence in the hidden Heaven, "where Christ sits at the right Hand of God." There lies our citizenship "in Jerusalem, the free, the mother of us all." Thither we are to send our hearts travelling—where our treasure is laid up, unstolen and incorruptible. In this Heavenly place, in all hours of blessing and thanksgiving, we sit with Christ our Master; we take a Heavenly Food; we lay our lives in His Hand, to hold fast for us against that day: and, for the hope so set before us, and in loyalty to that high calling, we struggle here on earth to take up our cross; to be crucified in the affections and lusts, mortifying the body; to die with Christ, to be already dead, that our life may be even now hid in Him; to hate father, mother, sisters, and brothers; to leave home, and land, and wife; to seek that city not made with hands, to enter the rest, the rest which remaineth. We are children of the Resurrection, for whom to die is gain, because it will restore us to the Bridegroom, now taken from us, and so shall we be with Christ, which is far better. So we wait groaning in this earthly tabernacle. So the heart of faith in Apostle and Saint beats its wings against withholding bars. So, as an exile by strange waters, it makes melody to itself in psalms, and hymns, and spiritual songs. But nevertheless, on the other side, not in spite of the homeward yearning, but by virtue of it; not in forgetfulness of the hidden Lord, but in very faithfulness to His honour; that same heart, fed with bread from Heaven, turns, with a warmer love and a fresher zeal, and a more tender patience, to the scene of its dying Master's toils. It pours out its devotions, its pains, its tears, its strength, upon all that hungers and suffers here. It lends itself to the world's pursuits, closes with the world's interests, and labours at the world's business with all the fervour of men who have the possessions committed to them of their Master to be used on His behalf. With a sharp reckoning ahead, and a short time in which to prepare for it, their faith in a risen and remote Lord intensifies the pleasure of the work to be got through on earth before He returns; and so we have already been considering those familiar motives which make the very absence of the Master beyond the grave the reason for quickening interest in the things to be done on this side of death.

And yet the picture may seem, to some, fantastic and fanciful. It may look very unlike human nature to be dragged in two directions at once. Men may say, " I can understand one line or the other. I can understand a Saint, a Hermit, an Apostle, possessed with the one longing to be with Christ; but to such an one this earthly tabernacle must remain as a prison house,—mean, contemptible, and unkind. Or I can imagine the man to whom the active business of this life and the development of his present energies is an absorbing occupation, to which he willingly gives his utmost skill; but then, to him Heaven must seem a far-off and strange dream, which he finds it very difficult to people or to conceive, and which he cannot bring to bear upon his daily business with any force or decision. He finds himself compelled to leave off imagining it, and to hope for the best. He prays for entry there hereafter, but in no practical sense can he manage to introduce its hope into the thick of actual and occupied days." " These two worlds," it may be said, " cannot well be pictured to belong to one another—Earth here and Heaven hereafter; they cannot be imagined intermingling or interlacing. They cannot cross each other's lines; they are too violently alien in type and features to be brought together in the intimate fashion which this account of the Christian faith requires. How can a fitness to sit in Heavenly places with Christ of itself adapt us to act among our fellows on earth? If our treasure is in Heaven, then our hearts cannot be here. True, you can give us some romantic reasons why we should value this earth out of love for a Master Who has left it in our charge, but it remains that we are to be dead to this life, and to live in the belief that it will all be put away from us at the last;

and no romantic loyalty to a lost Master's memory will finally sustain our interest in earth in face of that, its utter worthlessness. Surely, it is an unnatural pretence to profess that you love father, and mother, and sisters, and brothers, and house, and land, all the more because for Christ's sake you have learned to despise, hate, and forsake them."

Now, that is the criticism of common sense on the mysticism of the Christian position. It divides itself into two great heads.

First, it declares that there is not sufficient unity of kind between our life here and life hereafter to allow of this identity of interest; and then it supposes that this strange doctrine by which we are called upon to live in two worlds at once is in collision with human nature as we find it. Let us ask, Is it true that there is no unity of kind between our life here and life hereafter? Let us consider what is it that will certainly be the same with us here and hereafter. What is there that we shall carry away with us when we die, when everything else falls away from us? What is it which we shall still be—that which no conditions can change or efface; which will abide there under the awful Eyes, before the Throne, in the sight of Heaven? We know that it is *our character*. That must stand. Strip it as you will of all that encumbers it here, there it will still be all the more sure and visible for this nakedness. Our character—a certain moral structure which has come together with the growth of years, a certain combination of ruling motives, a certain bend of will, a peculiar set of emotional currents, a peculiar sentiment, taste, judgment, cast of feeling, movements, and desires,—all that which grows more and more fixed and distinct in us as the days pass, and which our friends mark and note, and discuss and classify, and criticise and estimate,—our personal character, that is what will and must abide. We can be quite sure of it. No change can cancel it except one that would annihilate us. So long as we exist we remain of the same character as now; it may be improved or worsened, but it is impossible that it should continue to exist without retaining its unbroken identity with itself.

Now, here is a very distinct bit of information about the other world. We may be utterly unable to shape a picture of it; yet this we know,—we shall be, on the day we enter it, in character and moral type exactly what we are to-day. We shall judge in the same kind of fashion, have the same likes and dislikes, the same standards of approval and disapproval, the same sentiments, the same tone, the same tendencies, the same movements of feeling, the same peculiarities, characteristics, mannerisms. Our friends, if they were watching us before the Judgment Bar, would be able to say at once, "There is the man I always knew. How like himself!" If so, you see we need not trouble ourselves because our imagination can shape for us no Heavenly scene, no Heavenly city, for neither can our imagination now shape for us our personal character. It has no form with which we can identify it, but that does not hinder at all the distinctness with which we know it. There is nothing that is more real, or near, or definite to us; and, if so, if our character is most real, and near, and definite, and known, then that which we shall be in Heaven hereafter, shapeless and hidden though it may be, is perfectly real, and near, and known to us now.

Our character, that we shall most assuredly carry away with us when we die. Here, then, is a real ground of unity between the life here and the life hereafter.

And what is character? What are its essential features?

The core of all character lies in individuality. Character is a moral fact: and, until life is individual, it is not moral. And by individual we mean something single, separate, and alone, that cannot be accounted for from outside, cannot be grouped under any general laws, cannot be extracted out of outside conditions. Its actions must spring from out of itself, it makes them happen; and you have to enter into its inner life and secrets if you would know why it does anything. However alike the circumstances may be, no other being would do exactly what this character does, or say what it says. It is this seal of individuality which it sets on everything that comes out from it, which makes it a character. Sometimes it stamps it weakly, and then we say a person has little or no character; or sometimes it stamps it forcibly, and then we say, "That is a man of character." At all costs, character must show itself to be free and above its circumstances. If a man is the creature of circumstances we call him a man without character; changing with all the changing hours, he has no self-identity; and character is that with which we identify a man. Character is vital and vigorous so far only as it insists on making itself free room for action amid the thronging events, and it dies down as soon as it fails to hold itself aloof and separate from circumstances. Character is the reaction from circumstances. It is the inner movement which encounters and withstands the shock of change and outward things. And it must, therefore, issue from a life that directs itself. Character, that is, must be personal. If men were machines moved from without, they could have no character. If the soul were a function of the body, it could have no character. Whenever we impute character to material things we do it by a metaphor. Individuality, self-identity, these are the secrets which constitute and create character; and character, therefore, supposes always a central core of individual life which is cut off from all its surroundings, a stranger that this outward world cannot own nor any web of circumstances explain; a mysterious, unearthly presence, which is intended to creep forward, out of its dim wrapping of flesh and feelings, and slowly to emerge like a plant, disclosing itself petal after petal like a flower, detaching itself from all that encircles it, from country, home, father, mother, and sister and brother, asserting itself day by day with evergrowing distinctness as a separate and unique fact upon the earth; different from every other being that ever was born; something utterly and profoundly alone, a person with a character.

Character and circumstances—these, then, are at

deadly war with one another. And, now, how does this character show itself? By what methods does it grow? It grows by one way only—by acts, by choice, by judgments. Its decisions show what it is; each decision that it makes strengthens a bent, deepens a groove, determines a current, builds up a sentiment. Each decision that it forms creates the character. And what is it, then, that demands of it its decisions, its acts, its judgments? Its old foe—circumstance. Circumstances press upon it, they hustle and throng all round it, amid the throng it must judge and choose and decide. Circumstances are, therefore, essential to its growth, to its history. Without the necessity to act it could never come to a decision, and without coming to a decision character would be utterly unshapen, asleep. Circumstances must be there to evoke it, to force upon it alternatives, to wait upon its direction, to elicit its judgments.

This, then, is the situation; a situation of contrast. There is within each one of us a strange presence which sits alone, unfathered by any earthly parentage, a ghostly visitant which exists by defying circumstance, by holding itself aloof, a form obviously designed, in its fit measure, to become organic and free, self-directing, self-identical, a hidden spring of original life; that first. But then its career, its formation, its waking existence depends on its intimate contact with earthly circumstances; and the more changing and rapid the movement of circumstances the more alert must be the judgment, and the quicker and more vital the formation of character.

That is our situation.

And then, I would ask you, is not this is a situation to which our Christian faith exactly applies itself? Our Faith lays hold of these very points. It finds first a dim presence within man struggling to free itself from the fold and wraps of its earthly birth, struggling to get alone with itself, to lift itself out of the blind currents which swing it hither and thither. So Faith finds us, and passes the knife of the clean-cutting Spirit round that prisoner, and lifts it up, by the Resurrection, clear above all earthly circumstances, and separates it into its proper loneliness. It plucks it out of the soil, and puts it into the new body of Christ, and lo! now it is free, distinct; it is alive, it is alone. God gives His Blessed Son for it alone, and endows it with its own special and separate unction, and whispers in its ear its secret name which is known to God and to itself only. There, apart, separate, is a new seat from which character may spring; its withdrawal into Christ is the key to all its power of after-growth. Its root is hidden, but it is the seat of all its vitality.

Then there is the other side. The seed of character is there, but its growth is all to come. It must be buried deep again in circumstance, and be thrown into the very thick of actions; only so can it improve and reveal itself, and witness to its new secret. And it loves circumstance; it loves it, for it is alive now and eager to begin. Every touch of its renewal in Jesus has quickened its desire to improve itself. Oh that it may test its loyalty, may show what the Cross of God has in it, may witness to its hidden name! Oh that it may so bear witness to that Master that men may "see its good works, and glorify the Father Which is in Heaven!" How blest the command which sends it back from its withdrawn Master, and its hidden feast with Him, to the swarming herds of men, to the crowded earth, with the talents in its hands, and the sweet words in its ear, "Occupy till I come. Bear witness of Me."

What is its occupation, but to prove and develop character? Character is the gift committed. How is that to be proved and developed? By acts of choice. What does it signify, therefore, that the circumstances end and perish, that the earth does but offer occasions which disappear in blind death? Each, before it went, evoked a decision, and allowed time for a judgment; and, by that judgment, a work has gone forward, and a result remains. The character has grown; the gift has been improved; the five talents are on the way to become ten. We look up as each moment dies, and thank the Master that the choice made in it was one that would tend to restore Him His own with usury. What peace and freedom is ours! Circumstances, before we were released from our fetters, used to be so irritating and so uncertain; but now they have become doubly dear and precious, because now we live no longer inside them—wretched if they were wretched, yet more wretched at their rapid perishing if they were happy,—but live through them, and by means of them; and all of them are serviceable, and all can be turned to good account, and when they have served their purpose we can gladly afford to see them fly.

z

There is no circumstance, however mean and poor, however dry and dreary, which does not involve some judgment, some act of will, and it is impossible to make any such judgment or do any such act without its entering into and fashioning our characters. Every single judgment we come to must emphasise some tendency, must check some counter-motion; must repress one thing, impress and elicit another; must favour a certain bent, must fix a certain stamp. And every hour and every minute of our waking life is thick with these quick judgments. We are being made every minute, and we cannot help it,—you and I, as we walk and talk, eat and drink, marry and are given in marriage, work and play, go out and come in— we are being made and fashioned into that in which we shall pass out into the night of darkness and into the glory of God.

This is surely why our business hours, our social habits, are all included within our work for the hidden Master at God's right Hand. For it is just in the constant, habitual, hurried, routine acts of common life that that swarm of little judgments is made such as form the character. It is a literal and necessary fact and no romance, that it is these daily routine acts which finally settle what we shall be carrying in our hands when our Lord comes to make up the reckoning.

Let us recall, in our Lord's own vivid image, both the impotence and the potency of circumstance. "Two women shall be grinding at the mill; one shall be taken, and the other left." How powerless and immaterial is circumstances for those two! Every single circumstance of life is identical; together they rise at the same hour; together they begin the day's long labour; right through the day they grind together; at the same hour they go to the evening meal, and at the same hour they sleep. Everything, year after year, repeats itself. They dress alike, they were paid alike; life passed for both on the same level of low, unchanging poverty. To any one looking on they would be wholly alike, two poor women, of the same class, occupation, education, wage, interest, dress. Nothing from end to end of these earthly circumstances could be found to distinguish the one from the other. At the same mill they had turned and turned, to both the earth had been equally harsh and unkind, and no lights shone in upon them, and no changes ever surprised them. On and on together, hand in hand, and face to face, they had ground at the same mill up to the last; and, lo! one is for Heaven and one for Hell. Within they are as different as black from white, as good from evil; so dominant, so imperial is human character, so free it is from the control of circumstances.

Oh! what wide comfort. What can it matter what our conditions may be? Two grinding at the mill; one taken, and the other left. Is there any one who sinks under the sodden monotony of daily routine, who withers under the pressure of every-day sameness; who finds himself chained into that mean, petty, narrow block of circumstances which he knows to be killing out all spiritual emotions in those about him, and yet he cannot break from it, and he dreads to feel creeping over his soul the same melancholy dryness he sees in others? That which kills another may be life to him, if he will use it. He alone is the master. Nothing from without can hurt or soil it,—for not that which goeth in at the mouth doth soil a man. Though others die at the mill, yet any one who chooses, may find, as he turns at the same wheel, a Heaven or a Hell,—may be saved or lost.

Two women at the mill. So powerless is circumstance, and yet, on the other hand, so powerful is it! It is at the mill, at the grinding, there and nowhere else, that the thing has got to be done, the difference is to be created. There, as they ground and ground together, these two poor women built up bit by bit the wall of their separation. It was out of the doing of the same things that one grew daily readier for the Lord and the other darkened down to the slothful servant. At the mill, still grinding, the Lord finds them. No one, then, need leave his mill. In the field where men work—there our drama works itself out. Circumstances are nothing, but they are also everything; and we shall discover our weakness if we attempt to ignore them. Is there any one who has more zeal than he finds room for in his narrow circle, who is waiting always for some fair day to dawn when the faith in him will be given more chance and wider field? Nay! our field must be the present, and our circumstances as they stand are wide enough. Turn to them and begin. There are no circumstances so poor, but that character may display itself and make itself therein. Strength of character lies not in demanding special circumstances, but in mastering and using any that may be given. Our work and daily contact with our fellows form our scene of action, and God blesses with a peculiar blessing the efforts to put to profit, not some self-selected occasion, but the actual conditions in which we find ourselves.

"Two men shall be lying in one bed." Each in our bed; there is our discipline. Working in the field where we are set, there is our best growth. Blessed is that servant whom the Lord shall find in the bed made for him; blessed is that servant whom the Master may take straight to Himself from the field where he was set.

The one enduring interest of human life is character; and our faith brightens our lives by unearthing character, and it vitalises it under both those aspects of which we have been speaking. First, it proclaims that our "life is hid with Christ;" we are wholly free, nothing can hold us down; gifted with a refuge far above all accidents and risks, we have an indefeasible advantage over all earthly circumstances. "Hid with Christ; free with the freedom of the Son," nothing can thwart or terrify us; safe hid from the provoking of all men, no man can snatch us out of His Hand. We sit hidden with the Lord above the waterfloods. Here is the primary force faith insures to us all; and why is it, let each ask, that with this advantage secured to me, this indefeasible refuge, why is it my character has no more force than solidity? Hid with Christ; why, then, am I so afraid of men—why so afraid lest they think badly of me? why so nervous of my reputation, so anxious to keep in the run? "Hid with Christ;" why is it, then, I move up and down with the swing of popular opinions? why so unsteady in judgment? why do I say what all men say, and think what every body about me is thinking? Why have I so little sense of responsibility for my thoughts, words, and desires? How is it that I vary so strangely from day to day; that my temper is a mere index to my bodily health; why so moody? "Hid with Christ;" yet every tiny little disappointment upsets me. "Hid with Christ;" yet I succumb to every flattery, I am so easily beguiled with praise, I hunger for applause, I am miserable if people are not noticing me. Where is the unconquerable force, the high peace of those whose secret life is hid with the hidden Christ?

And then, our faith is not only the secret of self-reliance, but it ought to endue us with a new zeal with which to face and conquer our earthly circumstances. Fed with that hidden and inner force, we ought to be as those who burn to put it into action. We, my brethren, by our very security, should be made eager to display abroad, under the pressure of circumstances, the character with which we have been endued by Christ. We are sent down to be a spectacle to men and to Angels, and the eyes of the Heavenly hosts are upon us. They are saying over us, as they watch, "What will this man do? What is that hidden virtue now in his soul? What will he do, what will he prove himself, what excellences of character will come from him, as he meets the shock of circumstance?" That is our drama. Do we, then, shrink back from the test? do we decline the troubles and anxieties from which our character is to disclose itself, by which that which is told us of the Spirit in the secret chamber is to be made manifest on the housetops? Long, weary, plodding labour, this is the condition for which we have been gifted, these are the hours that tell our tale; it is thus we bear our witness. Life, this dull, working life, may become to us so favoured, so interesting, so precious if we take it all as the theatre on which we display before the eyes of God the glory of that hidden name which we have received from Him. That which we are in God's thought and intention, that is what we are discovering to ourselves and others at each passing hour. Let us ask ourselves, What is my name? what is the peculiar combination of moral qualities which is in me and no others? The seed cast into me of God—oh that I knew what mystery was hidden in its silent history! Let the rains of God come, and the winds and the clouds pass over me, if only this name may break out and open into shape of flower and fulness of fruit, and so my name may be written broad and clear on my forehead, and all men may see it, and say, " He is not his own, he is God's. Behold the seal is on him. He is in the image of his Father. He is of the family of Christ."

THE END.

A SELECTION

FROM THE

Recent Publications

OF

Messrs. RIVINGTON

WATERLOO PLACE, PALL MALL
LONDON

Goulburn's Gospels for Sundays.

Second Edition.   Two Vols.   Crown 8vo.   16s.

THOUGHTS UPON THE LITURGICAL GOSPELS FOR THE SUNDAYS, ONE FOR EACH DAY IN THE YEAR. With an Introduction on their origin, history, the modifications made in them by the Reformers and by the Revisers of the Prayer Book, the honour always paid to them in the Church, and the proportions in which they are drawn from the Writings of the four Evangelists.

By Edward Meyrick Goulburn, D.D., D.C.L.,
Dean of Norwich.

Goulburn's Gospels for Holy Days.

Crown 8vo.   8s. 6d.

MEDITATIONS UPON THE LITURGICAL GOSPELS.   For the minor Festivals of Christ, the two first week-days of the Easter and Whitsun Festivals, and the Red Letter Saints' Days.   To which is prefixed some account of the origin of Saints' Days, and their Evens or Vigils ; of the pruning of the Calendar of the English Church by the Reformers ; and of the re-introduction of the Black-Letter Festivals, with separate notices of the Four which were re-introduced in the Prayer-Book of 1552.

By Edward Meyrick Goulburn, D.D., D.C.L.,
Dean of Norwich.

Goulburn's Holy Week Lectures.

Crown 8vo.   5s.

HOLY WEEK IN NORWICH CATHEDRAL ; being Seven Lectures on the several Members of the Most Sacred Body of our Lord Jesus Christ.   Delivered at Evensong on each Day of the Holy Week in the Cathedral Church of the Holy and Undivided Trinity of Norwich.

By Edward Meyrick Goulburn, D.D., D.C.L.,
Dean of Norwich.

The Altar Book.

With Rubrics in Red.   Large Type.   Royal 8vo.   10s. 6d.

THE ORDER OF THE ADMINISTRATION OF THE HOLY COMMUNION, AND THE FORM OF SOLEMNIZATION OF MATRIMONY, according to the Use of the Church of England.

May also be had bound in Morocco.

À Kempis' Of the Imitation of Christ.

Large Type Edition.   Crown 8vo.   3s. 6d.

OF THE IMITATION OF CHRIST.   In Four Books.

By Thomas à Kempis.

Translated and Edited by the Rev. W. H. Hutchings, M.A.,
Rector of Kirkby Misperton, Yorkshire.

Knox Little's Hopes of the Passion.

Crown 8vo.   3s. 6d.

THE HOPES AND DECISIONS OF THE PASSION OF OUR MOST HOLY REDEEMER.

By the Rev. W. J. Knox Little, M.A.,
Canon Residentiary of Worcester, and Vicar of Hoar Cross, Burton-on-Trent.

Newbolt's Man of God.

Small 8vo.   1s. 6d.

THE MAN OF GOD.   Being Six Addresses delivered at the Primary Ordination of the Right Rev. Lord Alwyne Compton, Lord Bishop of Ely, Lent, 1886.

By the Rev. W. C. E. Newbolt, M.A.,
Vicar of Malvern Link.

Waterloo Place, London.

Woodford's Great Commission.

Crown 8vo. 5s.

THE GREAT COMMISSION.   Twelve Addresses on the Ordinal.

By James Russell Woodford, D.D.,
Sometime Lord Bishop of Ely.

Edited, with an Introduction on the Ordinations of his Episcopate,

By Herbert Mortimer Luckock, D.D.,
One of his Examining Chaplains.

Luckock's Bishops in the Tower.

Crown 8vo. 6s.

THE BISHOPS IN THE TOWER.   A Record of Stirring Events affecting the Church and Nonconformists from the Restoration to the Revolution.

By Herbert Mortimer Luckock, D.D.,
Canon of Ely, etc.

The Book of Church Law.

Fourth Edition, revised.   Crown 8vo.   7s. 6d.

THE BOOK OF CHURCH LAW: being an Exposition of the Legal Rights and Duties of the Parochial Clergy and the Laity of the Church of England.

By the late Rev. John Henry Blunt, D.D.,

Revised by Sir Walter G. F. Phillimore, Bart., D.C.L.,
Barrister-at-Law, and Chancellor of the Diocese of Lincoln.

Waterloo Place, London.

Holland's Creed and Character.

Crown 8vo.   7s. 6d.

CREED AND CHARACTER.   A Volume of Sermons.

By the Rev. H. S. Holland, M.A.,
Canon of St. Paul's.

Contents.

The Story of an Apostle's Faith—The Story of a Disciple's Faith—The Rock ; The Secret ; The Fellowship ; The Witness ; The Resources ; The Mind ; The Ministry of the Church—The Solidarity of Salvation—The Freedom of Salvation—The Gift of Grace—The Law of Forgiveness—The Coming of the Spirit—The Beauty of Holiness—The Energy of Unselfishness—The Fruit of the Spirit—Thanksgiving—The Activity of Service—Character and Circumstance.

Holland's Logic and Life.

Third Edition.   Crown 8vo.   7s. 6d.

LOGIC AND LIFE, with other Sermons.

By the Rev. H. S. Holland, M.A.,
Canon of St. Paul's.

' Some of these sermons are as powerful as any preached in this generation, and, indeed, full of genius, original thought, and spiritual veracity.   Of the three first, it would be hard to speak in terms too high.'—*Spectator.*

' These [two last-named] sermons exhibit at the full the real greatness of Mr. Holland's power—his originality, his insight, his range of experience, observation, and sympathies ; and, above all, his never-failing elevation of spiritual feeling and judgment, speaking in language brilliant, forcible, copious, rising often to splendour and magnificence.'—*Church Quarterly Review.*

' The sermons are thoughtful, earnest, and often eloquent and powerful.   They fully bear out the high reputation Mr. Holland has obtained as a preacher of considerable acceptableness and influence with hearers of education and culture.'—*Guardian.*

Holland's Good Friday Addresses.

Small 8vo.   2s.

GOOD FRIDAY : being Addresses on the Seven Last Words, delivered at St. Paul's Cathedral, on Good Friday 1884.

By the Rev. H. S. Holland, M.A.,
Canon of St. Paul's.

Waterloo Place, London.

The Missioner's Hymnal.

Royal 32mo, 1d. Sewed; 3d. Cloth Boards.
With Music. Small 4to. 2s. 6d.

THE MISSIONER'S HYMNAL.

Edited by the Rev. A. G. Jackson,
Warden of the Farm School, Redhill, Surrey.

Wakeman's History of Religion.

Small 8vo. 1s. 6d.

THE HISTORY OF RELIGION IN ENGLAND.

By H. O. Wakeman, M.A.,
Fellow of All Souls' College, Bursar, and Tutor of Keble College, Oxford.

Constitutional Essays.

Crown 8vo. 6s.

ESSAYS INTRODUCTORY TO THE STUDY OF ENGLISH
CONSTITUTIONAL HISTORY.

By Resident Members of the University of Oxford.

Edited by Henry Offley Wakeman, M.A.,
Fellow of All Souls' College;

And Arthur Hassall, M.A.,
Student of Christ Church.

Crake's Church History.

New Edition. Crown 8vo. 7s. 6d.

HISTORY OF THE CHURCH UNDER THE ROMAN EMPIRE, A.D. 30-476.

By the Rev. A. D. Crake, B.A.,
Fellow of the Royal Historical Society, Vicar of Cholsey, Berks.

Waterloo Place, London.

Mercier's By the King and Queen.

Crown 8vo, with Frontispiece. 2s.

BY THE KING AND QUEEN : A Story of the Dawn of Religion
in Britain.

By Mrs. Jerome Mercier,
Author of ' Our Mother Church,' etc.

Crake's Chronicles of Æscendune.

Three Vols. Crown 8vo. 3s. 6d. each. Sold separately.

By the Rev. A. D. Crake, B.A.,
Author of the ' History of the Church under the Roman Empire, etc., etc.

EDWY THE FAIR ; OR, THE FIRST CHRONICLE OF ÆSCENDUNE.
A Tale of the Days of St. Dunstan.

ALFGAR THE DANE ; OR, THE SECOND CHRONICLE OF ÆSCENDUNE.
A Tale of the Days of Edmund Ironside.

THE RIVAL HEIRS ; BEING THE THIRD AND LAST CHRONICLE
OF ÆSCENDUNE.

Crake's House of Walderne.

Crown 8vo. 3s. 6d.

THE HOUSE OF WALDERNE : A Tale of the Cloister and the Forest
in the Days of the Barons' Wars.

By the Rev. A. D. Crake, B.A.,
Fellow of the Royal Historical Society, Author of the ' Chronicles of Æscendune,' etc.

Waterloo Place, London.

Mozley on the Old Testament.

Third Edition.   8vo.   10s. 6d.

RULING IDEAS IN EARLY AGES AND THEIR RELATION TO OLD TESTAMENT FAITH.   Lectures delivered to Graduates of the University of Oxford.

By J. B. Mozley, D.D.,

Late Canon of Christ Church, and Regius Professor of Divinity in the University of Oxford.

Contents.

Abraham—Sacrifice of Isaac—Human Sacrifices—Exterminating Wars—Visitation of the Sins of Fathers upon Children—Jael—Connection of Jael's Act with the Morality of her Age—Law of Retaliation—Retaliation: Law of Goël—The End the Test of a Progressive Revelation—The Manichæans and the Jewish Fathers.

Mozley's University Sermons.

Fifth Edition.   Crown 8vo.   7s. 6d.

SERMONS PREACHED BEFORE THE UNIVERSITY OF OXFORD AND ON VARIOUS OCCASIONS.

By J. B. Mozley, D.D.,

Late Canon of Christ Church, and Regius Professor of Divinity, Oxford.

Contents.

The Roman Council—The Pharisees—Eternal Life—The Reversal of Human Judgment—War—Nature—The Work of the Spirit on the Natural Man—The Atonement—Our Duty to Equals—The Peaceful Temper—The Strength of Wishes—The Unspoken Judgment of Mankind—The True Test of Spiritual Birth—Ascension Day—Gratitude—The Principle of Emulation—Religion the First Choice—The Influence of Dogmatic Teaching on Education.

Waterloo Place, London.

Mozley's Essays.

Second Edition.   Two Vols.   8vo.   24s.
ESSAYS, HISTORICAL AND THEOLOGICAL.
By J. B. Mozley, D.D.,
*Late Canon of Christ Church, and Regius Professor of Divinity in the
University of Oxford.*

Contents.

VOLUME I.—Introduction and Memoir of the Author—Lord Strafford—Arch-
bishop Laud—Carlyle's Cromwell—Luther.
VOLUME II.—Dr. Arnold—Blanco White—Dr. Pusey's Sermon—The Book of
Job—Maurice's Theological Essays—Indian Conversion—The Argument of
Design—The Principle of Causation considered in opposition to Atheistic
Theories—In Memoriam—The Author's Articles and Works.

Mozley on Miracles.

Seventh Edition.   Crown 8vo.   7s. 6d.
EIGHT LECTURES ON MIRACLES: being the Bampton Lectures for
1865.
By J. B. Mozley, D.D.,
*Late Canon of Christ Church, and Regius Professor of Divinity in the
University of Oxford.*

Mozley's Parochial Sermons.

Second Edition.   Crown 8vo.   7s. 6d.
SERMONS, PAROCHIAL AND OCCASIONAL.
By J. B. Mozley, D.D.,
*Late Canon of Christ Church, and Regius Professor of Divinity in the
University of Oxford.*

Contents.

The Right Eye and the Right Hand—Temptation treated as Opportunity—The
Influences of Habit on Devotion—Thought for the Morrow—The Relief of
Utterance—Seeking a Sign—David Numbering the People—The Heroism of
Faith—Proverbs—The Teaching of Events—Growing Worse—Our Lord the
Sacrifice for Sin—The Parable of the Sower—The Religious Enjoyment of
Nature—The Threefold Office of the Holy Spirit—Wisdom and Folly Tested by
Experience—Moses, a Leader—The Unjust Steward—Sowing to the Spirit—
True Religion, a Manifestation—St. Paul's Exaltation of Labour—Jeremiah's
Witness against Idolatry—Isaiah's Estimate of Worldly Greatness—The Short-
ness of Life—The Endless State of Being—The Witness of the Apostles—Life
a Probation—Christian Mysteries, the Common Heritage—Our Lord's Hour—
Fear—The Educating Power of Strong Impressions—The Secret Justice of
Temporal Providence—Jacob as a Prince Prevailing with God.

Waterloo Place, London.

Mozley's Lectures.

8vo. 10s. 6d.

LECTURES AND OTHER THEOLOGICAL PAPERS.

By J. B. Mozley, D.D.,
Late Canon of Christ Church, and Regius Professor of Divinity in the University of Oxford.

The Prayer Book in Latin.

With Rubrics in Red. Small 8vo. 7s. 6d.

LIBER PRECUM PUBLICARUM ECCLESIÆ ANGLICANÆ.

A Gulielmo Bright, S.T.P.,
Ædis Christi apud Oxon. Canonico, Historiæ Ecclesiasticæ, Professore Regio,

et

Petro Goldsmith Medd, A.M.,
Collegii Universitatis apud Oxon. Socio Seniore.

LATINE REDDITUS. Editio Tertia, cum Appendice.

[In hac Editione continentur Versiones Latinæ—1. Libri Precum Publicarum Ecclesiæ Anglicanæ; 2. Liturgiæ Primæ Reformatæ; 3. Liturgiæ Scoticanæ; 4. Liturgiæ Americanæ.]

Blunt's Household Theology.

New Edition. Small 8vo. 3s. 6d.

HOUSEHOLD THEOLOGY: a Handbook of Religious Information respecting the Holy Bible, the Prayer Book, the Church, the Ministry, Divine Worship, the Creeds, etc., etc.

By the Rev. John Henry Blunt, D.D.,
Editor of the 'Annotated Book of Common Prayer,' etc., etc.

Also a Cheap Edition. 16mo. 1s.

Waterloo Place, London.

Selections from Liddon.

Second Edition.   Crown 8vo.   3s. 6d.

SELECTIONS from the Writings of H. P. LIDDON, D.D., D.C.L.,
Chancellor and Canon of St. Paul's.

Selections from Keble.

Crown 8vo.   3s. 6d.

SELECTIONS from the Writings of JOHN KEBLE, M.A.,
Author of 'The Christian Year.'

Selections from Pusey.

Second Edition.   Crown 8vo.   3s. 6d.

SELECTIONS from the Writings of EDWARD BOUVERIE PUSEY, D.D.,
Late Regius Professor of Hebrew, and Canon of Christ Church, Oxford.

Selections from Neale.

Crown 8vo.   3s. 6d.

SELECTIONS from the Writings of JOHN MASON NEALE, D.D.,
Late Warden of Sackville College.

Waterloo Place, London.

Corpus Christi.

With Red Borders.   Royal 32mo.   2s.

CORPUS CHRISTI: A Manual of Devotion for the Blessed Sacrament.

With a Preface by the Rev. H. Montagu Villiers,
Vicar of St. Paul's, Wilton Place.
Also a Cheap Edition, without the Red Borders, 1s.

Williams on the Catechism.

New Edition.   Two Vols.   Crown 8vo.   5s. each.   Sold separately.

PLAIN SERMONS ON THE CATECHISM.

By the Rev. Isaac Williams, B.D.,
Late Fellow of Trinity College, Oxford; Author of a 'Devotional Commentary on the Gospel Narrative.'

Bickersteth's Yesterday, To-day, and For Ever.

One Shilling Edition.   18mo.
With Red Borders.   16mo.   2s. 6d.

YESTERDAY, TO-DAY, AND FOR EVER : a Poem in Twelve Books.

By Edward Henry Bickersteth, D.D.,
Bishop of Exeter.

'This blank-verse poem, in twelve books, has made its way into the religious world of England and America without much help from the critics.'—*Times.*

'The most simple, the richest, and the most perfect sacred poem which recent days have produced.'—*Morning Advertiser.*

'A poem worth reading, worthy of attentive study; full of noble thoughts, beautiful diction, and high imagination.'—*Standard.*

'In these light Miscellany days there is a spiritual refreshment in the spectacle of a man girding up the loins of his mind to the task of producing a genuine epic. And it is true poetry. There is a definiteness, a crispness about it, which in these moist, viewy, hazy days is no less invigorating than novel.'—*Edinburgh Daily Review.*

'Mr. Bickersteth writes like a man who cultivates at once reverence and earnestness of thought.'—*Guardian.*

The Larger Edition, 5s., may be had.

Waterloo Place, London.

The Annotated Prayer Book.

In One Volume. Quarto. £1, 1s.
Or Half-bound in Morocco. £1, 11s. 6d.

THE ANNOTATED BOOK OF COMMON PRAYER : being an Historical, Ritual, and Theological Commentary on the Devotional System of the Church of England.

Edited by the Rev. John Henry Blunt, D.D., F.S.A.

The reception which the Annotated Book of Common Prayer has met with during an issue of eight editions in sixteen years has led the publishers to believe that a new edition, carefully revised and enlarged, in accordance with our advanced knowledge, would be acceptable. The present edition has therefore been prepared with, among others, the following improvements :—

1. A thoroughly trustworthy text of the whole Prayer Book, such as has not hitherto been accessible.

2. A much enlarged Introduction, embracing in a compact form all that is now known respecting the history of the Prayer Book.

3. The Epistles and Gospels, with all other portions of Holy Scripture, are now printed at length.

4. The Notes on the Minor Saints' Days have been carefully revised, and in most cases re-written.

Maxims from Carter.

Crown 16mo. 2s.

MAXIMS AND GLEANINGS from the Writings of T. T. CARTER, M.A.

Selected and arranged for Daily Use by C. M. S.,

Compiler of ' Daily Gleanings of the Saintly Life,' ' Under the Cross,' etc.

With an Introduction by the Rev. M. F. Sadler,

Rector of Honiton, Devon.

Waterloo Place, London.

Luckock on the Prayer Book.

Second Edition.   Crown 8vo.   6s.

STUDIES IN THE HISTORY OF THE BOOK OF COMMON PRAYER. The Anglican Reform—The Puritan Innovations—The Elizabethan Reaction—The Caroline Settlement.   With Appendices.

By Herbert Mortimer Luckock, D.D.,

Canon of Ely, etc.

'This able and helpful book—recommending it emphatically to all educated members of the entire Anglican community.' —*Church Quarterly Review.*

' We heartily commend this very interesting and very readable book.'—*Guardian.*

'Dr. Luckock's compact and clearly arranged volume is a valuable contribution to liturgical history, which will prove interesting to all readers and almost indispensable to the theological student who has to master the history and *rationale* of the Book of Common Prayer.'—*Notes and Queries.*

Knox Little's Mystery of the Passion.

Third Edition.   Crown 8vo.   3s. 6d.

THE MYSTERY OF THE PASSION OF OUR MOST HOLY REDEEMER.

By the Rev. W. J. Knox Little, M.A.,

Canon Residentiary of Worcester and Vicar of Hoar Cross.

The Treasury of Devotion.

Fourteenth Edition.   18mo, 2s. 6d.; Cloth limp, 2s.; or bound with the Book of Common Prayer, 3s. 6d.

THE TREASURY OF DEVOTION : a Manual of Prayers for General and Daily Use.

Compiled by a Priest.

Edited by the Rev. T. T. Carter, M.A.

Also an Edition in Large Type.   Crown 8vo.   5s.

Waterloo Place, London.

Williams's Female Scripture Characters.

New Edition.   Crown 8vo.   5s.

FEMALE CHARACTERS OF HOLY SCRIPTURE.   A Series of Sermons.

By the Rev. Isaac Williams, B.D.,
Formerly Fellow of Trinity College, Oxford.

Contents.

Eve—Sarah—Lot's Wife—Rebekah—Leah and Rachel—Miriam—Rahab—Deborah—Ruth—Hannah—The Witch of Endor—Bathsheba—Rizpah—The Queen of Sheba—The Widow of Zarephath—Jezebel—The Shunammite—Esther—Elisabeth—Anna—The Woman of Samaria—Joanna—The Woman with the Issue of Blood—The Woman of Canaan—Martha—Mary—Salome—The Wife of Pilate—Dorcas—The Blessed Virgin.

Blunt's Dictionary of Sects.

Imperial 8vo.   36s. ; or in half-morocco, 48s.

DICTIONARY OF SECTS, HERESIES, ECCLESIASTICAL PARTIES, AND SCHOOLS OF RELIGIOUS THOUGHT.   By Various Writers.

Edited by the Rev. John Henry Blunt, D.D.,
Editor of the 'Dictionary of Theology,' 'Annotated Book of Common Prayer,' etc., etc.

Body's Life of Temptation.

Sixth Edition.   Crown 8vo.   4s. 6d.

THE LIFE OF TEMPTATION.   A Course of Lectures delivered in substance at St. Peter's, Eaton Square ; also at All Saints', Margaret Street.

By the Rev. George Body, M.A.,
Canon of Durham.

Contents.

The Leading into Temptation—The Rationale of Temptation—Why we are Tempted—Safety in Temptation—With Jesus in Temptation—The End of Temptation.

Waterloo Place, London.

Knox Little's Manchester Sermons.

Second Edition. Crown 8vo. 7s. 6d.

SERMONS PREACHED FOR THE MOST PART IN MANCHESTER.

By the Rev. W. J. Knox Little, M.A.,
Canon Residentiary of Worcester, and Vicar of Hoar Cross.

Contents.

The Soul instructed by God—The Claim of God upon the Soul—The Super-natural Powers of the Soul—The Soul in its Inner Life—The Soul in the World and at the Judgment—The Law of Preparation—The Principle of Preparation—The Temper of Preparation—The Energy of Preparation—The Soul's Need and God's Nature—The Martyr of Jesus—The Secret of Prophetic Power—The Law of Sacrifice—The Comfort of God—The Symbolism of the Cross—The Beatitude of Mary, the Mother of the Lord.

Knox Little's Christian Life.

Third Edition. Crown 8vo. 3s. 6d.

CHARACTERISTICS AND MOTIVES OF THE CHRISTIAN LIFE. Ten Sermons preached in Manchester Cathedral in Lent and Advent 1877.

By the Rev. W. J. Knox Little, M.A.,
Canon Residentiary of Worcester, and Vicar of Hoar Cross.

Contents.

Christian Work—Christian Advance—Christian Watching—Christian Battle—Christian Suffering—Christian Joy—For the Love of Man—For the sake of Jesus—For the Glory of God—The Claims of Christ.

Knox Little's Witness of the Passion.

Crown 8vo. 3s. 6d.

THE WITNESS OF THE PASSION OF OUR MOST HOLY REDEEMER.

By the Rev. W. J. Knox Little, M.A.,
Canon Residentiary of Worcester, and Vicar of Hoar Cross.

Waterloo Place, London.

B

Williams's Devotional Commentary.

New Edition.   Eight Vols.   Crown 8vo.   5s. each.   Sold separately.

A DEVOTIONAL COMMENTARY ON THE GOSPEL NARRATIVE.

By the Rev. Isaac Williams, B.D.,
Formerly Fellow of Trinity College, Oxford.

THOUGHTS ON THE STUDY OF THE HOLY GOSPELS.
A HARMONY OF THE FOUR EVANGELISTS.
OUR LORD'S NATIVITY.
OUR LORD'S MINISTRY (SECOND YEAR).
OUR LORD'S MINISTRY (THIRD YEAR).
THE HOLY WEEK.
OUR LORD'S PASSION.
OUR LORD'S RESURRECTION.

Voices of Comfort.

Sixth Edition.   Crown 8vo.   7s. 6d.

VOICES OF COMFORT.

Edited by the Rev. Thomas Vincent Fosbery, M.A.,
Sometime Vicar of St. Giles's, Oxford.

This Volume of prose and poetry, original and selected, aims at revealing the fountains of hope and joy which underlie the griefs and sorrows of life. It is so divided as to afford readings for a month.   The keynote of each day is given to the title prefixed to it, such as : 'The Power of the Cross of Christ, Day 6.   Conflicts of the Soul, Day 17.   The Communion of Saints, Day 20. The Comforter, Day 22.   The Light of Hope, Day 25.   The Coming of Christ, Day 28.'   Each day begins with passages of Holy Scripture.   These are followed by articles in prose, which are succeeded by one or more short prayers. After these are poems or passages of poetry, and then very brief extracts in prose or verse close the section.   The book is meant to meet, not merely cases of bereavement or physical suffering, but 'to minister specially to the hidden troubles of the heart, as they are silently weaving their dark threads into the web of the seemingly brightest life.'

Also a Cheap Edition.   Small 8vo.   3s. 6d.

Waterloo Place, London.

The Star of Childhood.

Fourth Edition. Royal 16mo. 2s. 6d.

THE STAR OF CHILDHOOD : a First Book of Prayers and Instruction for Children.

**Compiled by a Priest.
Edited by the Rev. T. T. Carter, M.A.**

With Illustrations after Fra Angelico.

The Guide to Heaven.

New Edition. 18mo. 1s. 6d.; Cloth limp, 1s.

THE GUIDE TO HEAVEN : a Book of Prayers for every Want. For the Working Classes.

**Compiled by a Priest.
Edited by the Rev. T. T. Carter, M.A.**

An Edition in Large Type. Crown 8vo. 1s. 6d.; Cloth limp, 1s.

H. L. Sidney Lear's For Days and Years.

New Edition. 16mo. 2s. 6d.

FOR DAYS AND YEARS. A Book containing a Text, Short Reading and Hymn for Every Day in the Church's Year.

Selected by H. L. Sidney Lear.

Also a Cheap Edition. 32mo, 1s.: or Cloth gilt, 1s. 6d.

Williams on the Epistles and Gospels.

*New Edition. Two Vols. Crown 8vo. 5s. each.
Sold separately.*

SERMONS ON THE EPISTLES AND GOSPELS FOR THE SUNDAYS AND HOLY DAYS THROUGHOUT THE YEAR.

By the Rev. Isaac Williams, B.D.,

Author of a ' Devotional Commentary on the Gospel Narrative.'

Waterloo Place, London.

Moberly's Parochial Sermons.

Crown 8vo.   7s. 6d.

PAROCHIAL SERMONS, chiefly preached at Brighstone, Isle of Wight.

By George Moberly, D.C.L.,
Late Bishop of Salisbury.

Contents.

The Night is far spent, the Day is at hand—Elijah, the Warner of the Second Advent of the Lord—Christmas—Epiphany—The Rich Man and Lazarus—The Seventh Day Rest—I will arise and go to my Father—Confirmation, a Revival—Korah—The Law of Liberty—Buried with Him in Baptism—The Waiting Church of the Hundred and Twenty—Whitsun Day. I will not leave you comfortless—Whitsun Day. Walking after the Spirit —The Barren Fig Tree—Depart from me; for I am a sinful man, O Lord— Feeding the Four Thousand—We are debtors—He that thinketh he standeth —The Strength of Working Prayer—Elijah's Sacrifice—If thou hadst known, even thou—Harvest Thanksgiving—Jonadab, the Son of Rechab—The Transfiguration; Death and Glory—Welcome to Everlasting Habitations—The Question of the Sadducees.

Moberly's Plain Sermons.

New Edition.   Crown 8vo.   5s.

PLAIN SERMONS, PREACHED AT BRIGHSTONE.

By George Moberly, D.C.L.,
Late Bishop of Salisbury.

Contents.

Except a man be born again—The Lord with the Doctors—The Draw-Net—I will lay me down in peace—Ye have not so learned Christ—Trinity Sunday— My Flesh is Meat indeed—The Corn of Wheat dying and multiplied—The Seed Corn springing to new life—I am the Way, the Truth, and the Life—The Ruler of the Sea—Stewards of the Mysteries of God—Ephphatha—The Widow of Nain—Josiah's discovery of the Law—The Invisible World : Angels—Prayers, especially Daily Prayers—They all with one consent began to make excuse— Ascension Day—The Comforter—The Tokens of the Spirit—Elijah's Warning, Fathers and Children—Thou shalt see them no more for ever—Baskets full of fragments—Harvest—The Marriage Supper of the Lamb—The Last Judgment.

Waterloo Place, London.

Luckock's Footprints of the Son of Man.

Third Edition.   Two Vols   Crown 8vo.   12s.

FOOTPRINTS OF THE SON OF MAN AS TRACED BY SAINT MARK: being Eighty Portions for Private Study, Family Reading, and Instructions in Church.

By Herbert Mortimer Luckock, D.D.,
Canon of Ely; Examining Chaplain to the Bishop of Ely; and Principal of the Theological College.

With an Introduction by the late Bishop of Ely.

Goulburn's Thoughts on Personal Religion.

New Edition.   Small 8vo.   6s. 6d.

THOUGHTS ON PERSONAL RELIGION : being a Treatise on the Christian Life in its two Chief Elements—Devotion and Practice.

By Edward Meyrick Goulburn, D.D., D.C.L.,
Dean of Norwich.

Also a Cheap Edition.   3s. 6d.

Presentation Edition, elegantly printed on Toned Paper.
Two Vols.   Small 8vo.   10s. 6d.

Goulburn's Pursuit of Holiness.

Seventh Edition.   Small 8vo.   5s.

THE PURSUIT OF HOLINESS: a Sequel to 'Thoughts on Personal Religion,' intended to carry the Reader somewhat farther onward in the Spiritual Life.

By Edward Meyrick Goulburn, D.D., D.C.L.,
Dean of Norwich.

Also a Cheap Edition.   3s. 6d.

Waterloo Place, London.

Goulburn on the Lord's Supper.

Sixth Edition. Small 8vo. 6s.

A COMMENTARY, Expository and Devotional, on the Order of the Administration of the Lord's Supper, according to the Use of the Church of England ; to which is added an Appendix on Fasting Communion, Non-communicating Attendance, Auricular Confession, the Doctrine of Sacrifice, and the Eucharistic Sacrifice.

By Edward Meyrick Goulburn, D.D., D.C.L.,
Dean of Norwich.

Also a Cheap Edition, uniform with ' Thoughts on Personal Religion,' and 'The Pursuit of Holiness.' 3s. 6d.

Goulburn's Holy Catholic Church.

Second Edition. Crown 8vo. 6s. 6d.

THE HOLY CATHOLIC CHURCH : its Divine Ideal, Ministry, and Institutions. A short Treatise. With a Catechism on each Chapter, forming a Course of Methodical Instruction on the subject.

By Edward Meyrick Goulburn, D.D., D.C.L.,
Dean of Norwich.

Contents.

What the Church is, and when and how it was founded—Duty of the Church towards those who hold to the Apostles' Doctrine, in separation from the Apostles' fellowship—The Unity of the Church and its Disruption—The Survey of Zion's towers, bulwarks, and palaces—The Institution of the Ministry, and its relation to the Church—The Holy Eucharist at its successive Stages—On the Powers of the Church in Council—The Church presenting, exhibiting, and defending the Truth—The Church guiding into and illustrating the Truth—On the Prayer Book as a Commentary on the Bible—Index.

Waterloo Place, London.

Goulburn's Collects of the Day.

Third Edition.   Two Vols.   Crown 8vo.   8s. each.   Sold separately.

THE COLLECTS OF THE DAY : an Exposition, Critical and Devotional, of the Collects appointed at the Communion. With Preliminary Essays on their Structure, Sources, and General Character, and Appendices containing Expositions of the Discarded Collects of the First Prayer Book of 1549, and of the Collects of Morning and Evening Prayer.

By Edward Meyrick Goulburn, D.D., D.C.L.,
Dean of Norwich.

Contents.

VOLUME I. BOOK I. *Introductory.*—On the Excellencies of the Collects–On the Origin of the word Collect—On the Structure of a Collect, as illustrated by the Collect in the Burial Service—Of the Sources of the Collects : Of the Sacramentary of Leo, of the Sacramentary of Gelasius, of Gregory the Great and his Sacramentary, of the Use of Sarum, and of S. Osmund its Compiler—On the Collects of Archbishop Cranmer—Of the Restoration Collects, and of John Cosin, Prince-Bishop of Durham—Of the Collects, as representing the Genius of the English Church. BOOK II. Part I.—*The Constant Collect.* Part II.—*Collects varying with the Ecclesiastical Season*—Advent to Whitsunday.

VOLUME II. BOOK II. *contd.*—Trinity Sunday to All Saints' Day. BOOK III. —*On the Collects after the Offertory.* APPENDIX A.—*Collects in the First Reformed Prayer Book of* 1549 *which were suppressed in* 1552—The Collect for the First Communion on Christmas Day—The Collect for S. Mary Magdalene's Day (July 22). APPENDIX B.—*Exposition of the Collects of Morning and Evening Prayer*—The Second at Morning Prayer, for Peace—The Third at Morning Prayer, for Grace—The Second at Evening Prayer, for Peace— The Third at Evening Prayer, for Aid against all Perils.

Knox Little's Good Friday Addresses.

New Edition.   Small 8vo.   2s. ; or in Paper Cover, 1s.

THE THREE HOURS' AGONY OF OUR BLESSED REDEEMER : being Addresses in the form of Meditations delivered in S. Alban's Church, Manchester, on Good Friday 1877.

By the Rev. W. J. Knox Little, M.A.,
Canon Residentiary of Worcester, and Vicar of Hoar Cross.

Waterloo Place, London.

Luckock's After Death.

Fifth Edition. Crown 8vo. 6s.

AFTER DEATH. An Examination of the Testimony of Primitive Times respecting the State of the Faithful Dead, and their relationship to the Living.

By Herbert Mortimer Luckock, D.D.,
Canon of Ely, etc.

Contents.

PART I.—The Test of Catholicity—The Value of the Testimony of the Primitive Fathers—The Intermediate State—Change in the Intermediate State—Prayers for the Dead : Reasons for Our Lord's Silence on the Subject—The Testimony of Holy Scripture—The Testimony of the Catacombs—The Testimony of the Early Fathers—The Testimony of the Primitive Liturgies—Prayers for the Pardon of Sins of Infirmity, and the Effacement of Sinful Stains—The Inefficacy of Prayer for those who died in wilful unrepented Sin.

PART II.—Primitive Testimony to the Intercession of the Saints—Primitive Testimony to the Invocation of the Saints—The Trustworthiness of the Patristic Evidence for Invocation tested—The Primitive Liturgies and the Roman Catacombs—Patristic Opinions on the Extent of the Knowledge possessed by the Saints—The Testimony of Holy Scripture upon the same Subject—The Beatific Vision not yet attained by any of the Saints—Conclusions drawn from the foregoing Testimony.

SUPPLEMENTARY CHAPTERS.—(*a.*) Is a fuller Recognition of the Practice of Praying for the Dead desirable or not?—(*b.*) Is it lawful or desirable to practise Invocation of Saints in any form or not?—Table of Fathers, Councils, etc. – Passages of Scripture explained or quoted—General Index.

S. Bonaventure's Life of Christ.

Crown 8vo. 7s. 6d.

THE LIFE OF CHRIST.

By S. Bonaventure.
Translated and Edited by the Rev. W. H. Hutchings,
Rector of Kirkby Misperton, Yorkshire.

'The whole volume is full of gems and rich veins of thought, and whether as a companion to the preacher or to those who seek food for their daily meditations, we can scarcely imagine a more acceptable book.' —*Literary Churchman.*

Waterloo Place, London.

Newman's Selection from Sermons.

Third Edition.   Crown 8vo.   5s.

SELECTION, adapted to the Seasons of the Ecclesiastical Year, from the 'Parochial and Plain Sermons' of JOHN HENRY NEWMAN, B.D., sometime Vicar of S. Mary's, Oxford.

Edited by the Rev. W. J. Copeland, B.D.,
Late Rector of Farnham, Essex.

Contents.

Advent:—Self-denial the Test of Religious Earnestness—Divine Calls—The Ventures of Faith—Watching. *Christmas Day:*—Religious Joy. *New Year's Sunday:*—The Lapse of Time. *Epiphany:*—Remembrance of Past Mercies—Equanimity—The Immortality of the Soul—Christian Manhood—Sincerity and Hypocrisy—Christian Sympathy. *Septuagesima:*—Present Blessings. *Sexagesima:*—Endurance, the Christian's Portion. *Quinquagesima:*—Love, the One Thing Needful. *Lent:*—The Individuality of the Soul—Life the Season of Repentance—Bodily Suffering—Tears of Christ at the Grave of Lazarus—Christ's Privations a Meditation for Christians—The Cross of Christ the Measure of the World. *Good Friday:*—The Crucifixion. *Easter Day:*—Keeping Fast and Festival. *Easter-Tide:*—Witnesses of the Resurrection—A Particular Providence as Revealed in the Gospel—Christ Manifested in Remembrance—The Invisible World—Waiting for Christ. *Ascension:*—Warfare the Condition of Victory. *Sunday after Ascension:*—Rising with Christ. *Whitsunday:*—The Weapons of Saints. *Trinity Sunday:*—The Mysteriousness of our Present Being. *Sundays after Trinity:*—Holiness Necessary for Future Blessedness—The Religious Use of Excited Feelings—The Self-wise Inquirer—Scripture a Record of Human Sorrow—The Danger of Riches—Obedience without Love as instanced in the Character of Balaam—Moral Consequences of Single Sins—The Greatness and Littleness of Human Life—Moral Effects of Communion with God—The Thought of God the Stay of the Soul—The Power of the Will—The Gospel Palaces—Religion a Weariness to the Natural Man—The World our Enemy—The Praise of Men—Religion Pleasant to the Religious—Mental Prayer—Curiosity a Temptation to Sin—Miracles no Remedy for Unbelief—Jeremiah, a Lesson for the Disappointed—The Shepherd of our Souls—Doing Glory to God in Pursuits of the World.

Waterloo Place, London.

Early Influences.

Crown 8vo. 3s. 6d.

EARLY INFLUENCES. New Edition.

With a Preface by Mrs. Gladstone.

Chapter I.—Infancy. Chapter II.—Watchfulness and Affection. Chapter III.—The Faults of Childhood and the Influence of Religious Instruction. Chapter IV.—Good Impulses and Moral Influence. Chapter V.—Manner and Accomplishments. Chapter VI.—The Mental Powers of Childhood—Instruction in General. Chapter VII.—Home—The Influence of Domestic Life upon the Country in General. Chapter VIII.—The Difficulty and the Reward.

The School of Life.

Crown 8vo. 4s. 6d.

THE SCHOOL OF LIFE. Seven Addresses delivered during the London Mission, 1885, in St. Paul's Church, Knightsbridge, to Public School Men, by late and present Head Masters.

With an Introduction by C. J. Vaughan, D.D.,

Dean of Llandaff and Master of the Temple. Formerly Head Master of Harrow School.

H. L. Sidney Lear's Precious Stones.

Three Vols. 32mo. 1s. each; or in Paper Covers, 6d. each.

Precious Stones, collected by H. L. Sidney Lear.

I. PEARLS—GRACE.

II. RUBIES—NATURE.

III. DIAMONDS—ART.

Also a Superior Edition, 16mo, with Red Borders, 2s. each.

'*Diamonds* contains extracts having reference to Art. Many will appreciate the beautiful passages from Ruskin; and the carefully chosen thoughts from the writings of Newman, Faber, and Sir Joshua Reynolds will give pleasure. An undercurrent of devotional feeling has guided the choice of these extracts. In *Pearls* the compiler has taken a wider range. We find valuable meditations from Thomas à Kempis, Bishop Jeremy Taylor, Faber, Newman, Emerson, while one or two reflections fraught with practical wisdom have been gathered from Lord Chesterfield. The collection called *Rubies* contains reflections on Nature from S. Augustine, S. Francis de Sales, and S. Gregory, besides extracts from Ruskin, Neale, Hugh Macmillan, and Charles Kingsley.'—*Times.*

An Edition complete in One Volume, 16mo, with Red Borders, 3s. 6d.

Jennings' Ecclesia Anglicana.

Crown 8vo. 7s. 6d.

ECCLESIA ANGLICANA. A History of the Church of Christ in England, extending from the Earliest to the Present Times.

By the Rev. Arthur Charles Jennings, M.A.,

Jesus College, Cambridge, sometime Tyrwhitt Scholar, Crosse Scholar, Hebrew University Prizeman, Fry Scholar of S. John's College, Carus and Scholefield Prizeman, and Rector of King's Stanley,

---

Bickersteth's The Lord's Table.

Second Edition. 16mo. 1s. ; or Cloth extra, 2s.

THE LORD'S TABLE ; or, Meditations on the Holy Communion Office in the Book of Common Prayer.

By E. H. Bickersteth, D.D.,

Bishop of Exeter.

'We must draw our review to an end, without using any more of our own words, except one parting expression of cordial and sincere thanks to Mr. Bickersteth for this goodly and profitable "Companion to the Communion Service." '—*Record.*

Manuals of Religious Instruction.

New and Revised Editions. Small 8vo. 3s. 6d. each. Sold separately.

MANUALS OF RELIGIOUS INSTRUCTION.

Edited by John Pilkington Norris, D.D.,

Archdeacon of Bristol and Canon Residentiary of Bristol Cathedral.

I. THE CATECHISM AND PRAYER BOOK.
II. THE OLD TESTAMENT.
III. THE NEW TESTAMENT.

Waterloo Place, London.

Aids to the Inner Life.

*Five Vols.   32mo, Cloth limp, 6d. each : or Cloth extra, 1s. each.
Sold separately.*

*These Five Volumes, Cloth extra, may be had in a Box, price 7s.
Also an Edition with Red Borders, 2s. each.*

AIDS TO THE INNER LIFE.

Edited by the Rev. W. H. Hutchings, M.A.,
Rector of Kirkby Misperton, Yorkshire.

These books form a series of works provided for the use of members of the English Church.   The process of adaptation is not left to the reader, but has been undertaken with the view of bringing every expression, as far as possible, into harmony with the Book of Common Prayer and Anglican Divinity.

OF THE IMITATION OF CHRIST.   In Four Books.   By THOMAS À KEMPIS.

THE CHRISTIAN YEAR.   Thoughts in Verse for the Sundays and Holy Days throughout the Year.

INTRODUCTION TO THE DEVOUT LIFE.   From the French of S. FRANCIS DE SALES, Bishop and Prince of Geneva.

THE HIDDEN LIFE OF THE SOUL.   From the French of JEAN NICOLAS GROU.

THE SPIRITUAL COMBAT.   Together with the Supplement and the Path of Paradise.   By LAURENCE SCUPOLI.

'We heartily wish success to this important series, and trust it may command an extensive sale.   We are much struck, not only by the excellent manner in which the design has been carried out in the Translations themselves, but also by the way in which Messrs. Rivington have done their part.   The type and size of the volumes are precisely what will be found most convenient for common use.   The price at which the volumes are produced is marvellously low.   It may be hoped that a large circulation will secure from loss those who have undertaken this scheme for diffusing far and wide such valuable means of advancing and deepening, after so high a standard, the spiritual life.'—*Literary Churchman.*

Blunt's Theological Dictionary.

Second Edition.   Imperial 8vo.   42s. : or in half-morocco, 52s. 6d.

DICTIONARY OF DOCTRINAL AND HISTORICAL THEOLOGY.
By Various Writers.

Edited by the Rev. John Henry Blunt, D.D.,
Editor of the ' Annotated Book of Common Prayer,' etc., etc.

Waterloo Place, London.

Norris's Rudiments of Theology.

Second Edition, revised.   Crown 8vo.   7s. 6d.

RUDIMENTS OF THEOLOGY.   A First Book for Students.

By John Pilkington Norris, D.D.,

Archdeacon of Bristol, and Canon Residentiary of Bristol Cathedral.

Contents.

PART I.—FUNDAMENTAL DOCTRINES:—The Doctrine of God's Existence—The Doctrine of the Second Person of the Trinity—The Doctrine of the Atonement—The Doctrine of the Third Person of the Trinity—The Doctrine of The Church—The Doctrine of the Sacraments.

PART II.—THE SOTERIOLOGY OF THE BIBLE:—The Teaching of the Old Testament—The Teaching of the Four Gospels—The Teaching of S. Paul—The Teaching of the Epistle to the Hebrews, of S. Peter and S. John—Soteriology of the Bible (concluded).

APPENDIX—ILLUSTRATIONS OF PART I. FROM THE EARLY FATHERS:—On the Evidence of God's Existence—On the Divinity of Christ—On the Doctrine of the Atonement—On the Procession of the Holy Spirit—On The Church—On the Doctrine of the Eucharist—Greek and Latin Fathers quoted or referred to in this volume, in their chronological order—Glossarial Index.

Medd's Bampton Lectures.

8vo.   16s.

THE ONE MEDIATOR.   The Operation of the Son of God in Nature and in Grace.   Eight Lectures delivered before the University of Oxford in the year 1882, on the Foundation of the late Rev. John Bampton, M.A., Canon of Salisbury.

By Peter Goldsmith Medd, M.A.,

Rector of North Cerney; Hon. Canon of S. Alban's, and Examining Chaplain to the Bishop; late Rector of Barnes; Formerly Fellow and Tutor of University College, Oxford.

Waterloo Place, London.

H. L. Sidney Lear's Christian Biographies.

Eight Vols.   Crown 8vo.   3s. 6d. each.   Sold separately.

CHRISTIAN BIOGRAPHIES.

By H. L. Sidney Lear.

MADAME LOUISE DE FRANCE, Daughter of Louis xv., known also as the Mother Térèse de S. Augustin.

A DOMINICAN ARTIST: a Sketch of the Life of the Rev. Père Besson, of the Order of S. Dominic.

HENRI PERREYVE. By A. GRATRY. Translated by special permission. With Portrait.

S. FRANCIS DE SALES, Bishop and Prince of Geneva.

THE REVIVAL OF PRIESTLY LIFE IN THE SEVENTEENTH CENTURY IN FRANCE. Charles de Condren—S. Philip Neri and Cardinal de Berulle—S. Vincent de Paul—Saint Sulpice and Jean Jacques Olier.

A CHRISTIAN PAINTER OF THE NINETEENTH CENTURY: being the Life of Hippolyte Flandrin.

BOSSUET AND HIS CONTEMPORARIES.

FÉNELON, ARCHBISHOP OF CAMBRAI.

H. L. Sidney Lear's Five Minutes.

Third Edition.   16mo.   3s. 6d.

FIVE MINUTES.   Daily Readings of Poetry.

Selected by H. L. Sidney Lear.

Pusey's Private Prayers.

Second Edition.   Royal 32mo.   2s. 6d.

PRIVATE PRAYERS.

By the Rev. E. B. Pusey, D.D.
Edited, with a Preface, by H. P. Liddon, D.D., D.C.L.
Chancellor and Canon of St. Paul's.

Half-a-Crown Editions of Devotional Works.

New and Uniform Editions.
Seven Vols. 16mo. 2s. 6d. each. Sold separately.

HALF-A-CROWN EDITIONS OF DEVOTIONAL WORKS.

Edited by H. L. Sidney Lear.

SPIRITUAL LETTERS TO MEN. By ARCHBISHOP FÉNELON.

SPIRITUAL LETTERS TO WOMEN. By ARCHBISHOP FÉNELON.

A SELECTION FROM THE SPIRITUAL LETTERS OF S. FRANCIS DE SALES, BISHOP AND PRINCE OF GENEVA.

THE SPIRIT OF S. FRANCIS DE SALES, BISHOP AND PRINCE OF GENEVA.

THE HIDDEN LIFE OF THE SOUL.

THE LIGHT OF THE CONSCIENCE. With an Introduction by the Rev. T. T. CARTER, M.A.

SELF-RENUNCIATION. From the French. With an Introduction by the Rev. T. T. CARTER, M.A.

H. L. Sidney Lear's Weariness.

Large Type. Fourth Edition. Small 8vo. 5s.

WEARINESS. A Book for the Languid and Lonely.

By H. L. Sidney Lear,
Author of 'For Days and Years,' 'Christian Biographies,' etc., etc.

Maxims from Pusey.

Third Edition. Crown 16mo. 2s.

MAXIMS AND GLEANINGS from the Writings of EDWARD BOUVERIE PUSEY, D.D.

Selected and arranged for Daily Use, by C. M. S.,
Compiler of 'Daily Gleanings of the Saintly Life,' 'Under the Cross,' etc.

With an Introduction by the Rev. M. F. Sadler,
Prebendary of Wells, and Rector of Honiton.

Waterloo Place, London.

Body's Life of Justification.

Sixth Edition.   Crown 8vo.   4s. 6d.

THE LIFE OF JUSTIFICATION.   A Series of Lectures delivered in
substance at All Saints', Margaret Street.

By the Rev. George Body, M.A.,
Canon of Durham.

Contents.

Justification the Want of Humanity—Christ our Justification—Union with
Christ the Condition of Justification—Conversion and Justification—The Life of
Justification—The Progress and End of Justification.

Keys to Christian Knowledge.

Seven Volumes.   Small 8vo.   1s. 6d. each.   Sold separately.
The 2s. 6d. Edition may still be had.

Edited by the Rev. John Henry Blunt, D.D.,
Editor of the 'Annotated Bible,' 'Annotated Book of Common Prayer,' etc., etc.

THE HOLY BIBLE.
THE BOOK OF COMMON PRAYER.
CHURCH HISTORY (ANCIENT).
CHURCH HISTORY (MODERN).
CHRISTIAN DOCTRINE AND PRACTICE (founded
on the Church Catechism).

Edited by John Pilkington Norris, D.D.,
Archdeacon of Bristol, and Canon Residentiary of Bristol Cathedral.
Editor of the 'New Testament with Notes,' etc.

THE FOUR GOSPELS.
THE ACTS OF THE APOSTLES.

Waterloo Place, London.